CLARENDON ARISTOTLE SERIES

General Editor: J. L. ACKRILL

CLARENDON ARISTOTLE SERIES

CATEGORIES and *DE INTERPRETATIONE*
J. L. ACKRILL

DE ANIMA, Books II and III
D. W. HAMLYN

METAPHYSICS, Books Γ, Δ, E
CHRISTOPHER KIRWAN

POSTERIOR ANALYTICS
JONATHAN BARNES

METAPHYSICS, Books *M* and *N*
JULIA ANNAS

ARISTOTLE'S
EUDEMIAN ETHICS

BOOKS *I*, *II*, and *VIII*

*Translated
with a Commentary*

by

MICHAEL WOODS

*Fellow of Brasenose College,
Oxford*

CLARENDON PRESS · OXFORD
1982

Oxford University Press, Walton Street, Oxford OX2 6DP

London Glasgow New York Toronto
Delhi Bombay Calcutta Madras Karachi
Kuala Lumpur Singapore Hong Kong Tokyo
Nairobi Dar es Salaam Cape Town
Melbourne Auckland
and associates in
Beirut Berlin Ibadan Mexico City Nicosia

Published in the United States by
Oxford University Press, New York

British Library Cataloguing in Publication Data
Aristotle
[Ethics. English] . Aristotle's Eudemian ethics,
Books I, II, and VIII. – (Clarendon Aristotle series)
1. Aristotle. Eudemian ethics
I. Title   II. Aristotle's Eudemian ethics,
Books I, II and VIII   III. Woods, Michael
170   B422
ISBN 0-19-872060-2
ISBN 0-19-872061-0 Pbk

Typeset by Hope Services, Abingdon
and printed in Great Britain
at the University Press, Oxford
by Eric Buckley
Printer to the University

To

My Parents

PREFACE

The purpose of this volume, as of others in the series, is to provide a new translation of a philosophical text of Aristotle, of a kind to serve the needs of philosophers without knowledge of Greek, and a philosophical commentary. Of the five books of the *Eudemian Ethics* that do not overlap with the *Nicomachean Ethics*, the three translated in this volume are likely to be of the greatest interest to readers of the present day.

This work of Aristotle's presents special difficulties to a translator, because the text is in an extremely poor state, especially in Book VIII, and in many passages it is not possible to reconstruct what Aristotle wrote with any confidence. Although in many passages at least the general sense is clear, in some cases doubts about readings are the source of uncertainty about major points of interpretation. In consequence, a large number of passages have had to be mentioned in the Notes on the Text and Translation, and I have found it necessary, for reasons of space, often simply to give the text adopted for the translation, without offering a full defence of my choice, or referring to alternative proposals. Where a point of major philosophical interest turns on the textual reading adopted, I have tried to make this clear in the Commentary. It was not possible, with this work, to take one edition of the Greek text as a base and simply note deviations.

In the translation, in accordance with the policy of the series, I have aimed at producing a version as close as possible to the original, even at the cost, sometimes, of elegance and conformity to English idiom. In the Glossary are given the renderings of some of the more philosophically important Greek words and phrases. Wherever possible, a uniform rendering of a given expression has been used in the translation.

It is a pleasure to record a debt of gratitude to many people with whom I have discussed Aristotle's ethics, and this work in particular, over a number of years. I benefited from attending the meetings of the Symposium Aristotelicum, held in Oosterbeek, Holland, in 1969. The late Richard Walzer made available to me his draft for an Oxford

Classical Text of the *E.E.*, making use of earlier work of the late Sir David Ross. More recently, after Walzer's death, Mr D. A. F. M. Russell has allowed me to see some further documents, including some textual proposals of his own, and comments on the suggestions of Ross and Walzer. As will be apparent from the Notes, I have often thought that these proposals were superior to anything proposed previously, and have been glad to adopt them for my translation.

I have learned a good deal from Dr A. J. P. Kenny, with whom I gave a seminar on this work in Oxford a few years ago. Although a discussion of the relative priority of the Eudemian and Nicomachean books and the problem of the 'common books' is outside the scope of this volume, I have taken account of his interpretations of a number of passages in the *E.E.* in his book *The Aristotelian Ethics*. His more recent book, *Aristotle's Theory of the Will*, appeared when the work for this volume was already completed. (The same is true of the new French translation of the *E.E.* by Vianney Décarie.)

I must record a great debt to Professor J. L. Ackrill, the General Editor of this Series, who has been extremely generous with his time in reading drafts of this book and discussing them with me. He has made many suggestions for the improvement of the translation, and for making the Commentary clearer and less prolix, which in most cases I have gratefully adopted. Mr. Douglas Hutchinson has also made a number of useful suggestions.

Finally, I must express my gratitude to the Radcliffe Fund for a Fellowship during which much of the work for this volume was done, and to the Governing Body of Brasenose College for allowing me to accept it.

Brasenose College, Oxford MICHAEL WOODS
October 1979

CONTENTS

INTRODUCTION

Four ethical works attributed to Aristotle have survived from antiquity: the *Nicomachean Ethics*, the *Eudemian Ethics*, and two shorter works, the *Magna Moralia* and *On Virtues and Vices*. The last of these is now universally condemned as spurious, and the majority of scholars still reject the authenticity of the *Magna Moralia*, although there has been some recent work arguing for the contrary view. Of the two longer works, the *Nicomachean Ethics* has almost monopolized the attention of Aristotelian scholars over the centuries, and incomparably more commentaries have been published on the Nicomachean than on the Eudemian treatise. It is a reflection of this that many more manuscripts survive of the *N.E.*, and, as a result, the textual problems presented by the *E.E.* are much greater. For a time, during the nineteenth century, the *E.E.* was also held to be spurious, perhaps being a compilation of Eudemus of Rhodes after Aristotle's death; but, early in the present century, as a result of the work of Kapp and others who sought to trace the development of Aristotle's thought, it has been recognized that there are no serious reasons for doubting the Aristotelian authorship of the Eudemian work, and that view still prevails. The reasons for the traditional title 'Eudemian' remain obscure.

Controversy still flourishes over two connected problems: the relative priority of composition of the two treatises, and the origin of the 'common books'. The *E.N.* is in ten books, the *E.E.* in eight, but according to the manuscript tradition, the fourth, fifth, and sixth books of the *E.E.* are identical with the fifth, sixth, and seventh of the *E.N.* Although, owing to the pre-eminence that has attached to the Nicomachean treatise, these three books have been commonly considered as belonging to, and an integral part of, the *E.N.*, it is a serious question, to which the answer is far from obvious, whether these books were intended for, or at any rate belong chronologically with, the one work or the other. (Alternative hypotheses are that some parts of these books belong to one work and some to the other, or that they belong chronologically to a period intermediate between the composition of the *E.N.* and the *E.E.*) Despite the traditional Nicomachean attribution, certain features of these books, such as the existence of an apparently independent discussion of pleasure in the third of them, duplicating the discussion of that subject in *E.N.* X, would suggest that they have a Eudemian origin.

From the time that the *E.E.* has been accepted as a genuine work of Aristotle, it has been generally held that the *E.E.* is an earlier and philosophically less mature work than the *E.N.* This view has been recently challenged by Allan, Monan, and Kenny. Kenny argues, on the basis of a systematic comparison of the style and vocabulary of *E.N.* V–VII, that the common books are Eudemian, and that the *E.N.* is earlier than the *E.E.* As Kenny points out, the problem of the common books ought to be settled before any attempt is made to decide the question of priority, as the view to be taken of the general philosophical position of the two treatises, and the interpretation of many passages in the remaining books of each work, will depend on the origin of the common books.

These two issues cannot be discussed in a volume of this kind. My own opinion is that Kenny has made a powerful case for the Eudemian attribution of the common books, but I remain convinced by the arguments of Rowe and others for the priority of the *E.E.* But it is now generally agreed that, whatever view is taken about the issues of chronology and the common books, anyone seriously interested in Aristotle's work in ethics must attend to both treatises. Despite the broad similarities between the two books, many discussions occur in each to which there is no parallel in the other, and many themes receive a far more extended treatment in one book than in the other. I have assumed that readers of this book will want to compare parallels in the *E.N.*, and have accordingly provided, in the Commentary, cross-references to it (less often to the *M.M.*). Inevitably, in some cases the existence or closeness of the parallel is controversial. Of the three books of the *E.E.* translated in this volume, I corresponds broadly to the earlier part of *E.N.* I, II to the later part of *E.N.* I, and to parts of *E.N.* II and III; VIII can hardly be said to have a parallel in the other work.

TRANSLATION

The paragraphs in the translation correspond to sections of the Commentary. Marginal lineation (5, 10, etc.) is based on Susemihl's Teubner text. Works and phrases enclosed in angle brackets have been inserted in order to make the English intelligible, though nothing corresponds to them in the Greek.

BOOK 1

CHAPTER 1

The man who, in the shrine at Delos, published his opinion by com- **1214ᵃ** posing an inscription on the propylaeum of the temple of Leto, distinguished the good, the fine, and the pleasant as not all belonging to the same thing. These were his verses:

'The most just is finest, being healthy is best; most pleasant   5
is to achieve one's heart's desire.'

But we do not agree with him: for happiness, the finest and best thing of all, is the most pleasant.

There are many inquiries concerning each object and each branch 10 of nature which pose problems and require investigation; some contribute only to the attainment of knowledge; some have to do also with getting and doing. In regard to those things that belong solely to theoretical philosophy, we must say, when the occasion arises, whatever is relevant to the discipline.

But first we must consider what living well consists in and how it 15 is to be attained: Is it by nature that all those become happy who win this appellation at all—just as men are naturally tall, or short, or of different complexions? Or is it through learning,—happiness being a form of knowledge? Or again, is it through a kind of training? (Many things come the way of human beings neither in the course of nature, nor after learning, but after habituation — bad things to those 20 with the wrong sort of habituation, good to those with the right sort.) Or is it in none of *those* ways, but one of two further alternatives: either a divine dispensation, as if by divine inspiration, like

1

1214^a

those in the possession of a deity or supernatural powers, or is it
25 a matter of luck? After all, many say that happiness and good fortune are the same thing.

That happiness comes to men either through all, or through
some, or through just one of these means is evident. For virtually
all changes fall under these principles: actions resulting from thought
may all be classed along with those resulting from knowledge.

30 But to be happy, and to live the fine and divinely-happy life,
would seem to reside in three things above all, three things that
seem to be the most worth having there are. For some say that
wisdom is the greatest good, others virtue, others pleasure. And
some enter into dispute about the importance of those in relation
1214^b to happiness, claiming that one contributes more than another to
it: some hold wisdom to be a greater good than virtue, others the
reverse; while others again believe pleasure a greater good than
either. And again, some think that living happily is composed of
5 all of these, some of two of them, others that it consists in one of
them in particular.

CHAPTER 2

Taking note of these things, everyone who can live according to his
own choice should adopt some goal for the fine life, whether it be
honour or reputation or wealth or cultivation—an aim that he will
10 have in view in all his actions; for, not to have ordered one's life in
relation to some end is a mark of extreme folly. But, above all, and
before everything else, he should settle in his own mind,—neither in
a hurried nor in a dilatory manner—in which human thing living well
consists, and what those things are without which it cannot belong
to human beings.

For being healthy is not the same as the things without which it
15 is not possible to be healthy; and this holds likewise in many other
cases too. So, living well also is not the same as the things without
which living well is impossible. (Some things of this sort are not
specific to health or to the good life, but are common to more or
less everything, both dispositions and actions—for example, without
20 our breathing or being awake or sharing in movement, nothing either
good or bad could belong to us; whereas other things are specific to

2

each kind of thing. This is a point which must not be overlooked: the things just mentioned are not relevant to physical well-being in the same way as are the eating of meat and the taking of exercise after meals.) These are the reasons for the dispute over being happy —what it is and the means by which it comes about: things without 25 which it is not possible to be happy are thought by some to be parts of happiness.

CHAPTER 3

It would be superfluous to examine all the opinions about happiness that find adherents. Many opinions are held by children and by the 30 diseased and mentally unbalanced, and no sensible man would concern himself with puzzles about them; the holders of such views are in need, not of arguments, but of maturity in which to change their opinions, or else of correction of a civil or medical kind (for medical treatment is no less a form of correction than flogging is). Similarly, neither need we examine the views of the many; they speak in an **1215ᵃ** unreflective way on almost any topic, most of all when they speak about this; only the opinions of reasonable men should be examined; it would be strange to present argument to those who need not argument, but experience. But, as each inquiry has its own problems, so, evidently does that concerning the best and highest life. It is *these* 5 opinions, then, that it is right for us to investigate; for the refutation of those who dispute a certain position is a demonstration of the opposing view.

Moreover, clarity about such matters is helpful, but above all for the purpose that anyone must have who enquires how it is possible to live a fine and happy life (if it is unacceptable to say 10 'divinely-happy')—and for the prospect that reasonable men would have, with each alternative, of achieving it. If living well is to be found among those things which occur by luck or in the course of nature, for many it would be a hopeless aspiration; for in that case its possession would not be by their own efforts and in their own power, nor a matter of their own enterprise. But if it consists in the having of a certain character by oneself and one's 15 actions, the good will be at once a more common possession and a more divine one: more common because it will be possible for more people to have a share in it, more divine because happiness is there for those who cultivate a certain ...aracter in themselves and their actions.

CHAPTER 4

20 Most of the matters of controversy and puzzlement will become clear if what happiness should be thought to be is properly defined. Should we think that it consists only in the soul's having a certain character, as some older philosophers thought? Or must a man, 25 himself, or rather his actions, also have a certain character?

Various lives are distinguished. Some do not even enter the contest for such good fortune, but are engaged in in order to provide for the necessities of life. I have in mind those devoted to vulgar trades, and to commerce, and the banal occupations (by 'vulgar trades' I mean those engaged in only to obtain reputation, by 'banal occu- 30 pations', I mean those of a sedentary or wage-earning kind, and by 'commercial', those concerned with the marketing and selling of goods). Just as there are three things that are assigned to a happy conduct of life – the goods that we have in fact already mentioned as the greatest available for human beings, virtue, wisdom, and pleasure – 35 so too we see three lives which all who have the opportunity choose to live, the political, the philosophical, and the pleasure-loving.

1215^b Of these, the philosophical aspires to a concern with wisdom and speculation about truth, the political with fine actions, – actions that 5 result from virtue – and the pleasure-loving with physical pleasures. And so, as we have said before, one man is called happy by one person, another by another. Anaxagoras of Clazomenae, when asked who was happiest said: 'None of the people you think; he would seem a strange person to you.' He answered in this fashion because 10 he saw that his inquirer supposed that it was impossible for anyone who was not powerful and attractive, or rich, to win this appellation; whereas *he* perhaps thought that it was the man who led a life without pain and free from stigma in matters of justice, or participated in some divine speculation, who was, humanly speaking, divinely-happy.

CHAPTER 5

15 About many things it is not easy to judge correctly, but it is especially

difficult to do so in regard to that which everyone thinks is most
easy and within anyone's capacity to know; namely, which of the
things in life is worth choosing, and such that one who obtains it
will have his desire fulfilled. After all, many things that happen are
such as to induce people to abandon life – disease, extremes of pain, 20
storms, for example; so that it is evident that, on account of those
things at any rate, it would, given the choice, have been worth
choosing not to be born in the first place. Again, <there is> the life
which men lead while they are still children. For no one in his right
mind would tolerate a return to that sort of existence. Moreover,
many of the things that involve neither pleasure nor pain, or involve 25
pleasure, but of a reprehensible sort, are enough to make not existing
at all preferable to being alive. In general, if we put together all the
things that everyone does or undergoes, but not voluntarily (because
they are not done or undergone for their own sake), and an infinite
stretch of time were provided in addition, no one would choose in
order to have *them* to be alive, rather than not. Nor again would 30
anyone who was not a complete slave prefer to live solely for the
pleasure associated with nutrition and sex, if all the pleasures were
removed that knowing or seeing or any of the other senses bestow
upon human beings; for it is evident that, for a man who made such 35
a choice as *this* for himself, it would make no difference whether he
were born a beast or a man. Certainly the ox in Egypt, which they **1216ª**
honour as the god Apis, has a greater abundance of several of such
things than many sovereigns. Similarly, no one would prefer life for
the pleasure of sleep; for what difference is there between sleeping
without ever waking from one's first day to one's last, over a period
of ten thousand years – or however many one likes – and living the 5
life of a plant? Certainly plants seem to have a share in some such
sort of life, as do infants. Babies indeed when they first come to be
inside the mother exist in their natural state, but asleep all the time.
So all this makes it clear that what the well and the good is in life
eludes those who investigate the subject. 10

They say that Anaxagoras, when someone raised just these puzzles
and asked him what it was for which a person would choose to be
born rather than not, answered that it would be 'in order to appre-
hend the heavens and the order in the whole universe'. So *he* thought 15

5

1216ᵃ

that it was knowledge that made the choice of life worth making; on the other hand, those who admire Sardanapallus, or Smindurides of Sybara or one or other of those who live the pleasure-loving life, all appear to place happiness in enjoyment; but others again would
20 choose neither wisdom nor bodily pleasures of any kind in preference to virtuous actions. And certainly, they are done by some not only for a reputation but also when there is no prospect of fame. But in fact the majority of political men do not really win this appellation,
25 for in reality they are not political men. For the political man is one who chooses to perform fine actions for their own sake, but the majority of them take up this sort of life for profit and personal advancement.

From what we have said it is clear that everyone attributes happiness to three lives, the political, the philosophical, and the pleasure-
30 loving. In considering these, it is evident to all what pleasure is associated with the body and with physical enjoyments, what its character is, and how it is produced; so we do not need to inquire what those pleasures are, but whether or not they contribute in any way to happiness, how they contribute to it, and whether, if we ought to allot some pleasures to the good life, it is *those* that we should allot, or whether, although the happy man must share in them in some
35 *other* way, it is on account of other pleasures that it is reasonable to think that the happy man lives a pleasurable and not merely a painless life.

We must investigate these matters further in due course; but first we must look into virtue and wisdom, and discover the nature of
40 each. Are they parts of the good life, either themselves or the actions
1216ᵇ resulting from them? For they are ascribed to happiness, if not by everyone, at any rate by all the people worth taking account of.

The elder Socrates thought that the end <of life> was to know vir-
5 tue, and used to inquire what justice is, and courage, and each of virtue's parts. It was understandable that he should have proceeded in this way, as he thought that the virtues were all forms of knowledge, and therefore once a man knew justice, he would be a just man. After all, as soon as we have learned geometry and building, we are geom-
10 etricians and builders. And so Socrates used to inquire what virtue is, rather than how it arises and from what. This approach holds good

6

in the theoretical sciences: nothing belongs to astronomy or natural science or geometry except knowing and apprehending the nature of the objects which fall under these sciences; though incidentally they 15 may well be useful to us for many of the things we need.

Of the productive sciences, however, the end is distinct from the science <itself> and from understanding: health is the end of medicine, good social order – or something of the sort distinct <from the science itself>, – the end of political science. If something is fine, understanding it is fine also; but still, in the case of virtue, the most 20 valuable thing is not to have knowledge of it, but to know from what sources it arises. For what we wish is to be courageous, not to know what courage is; to be just, not to know what justice is; in the same way as <we wish> to be healthy rather than to know what being healthy is, and to be in a good state, rather than know what it is to 25 be in a good state.

CHAPTER 6

We must try, by argument, to reach a convincing conclusion on all these questions, using, as testimony and by way of example, what appears to be the case. For it would be best if everyone should turn out to agree with what we are going to say; if not that, that they should all agree in a way and *will* agree after a change of mind; for 30 each man has something of his own to contribute to the finding of the truth, and it is from such <starting-points> that we must demonstrate: beginning with things that are correctly said, but not clearly, as we proceed we shall come to express them clearly, with what is more perspicuous at each stage superseding what is customarily expressed in a confused fashion.

In every discipline, what is said in a philosophical manner and 35 what in an unphilosophical, is different. So the political man, also, should not regard as irrelevant the inquiry that makes clear not only the *that* but also the *why*. For it is *that* method of proceeding that is the philosophical, in every discipline; but great care is needed here. 40 For, because it appears to be the mark of the philosopher never to **1217ᵃ** speak in an unconsidered fashion, but always with reason, there are some who often go undetected when they produce arguments that are foreign to the inquiry and idle; they do this sometimes because

1217^a

of ignorance, sometimes because of charlatanry; by these are caught
5 even those who are experienced and of practical ability at the hands
of men who neither have nor are capable of architectonic or practical
thought. This happens to them through lack of training; for it is a
lack of training to be unable to distinguish, in regard to each subject,
between those arguments which are appropriate to it and those which
are foreign.

10 It is also a good thing to appraise separately the account of the
reason and what is being demonstrated, firstly because of what has
just been said, that we should not in all cases pay attention to what
emerges from arguments but often rather to what appears to be the
case, (as things are, whenever they cannot solve a problem, they are
forced to accept what has been said) and secondly because frequently
15 what seems to have been demonstrated by argument is true, but not
for the reason that the argument claims. It is possible to demonstrate
a truth through what is false, as is evident from the *Analytics*.

CHAPTER 7

After these preliminaries, let us proceed, starting first, as we have
20 said, with first opinions, which are not clearly expressed, seeking to
discover in a clear fashion what happiness is. Now happiness has
been agreed to be the greatest and best of human goods. We say
'human' because happiness may perhaps exist also for some other
being superior to us—a god, for example. None of the other animals
25 that are naturally inferior to human beings have any claim to this
description: no horse or bird or fish is happy, nor any other thing
that there is which does not, as the proverb has it, have a share by
its nature in the divine; it is by sharing in good things in some *other*
way that these things live well or badly, as the case may be.

30 However, that this is how things are we must see later; we say
now that among goods, some are realizable by human action, others
are not realizable. We put it this way because some of the things that
there are have no share in change, and so no share in realizable goods,
either (and these things may well be the best that there are in nature),
35 while some are indeed realizable, but by beings superior to us. Now
things are called realizable (*praktos*), in two ways (both those things
for whose sake we act and the things we do for their sake involve

8

action (*praxis*); for example, we class as realizable things both health and wealth, and the things that are done for their sake, things of a health-giving or wealth-producing sort). So it is evident that happiness also must be set down as best among things realizable by human 40 beings.

CHAPTER 8

So we must inquire what the best is, and in how many ways it is **1217ᵇ** <so> called. Now this appears chiefly in three opinions. For they say that the good-itself is the best thing of all, and the good-itself is that to which it belongs to be both first among goods, and the cause by its presence, for other things, of their being goods. Both 5 these things, they hold, belong to the Form of the good. By 'both', I mean being first among goods, and the cause by its presence in other things, of their being goods. For, they say that it is of *that* object, above all, that the good is truly predicated, – other things being goods through sharing in it, and similarity to it; and it is first 10 among goods – since, if the object in which things share were taken away, with it would go all the things that share in the Form, and are called <what they are called> through sharing in it; and that is the way that the first stands in relation to what comes after. And indeed, like the other Forms, the Form of the good is separate from the 15 things that share in it.

To examine this opinion thoroughly belongs to an investigation at once different from the present one, and in many ways, inevitably, approximating more to logic. (Arguments that are both destructive and general belong to no other science.) To speak in a summary fashion, we may say first that the thesis that there is a Form either 20 of good or indeed of anything else is verbal and vacuous. The matter has been studied in many places, both in the external discussions, and in the work *On Philosophy*.

Again, even if the Forms, including a Form of good exist, they are not of the least help either for a good life or for actions.

For the good is <so> called in many ways, indeed in as many 25 ways as being. 'Being', as has been set out elsewhere, signifies what-is, quality, quantity, when, and in addition that <being which is found> in being changed and in changing; and the good occurs in each one 30

1217^b

of these categories—in substance, intelligence and God; in quality, the just; in quantity, the moderate, in the when, the right occasion; and teaching and learning in the sphere of change. So, just as being is not a single thing embracing the things mentioned, the good is not either; nor is there a single science of being or the good.

35 But even those goods that are so called in a categorially similar way—for instance, the right occasion and the moderate,—do not belong to a single science to look into: different sciences look into the right occasion and the moderate in different cases. Thus medicine and gymnastics study the right occasion and the moderate in nutrition,

40 whereas, where military actions are concerned, it is generalship, and in the same way a different science for diverse activities; so that the good-itself, at least, can hardly belong to a single science to look into.

1218^a Further, with those things that have a prior and posterior, there is no common thing over and above, and separate from, them. For <if there were>, there would be something prior to the first thing. For the thing that is common and separate is prior because, if the com-

5 mon thing were taken away, with it would go the first thing. Thus, if the double is the first of the multiples, the multiple that is predicated <of these> in common cannot be separate <from them>; for <if it is>, it will be prior to the double . . . if it turns out that the common thing is the form—if, for example, the common thing is made

10 separate: for if justice is a good, so is courage. Thus there is, according to them, a good-itself, so the 'itself' is an additional element added to the common definition. What would that be, if not that it is eternal and separate? But that which is white for many days is no *more* white than that which is white for one; so that the good will not be more good, either, by being eternal; nor is the common good identical with the Form; for it is common to all goods.

15 They ought in fact to demonstrate <the existence of> the good-itself in the opposite way to that in which they do now. As things are, beginning with objects not agreed to possess the good, they demonstrate what are agreed to be goods; starting with numbers, <they prove> that justice is a good, and health, on the grounds that they are forms of order and numbers, good belonging to numbers

20 and monads because the one is the good-itself. They ought to start with agreed <goods>, such as health, strength, and temperance,

10

<in order to show> that the fine is present even more in unchanging things. For all those things are <examples of> order and state of equilibrium; so if <*they* are good>, those things must be even more so, as these properties belong even more to those things. Hazardous, too, is the demonstration that the one is the good-itself, on the 25 grounds that the numbers seek it; for one thing, they do not say clearly how they desire it—they say that too baldly; and further, how could inclination be thought to be present in things that lack life? They ought to take more trouble over this, and not to accept, without argument, things that are not easy to believe even *with* an argument. And it is not true that everything that there is seeks some 30 single good: each thing has an inclination for its own good, the eye for sight, the body for health, and so on.

So, in favour of the conclusion that there is no good-itself, we have the problems just mentioned, and further, it is not any help to political science; <what is useful is> some specific good, both 35 for political science and the others, as physical well-being is for gymnastics.

Further, <there is> what has been written in the treatise: either the Form of the good is useful for no science, or for all sciences alike. Further, it is not realizable.

Likewise, the common good is neither the good-itself (for it would 1218^b belong even to a small good) nor is it realizable. For medicine does not make it its business to see that what belongs to anything shall belong, but that health shall. The same holds of every other craft, also. But the good is <so> called in many ways and part of it is the fine, and again, one good is realizable, and another not. But what is 5 realizable is the sort of good that is that-for-the-sake-of-which; that does not exist among unchanging things.

It is clear that neither the Form of the good nor the common <good> is the good-itself that we are seeking, as the first is unchanging and not realizable, the second changing, yet still not realizable. But that-for-the-sake-of-which, as <it is> an end, is best, and cause 10 of the things falling under it, and first among all <goods>. This, therefore, is what the good-itself, the end of things realizable by man, must be. That is what falls under the science supreme among all sciences. That comprises political science, household management,

and practical wisdom. For these are distinguished from other states
15 in being of that sort; we shall have to see later whether they differ
at all from one another.

That the end serves as a cause for the things under it, is shown by
teaching: <teachers>, after defining the end, demonstrate, with
regard to everything else, that it is a good; for that-for-the-sake-of-
which is a cause. For example, given that so-and-so is what being
20 healthy is, such-and-such must exist, which is beneficial for it: the
healthy is an *efficient* cause of health, but an efficient cause of
health's existence, not of its being a good. Again, no one demonstrates that health is a good, any more than he demonstrates any
other starting-point, unless he is not a doctor but a sophist; for they
25 create sophistries by using arguments inappropriately. The good is an
end for human beings and the best among the things that are realizable
—we must see in how many ways the best thing of all is <so>
called, since the best is this, making a new start at this point.

CHAPTER 1

1218^{b}

We must now make a fresh start, and turn to the next topic of discussion. According to a distinction made also in the external discussions, all goods are either in the soul or outside it, and it is those in the soul that are more worthy of choice; for wisdom, virtue, and pleasure are in the soul, and some or all of these seem to be an end 35 for everyone. Of things in the soul, some are states or capacities, others activities and processes.

Let this be assumed; and about excellence, that it is the best disposition, state, or capacity of anything that has some employment 1219^{a} or function. This is evident from induction: in all cases this is what we suppose. For example, a cloak has an excellence—and a certain function and employment also; and the best state of the cloak is its excellence. Similarly too with a boat, a house, and other things. So the same is true also of the soul; for there is something which is its 5 function.

Let us assume that a better state has a better function; and that as the states stand in relation to one another, so do the functions deriving from them; and each thing's function is its end. From these considerations, then, it is clear that the function is better than the state. For the end, as it is the end, is best; for it is assumed that that which is best, and which is the final thing for whose sake everything else is chosen, is an end. So it is evident that the function is better than the state and the disposition.

But a function is <so> called in two ways. In the case of some things, the function is something distinct, over and above the employment, in the way that the function of house-building is a house, not the building of one, and of medicine health, not the act of curing 15 or applying treatment; but in some cases the employment is the function, in the way that, for example, seeing is the function of sight, and speculation the function of mathematical science. So it follows that, where a thing's employment is its function, the employment is better than the state.

Having made these distinctions, let us say that a thing and its

20 excellence have the same function, though in different ways. For example, a shoe is the function of the art of shoe-making and the activity of shoe-making. So if there is some excellence which is the excellence of shoe-making and of a good shoe-maker, its function is a good shoe. The same holds in the other cases also. Now let us assume that the function of the soul is to make things live, but that is an employment and a waking state, since sleep is an idle and inactive state.

25 So, as the function of the soul and of its excellence must be one and the same, the function of its excellence is a good life. This, then, is the final good, that we agreed to be happiness. It is evident from our assumptions: happiness was assumed to be the best thing, and

30 ends,—the best among goods—are in the soul; but things in the soul are states or activities, (since the activity is better than the disposition, and the best activity is of the best state, and virtue is the best state) —that the activity of virtue must be the best thing of the soul.

But happiness too was said to be the best thing: so happiness is

35 activity of a good soul. Now as happiness was agreed to be something complete, and life may be complete or incomplete—and this holds with excellence also (in the one case it is total, in the other partial)—and the activity of what is incomplete is itself incomplete, happiness must be activity of a complete life in accordance with complete virtue.

40 Evidence that we are giving the genus and definition of happiness

1219ᵇ correctly is provided by opinions that we all have: that both acting well and living well are the same thing as being happy, and each of these (both the living and the acting) is an employment and an activity (for the practical life is a life of employment: the copper-smith makes a bridle, but the horseman makes use of it); also that

5 one cannot be happy either for a single day, nor as a child, nor for a stage of one's life. (And so Solon's idea was right when he said that one should not felicitate a man on being happy when he is alive, only when his life attains completion; for nothing incomplete is happy, as it does not form a whole.)

Further, awards of praise for virtue are on account of deeds, and encomia are for deeds; and it is those who win that are crowned

10 with wreaths, not those who have the ability to win, but fail to do so.

14

And there is the fact that one judges from deeds what sort of person someone is.

Again, why is happiness not praised? Because it is the reason for which other things are praised, either through being referred to it <as a standard>, or being parts of it. That is why felicitation and praise and encomium are all different. An encomium speaks of a 15 particular deed; praise of the agent's having that character generally; felicitation is of the end.

These considerations clear up the puzzle sometimes raised, why virtuous men are no better than the bad for half their life, since all men are alike when asleep; the reason is that sleep is not activity, but inactivity, of the soul. For this reason, too, if there is some 20 other part of the soul, the nutritive, for example, its virtue is not a part of total virtue, any more than the body's is; for in sleep the nutritive is more active whereas the perceiving and desiring parts do not fulfil their function during sleep. However, in so far as they are involved in changes in a way, virtuous men have better dreams, unless owing to disease or degeneration they do not. 25

We must now investigate the soul: because virtue belongs to the soul, and does so not incidentally. As it is human virtue that is the object of our inquiry, let us assume that there are two parts of a soul that share in reason, but that they do not both share in reason in the same way: one's nature is to prescribe, the other to obey and 30 listen; if there is something that is non-rational in a different way from this, let us disregard that part. It makes no difference if the soul is divided into parts or lacks parts, as it certainly has distinct capacities, including the ones mentioned—just as in a curve the concave and convex are inseparable, and the white and the straight 35 may be, though the straight is not white, except incidentally, and it is not essentially the same.

Any other part of the soul that there may be, the vegetative for example, is removed from consideration. But the parts we have mentioned *are* peculiar to the human soul. (And so, the excellences of the nutritive and growing parts are not human virtues, either). For, if <virtue belongs> to a human being *qua* human being, it necessarily 40 includes reasoning, as a starting-point of action; but reasoning con- **1220ᵃ** trols inclination and the affections, not reasoning itself, so the human

15

soul must have those parts. And as physical well-being is made up of the virtues of the several parts, so is the virtue of the soul, in so far as it is a complete whole.

5   Virtue is of two forms, virtue of character, and intellectual virtue. For we praise not only the just, but also the intelligent and the wise. For virtue, or its function, was assumed to be commended, but those things are not actualizations, though there exist actualizations of them. The intellectual virtues, having, as they do, a rational principle, such virtues belong to the part that has reason and prescribes to the

10 soul in so far as it possesses reason, whereas the virtues of character belong to the part that is non-rational, but whose nature is to follow the rational part; for we do not say what a man's character is like when we say that he is wise or clever, but when we say that he is gentle or daring.

    We must next ask first what virtue of character is, and,—since that is what this amounts to—what parts it has, and by what means

15 it is produced. Just as in other cases everyone goes in search with something in hand, we must so conduct our search that we try to arrive at what is said truly and clearly through things said truly but not clearly. At the moment we are placed as we should be if we knew that health was the best disposition of the body and that

20 Coriscus was the swarthiest person in the market-place; we do not know what either of these things is, but it is helpful, in order to know what each of them is, to be so placed.

    Let it be laid down, first, that the best disposition is produced by the best things, and that, with each thing, the best things are done from that thing's excellence; for example, the best exertions and

25 nourishment are those from which physical well-being results, and it is from well-being that men best exert themselves; moreover that any disposition is produced and destroyed by the same things, applied in a certain way—as we see health is by nourishment, exercise, and time of life. These things are evident from induction.

    Virtue, therefore, is the sort of disposition which is produced by

30 the best processes to do with the soul, and from which are done the best functions of the soul and its best affections; and it is by the same things that it is, in one manner, produced, and, in another, destroyed, and its employment has to do with the same things as

those by which it is promoted and destroyed: those in relation to which it disposes things in the best way. <That is> evidence that both virtue and vice have to do with pleasant and unpleasant things: for punishment operates through these, being as it is a kind of 35 therapy that works through opposites, as in other cases.

CHAPTER 2

It is evident then, that virtue of character has to do with pleasant and unpleasant things. Now *character* (*ēthos*), as the word itself indicates, is that which is developed from habit (*ethos*); and any- 1220^b thing is habituated which, as a result of guidance which is not innate, through being changed a certain way repeatedly, is eventually capable of acting in that way—something we do not see in inanimate things. (A stone, even if you throw it upwards ten thousand times, will never do so except under compulsion.) So let character be thus defined: 5 a quality of the part of the soul that is non-rational, but capable of following reason, in accordance with a prescriptive principle.

We must say, then, what it is in the soul in respect of which character-traits are qualified in a certain way. They are <qualified in a certain way> in respect of capacities for affections—capacities in virtue of which people are said to be susceptible to the affection —and in respect of the states in virtue of which people are said to be immune or not to those affections, because they experience them 10 in some particular fashion. Next the division, established elsewhere, of the affections, capacities, and states. By affections I mean such things as anger, fear, shame, desire—in general anything which, as such, gives rise usually to perceptual pleasure and pain. Now in respect of *these* there does not exist a quality—the soul is <just> affected— 15 but in respect of *capacities* there does exist a quality. I mean those capacities in respect of which those who are active in accordance with the affections are called, for example, irascible, phlegmatic, lustful, bashful, or shameless. States are what are responsible for whether these <affections> occur in accordance with reason, or the reverse, e.g. bravery, temperance, cowardice, or intemperance. 20

CHAPTER 3

Now that we have made these distinctions, we must note that in

1220^b

every divisible continuum there exists excess, deficiency, and a mean, and those both relative to one another and relative to us; in, for example, gymnastics, medicine, building, navigation, and in any
25 action whatever, whether scientific or unscientific, skilled or unskilled. For change is continuous, and action is change.

In all cases the mean relative to us is best; for that is as knowledge and rational principle prescribe. And in all cases that also pro-
30 duces the best state. And this is evident from induction and argument. For opposites rule out one another; the extremes are opposed both to one another and to the mean, because the mean is each one of the opposites in relation to the other: the equal is larger than the smaller, but smaller than the larger. So it must be the case that
35 virtue of character is concerned with certain means and is itself a certain mean state. So we must note what sort of mean state is virtue, and what are the sorts of mean it is concerned with.

We may take, for the sake of illustration, and examine, the items set out in the following table:

	irascibility	impassivity	gentle temper
	foolhardiness	cowardice	bravery
1221^a	shamelessness	thin-skinnedness	shame
	intemperance	insensibility	temperance
	envy	(unnamed)	fair-mindedness
	gain	disadvantage	justice
5	prodigality	meanness	liberality
	boastfulness	mock-modesty	truthfulness
	flattery	churlishness	friendliness
	servility	unaccommodatingness	dignity
	[softness	imperviousness	endurance]
10	vanity	meanness of spirit	pride
	ostentatious extravagance	niggardliness	magnificence
	[unscrupulousness	unworldliness	practical wisdom]

These affections, and others like them, occur in the soul; all of them are so described because of excess, in some cases, or deficiency, in others.
15 Thus the man who get angry more than he should, and more

18

quickly, and at more things than he should, is irascible, while the man
who falls short in what he is angry at, and when, and how, is impass-
ive; again, the man who does not fear the things he should, and
neither when nor as he should, is foolhardy, the man who fears
things he should not, and when he should not, and in a manner he
should not, is cowardly. Similarly, the man who desires what he
should not and goes to excess in every possible way is intemperate, 20
the man who falls short and does not desire even the better and the
natural, but is unsusceptible of feeling, like a stone, is insensible. The
man who snatches gain wherever he can is acquisitive, one who
accepts it from no source at all, or from very few sources, is self-
harming. The man who pretends to more things than he really has 25
is boastful, the man who claims less is mock-modest. The man who
praises another for more things than is right is a flatterer, one who
praises a man for fewer is churlish. To be over-ready to please is
servility, to do so rarely, and hardly at all, is unaccommodatingness.
The man who can stand no pain at all, even when it would be better
if he did, is soft; one who puts up with every pain alike, lacks a name,
strictly speaking, but by a transfer of application, is called hard and 30
gnarled and miserable. The man who thinks more highly of himself
than he should is vain, the man who thinks less highly is mean in
spirit. Again, the man who goes to excess in every expenditure is
prodigal, the one who is always deficient is mean; similarly, the
niggardly man and the pretentious: the one oversteps what is decent, 35
the other falls below it. The unscrupulous person is after advantage
in every way and from every source, the unworldly not even from
the right source. A man is envious through being distressed at good
fortune in more cases than he should. (Even those who deserve to
do well upset the envious when they do so.) The opposite is name- 40
less, but there is the man who goes too far in not being distressed 1221^b
even when people do well undeservedly; he is easy-going, like gluttons
when food is concerned, while the other man is hard and grudging.

    It would be superfluous to add to the definition, in each case, the
stipulation that matters are thus not incidentally. For no science, 5
either theoretical or productive, either in its pronouncements or its
actions, includes this stipulation in its definitions; this is to meet the
verbal chicaneries of technical virtuosos. Let virtue be defined in

general terms in this way; we can define it more precisely when we are speaking of the opposing states.

10 These affections themselves have different forms named because of differences in excess of time or intensity, or according to which of the things that produce the affection is their object. I mean, a man is called sharp-tempered for being affected more quickly than he should, bad-tempered and choleric for being so more than he should, bitter for being prone to maintain his anger, violent and 15 truculent for the retaliation resulting from the anger. Men are classified as gourmets or gluttons or dipsomaniacs according to which form of nourishment they have an affectible capacity to enjoy against reason.

We should not fail to notice that certain things cannot be taken as a matter of *how*, if *how* is taken to be undergoing it too much. 20 A man is not an adulterer through seducing married women more than he ought (there is no such thing): that is already a vice. For the affection is at the same time called <the affection it is> and said to be of such-and-such a sort. Likewise in the case of personal assault. That is why people dispute the accusation, saying that they had intercourse but were not committing adultery, as they were acting 25 in ignorance or were forced; or that they struck someone but did not assault him; the same thing holds in the other cases of that kind.

CHAPTER 4

Having reached these conclusions, we must go on to say that, as the soul has two parts, and virtues are classified on that basis, those that belong to the rational part being intellectual virtues, whose 30 function is truth concerning how things are or how they come about, those belonging to the part that is non-rational but possesses inclination being virtues-of-character (for not every part of the soul possesses inclination, if the soul has parts)—it follows that character is virtuous or bad by pursuing or avoiding certain pleasures and pains. 35 This is evident from the divisions made of affections, capacities, and states: capacities and states are defined by the affections, and affections are differentiated by pleasure and pain; so it follows both from these considerations and from the things that have been asserted before, that every virtue of character has to do with pleasures and pains. For, with any state of the soul, those things whose nature it is to make it better or worse are the things to which the nature of 40 the state relates and with which it is concerned. It is on account of 1222ᵃ pleasures and pains that we call men bad, for pursuing or avoiding them as they should not, or those they they should not. That is why everyone actually defines virtues in an off-hand manner as being insusceptibility and lack of disturbance in the sphere of pleasures and pains, vices in opposite terms. 5

CHAPTER 5

Virtue has been taken to be the state which makes people doers of what is best and through which men are best disposed in regard to what is best, and the best is that which is in accord with the right principle, this being the mean between excess and deficiency relative to us. So it would follow that virtue of character is essentially a 10 mean state in each case, and concerns certain means in pleasures and pains, and things pleasant and unpleasant. The mean state will sometimes be a mean state in the matter of pleasures, as will the excess or deficiency also, sometimes in pains, and sometimes in both. For the man who goes to excess in enjoyment, goes to excess 15 in the pleasant, the man who goes to excess in suffering pain does so in the opposite – and that either without qualification or relative to some limit, as when they do so not as most people do; but the good man does so as he should.

As there is no state from which the man who is in it will in some cases admit excess, in others deficiency, of the same thing, it follows 20 that, just as these objects are opposed both to one another and to the mean, so the states in question are opposed to one another and to virtue.

It happens, however, that in some cases all the oppositions are perfectly clear, sometimes those involving excess are, in some cases those involving deficiency. The cause of the difference is that the inequality or similarity in relation to the mean is not always of the 25 same degree: sometimes a man will change more quickly from excess to the mean state, sometimes more from deficiency; and it is the one who is further away who seems more opposed to it, just as in the case of the body, too, where exertions are concerned,

1222ᵃ

excess is a more healthy thing than deficiency, and closer to the
30 mean, whereas in diet, deficiency is more so than excess. So, too,
the states governing choice will be more healthy according to which
sort of decision is involved—in the one case it is those who favour
exertion, in the other those who are more restrained, and in one
35 case it is the man who abstains from exercise only, and not both
deviators from the mean, who is opposed to the man who attains
it, and opposed to what reason prescribes, whereas in the other case
it is the man of indulgence, not the man who fasts.

That comes about because human nature, right from the start, is
not distant from the mean in the same fashion in all cases: we are
not keen enough on physical exertion, too much so on indulgence.
The same holds, too, in the case of the soul. We oppose <to the
40 mean> that state in the direction of which we, and most men, are
more inclined to err—for example, anger is opposed to gentle temper,
and the angry man to the gentle-tempered. The other deviant state is
overlooked, as if it did not exist; because it is so rare it is not observed.
1222ᵇ All the same, there is such a thing as excess even in the direction of
being accommodating and conciliatory, and not getting angry when
beaten. But such men are few; everyone is more inclined to the other
direction. And that is why anger tends to retaliate.

5 Now that the distinctions between the states in respect of each of
the affections have been made, both the excesses and deficiencies
and those of the opposed states in which people are in accord with
the right principle (what the right principle is, and what limit we
must look to in saying what the mean is, we must investigate later),
it is clear that all the virtues of character and vices have to do with
10 excesses and deficiencies of pleasures and pains, and pleasures and
pains result from the states and affections we have mentioned. Now
the best disposition in each case is the mean one. So it is evident that
all or some of these mean states will be virtues.

CHAPTER 6

15 Let us then take a new starting-point to the ensuing inquiry. All
substances are naturally starting-points of a sort, which is why each
one can actually generate many things of the same sort—for a human
being generates human beings, and, in general, an animal generates

animals and a plant plants. A human being, moreover, is a starting-point of some actions, and he alone of animals; for of nothing else should we say that it *acted*.

Among starting-points, those that are of that sort—those from 20 which changes first arise—are called *controlling* starting-points, and most correctly those from which results what cannot be otherwise, the sort of control with which the god perhaps governs. In the case of unchanging starting-points, mathematical ones, for instance, there is no *controlling*, though they are called 'starting-points' on the strength of a similarity; with these, too, if the starting-point were 25 different, everything demonstrated would change, though they do not change one another where one thing is refuted by another, except through refuting the hypothesis and demonstrating by means of it. A human being is the starting-point of a certain kind of change; for an action is a change.

Since, as in other cases, the starting-point is a cause of those things that are or come about because of it, we must understand it 30 as we do in the case of demonstrations. For if it is necessary, if a triangle contains two right angles, that a quadrilateral has four, it is clear that the cause of this is that a triangle has two. If a triangle is different, the quadrilateral must be different too; if the triangle has 35 three right angles, the quadrilateral has six, and if the triangle has four, the quadrilateral eight. And if a triangle is of such and such a character, and could not be different from that, the other must also be of such-and-such a character. It is evident from the *Analytics* that what we are attempting to show is necessarily the case; here we can say precisely neither that it is nor that it is not so, except this much: for if nothing else is the cause of a triangle's being so, this 40 must be a sort of starting-point and cause of what follows.

So that if some of the things that are are capable of being in opposite states, their starting-points must also be of that kind. For, what follows from what holds of necessity must itself be necessary, whereas **1223ᵃ** what results from these is capable of turning out in opposite ways, —and many of such things are in men's power and of such things they themselves are the starting-points. So it is clear that all those 5 actions that man is a starting-point of, and controls, are capable of coming about or not, and, with those things at least that he controls whether they are or are not, it is in his own power whether they come about or not. All those things that are in his own power either to do or not do he himself is the cause of, and all those things that he is the cause of, are in his own power.

Now since virtue and vice and the resulting deeds are in some
10 cases commended and in others blamed (for blame and commendation are given not to things that occur of necessity or by luck or in the course of nature, but to all the things we ourselves are a cause of; since for things that someone else is the cause of, he gets the praise and blame), it is evident that virtue and vice have to do with those things of which a man himself is the cause, a starting-point of
15 actions. So we must determine of which a man himself is the cause, and a starting-point. Now we all agree that all those things that are voluntary and in accordance with an individual's choice he is a cause of, while those that are involuntary, he is not a cause of. And all the things that he does having chosen to do them, he actually does
20 voluntarily. So it is evident that both virtue and vice must concern the things that are voluntary.

CHAPTER 7

So we must determine what the voluntary is and what the involuntary is, and what choice is, since these set limits to virtue and vice. We must first look into the voluntary and the involuntary. Now it would seem that it is one of three things—either inclination or choice or
25 thought—the voluntary being in accordance with one of them, the involuntary contrary to one of them. But inclination has three divisions—wish, spirit, and desire. So these must be distinguished; we first consider accordance with desire.

It would seem that everything in accordance with desire is volun-
30 tary. For everything involuntary seems to be compelled, and what is compelled is unpleasant, as is everything which man are forced to do or undergo, as Euenus says:

> For everything unpleasant is,
> That men are forced to do

So that if a thing is unpleasant, it is compelled, and if compelled, unpleasant. But anything contrary to desire is unpleasant (because

24

desire is for the pleasant), so it must be compelled and involuntary. 35
Thus that which is in accordance with desire is voluntary, the voluntary and the involuntary being opposed to one another.

Again, vice always makes a man less just; incontinence appears to be a vice; the incontinent man is of a sort to act against reason, in accordance with desire, and he acts incontinently when he is active in accordance with desire; and unjust action is voluntary. So that the incontinent man will act unjustly through acting in accordance with **1223^b** desire. So the incontinent man will act voluntarily, and what is in accordance with desire will be voluntary. It would indeed be strange if those who became incontinent thereby became more just.

In view of *those* considerations it would seem that what is in accordance with desire is voluntary, but if we look at *these* the opposite appears to be the case. Anything which a man does volun- 5
tarily he does wishing to do it, and what he wishes to do he does voluntarily. But no one wishes for what he believes to be bad. But the man who acts incontinently does not do what he wishes to do, as to act, as a result of desire, against what one believes to be best is to act incontinently. So it will follow that the same man acts voluntarily and involuntarily at the same time; which is impossible.

Again, the continent man will act justly, and more so than the 10
incontinent man. For continence is a virtue, and virtue makes men more just. A man acts continently when he acts in accordance with reasoning against desire. So, if acting justly is voluntary, as acting 15
unjustly is (for both of these seem to be voluntary, and, if one is voluntary, the other must be also), but what is against desire is involuntary, the same man will at the same time be acting voluntarily and involuntarily.

The same argument holds for spirit also. For continence and incontinence seem to concern spirit, as well as desire; and what is contrary to spirit is unpleasant, and its suppression is compelled, so 20
that if the compelled is involuntary, what is in accordance with spirit must all be voluntary. (It is likely that Heraclitus has in view the strength of spirit when he says that the restraining of it is unpleasant. 'For it's a hard thing', he says, 'to fight against spirit; for it buys victory at the price of life.') If it is impossible for the same man to 25
do the same thing voluntarily and involuntarily at the same time in

respect of the same <aspect of the situation>, what is in accordance with wish is voluntary rather than what is in accordance with spirit or desire. Evidence for that is that we do many things voluntarily without either anger or desire.

30 It remains therefore to investigate whether the wished for and the voluntary are the same thing. That too seems impossible, for it is our assumption, and seems to be the case, that vice makes people less just, and incontinence appears to be a form of vice, whereas <on the assumption under discussion> the opposite will follow. For no one wishes for things that he believes to be bad, yet a man who becomes incontinent does such things. If therefore acting unjustly is voluntary, and the voluntary is in accordance with wish, when a man

35 becomes incontinent, he will no longer act unjustly, but be more just than he was before he become incontinent. And that is impossible.

CHAPTER 8

So it is clear that the voluntary does not consist in acting in accordance with inclination, nor is that which is against it involuntary; that it is not acting in accordance with choice either, is evident from the following considerations: what is in accordance with wish has not

1224ᵃ been shown to be involuntary; rather everything that is wished for is also voluntary. (It has been demonstrated only that it is *possible* to act voluntarily even in the absence of wish; but many things that we wish to do, we do in a flash, yet no one chooses in a flash.)

5 If it is necessary that the voluntary should be one of those three things, being in accordance either with inclination or choice or thought, but it is not two of them, it follows that the voluntary consists in action accompanied by thought of some kind. Now let us carry the discussion foward a little and complete the task of distinguishing the voluntary and involuntary; for it seems that the doing of something under compulsion and doing it not under com-

10 pulsion are relevant to what has been said: we say that what is compelled is involuntary and what is involuntary is always compelled. So we must first investigate what *under compulsion* is and how it is related to the voluntary and involuntary.

It appears that the compelled and the forced and compulsion and force are opposed in the case of action to the voluntary and to

persuasion; though quite generally we speak of compulsion and force 15
also where inanimate things are concerned: after all, we say that
under compulsion, and when forced, a stone travels upwards and fire
downwards. When, however, they travel according to their nature
and their essential impulse, they are not said to travel under compulsion though not voluntarily either; that term of the opposition
lacks a name. When they travel against that impulse, we say that 20
they do so under compulsion. Similarly, with animate things, including animals, we see them doing and undergoing many things under
compulsion, when something external moves them against their internal impulse. In inanimate things the starting-point is single, in animate
things there is more than one; for inclination and reason are not
always in harmony. So, with animals other <than human beings>, 25
the compelled is all of one kind, as it is with inanimate things (they
do not have reason and inclination each opposed to the other—they
live by inclination); in a man, however, both elements are present, at
a certain age—that, in fact, to which action also is ascribed. For we
do not say that a child acts, or a brute either; only someone who is
already doing things from reasoning.

Now it appears that the compelled is always unpleasant: no one 30
acts under compulsion, but with enjoyment. That is why the most
controversy arises over the continent and the incontinent man. For
each of them acts with impulses contrary to himself; so that it is by
compulsion, as they say, that the continent man drags himself away
from desires for pleasant things (as he feels pain, when he drags him- 35
self away, against the opposing inclination) and under compulsion
the incontinent <goes> against reasoning. The incontinent man
seems to suffer less pain, in that desire is for the pleasant, which he
follows with enjoyment, and thus the incontinent man <acts> voluntarily rather, and not under compulsion, because it is not unpleasant. But persuasion is opposed to compulsion and force. It is
towards what he has already been persuaded to do that the continent
man proceeds, voluntarily, not under compulsion. Desire, on the **1224ᵇ**
other hand, as it has no share in reason, drives one without having
persuaded.

We have said that these men seem to be very close to acting
under compulsion and involuntarily, and the reason for that—a

5 certain similarity to that 'under compulsion' which we use of inanimate things also; all the same, if the further element in the earlier
definition is added, the problem we have stated is solved. For when
something is moved or kept at rest by something external, against
the internal impulse, it is, we say, under compulsion, and when that
is not so, it is not under compulsion. Now within the continent and
the incontinent man it is his own impulse that drives him (for he has

10 both tendencies); so neither is under compulsion, but, as far as the
above argument goes, <each> would be acting voluntarily, and
would not be forced to act. For we call force that external starting-
point of change which impedes or generates change against impulse,
as if a man seized another's hand and struck him in opposition both
to wish and desire; but when the starting-point is within, it is not
under compulsion.

15 Moreover, both pleasure and pain are present in both of them.
The man acting continently suffers pain in that he is even now acting
against his desire, and gets enjoyment from the expectation that he
will benefit in the future or from the fact that he is even now ben-
efiting from being healthy; while the incontinent man gets enjoy-

20 ment from getting what he desires when he acts incontinently, but
suffers pain from an expectation, as he thinks that he will fare ill.

Thus there is some reason to say that each of them acts under
compulsion, and that because of reasoning and because of inclination
each sometimes acts involuntarily; for each of those two, because
they are distinct, is overcome by the other. And so, they transfer

25 it to the whole soul when they see something of that sort among
the soul's elements. In the case of the parts it is possible to say this;
but the whole soul, both of the continent man and the incontinent,
acts voluntarily; neither acts under compulsion, though an element
in them does, given that by nature we possess both parts.

For reason is among the natural starting-points, since it will be

30 present if growth is allowed to proceed, and is not stunted; desire,
too, because it is there straightaway and present from birth. And it
is more or less by these two marks that we distinguish what <belongs>
naturally: everything that is there straightaway as soon as something
comes to be, and all that occurs to us if growth is allowed to proceed

35 normally—things such as greying hair, ageing, and the like. So that

each of the two men, in a way, does not act in accordance with nature, though, without qualification, each *does* act in accordance with it, but not the same nature <in each case>. These, then, are the problems over the incontinent and the continent man — whether both act under compulsion or one of them does, with the consequence that either they do not act voluntarily, or they act at the same time under compulsion and voluntarily, and that if what occurs under compulsion is involuntary, they act at the same time voluntarily and involuntarily. It is pretty evident from what has been said **1225ᵃ** how we should deal with this.

In another way, men are said to act under compulsion and to be forced to act though reason and inclination are *not* in disharmony, and when they do what they take to be both unpleasant and bad, yet, if they do not do it, flogging or imprisonment or death await 5 them. They certainly say they are forced to do these things. Or is that not so? Do they all rather do the thing itself voluntarily. For it is open to them not to do it, but to endure the other experience.

Alternatively, someone might assent to some of these things, but not to others. All things of that kind that are such that it is within someone's power whether they come about or not — even if he does 10 things that he does not wish to do — he does voluntarily and not under compulsion; but things of that sort which are not within his power are, in a way, under compulsion, though not so without qualification, because he does not choose the actual thing that he does, but the thing for the sake of which he does it; since in these, also, there is some difference. If someone kills in order to prevent someone from catching hold of him, it would be absurd if he said 15 that he did so under compulsion, and because he was forced to do it; the evil which he is going to suffer if he does not do the thing has to be greater and more unpleasant. For a man will, in this way, be acting because he is forced, and under compulsion, or not naturally at any rate, whenever he does evil for the sake of a good, or the removal of a greater evil, and he will be acting involuntarily, as those things are not within his control.

That is why many classify even love as involuntary, and certain 20 cases of anger and certain natural states as being too strong for <human> nature; and we regard them as being pardonable, as being of

1225^a

such a nature as to constrain nature. And a man would appear to be acting under compulsion and involuntarily more when he does so to avoid suffering a severe pain than when he does so to avoid a slight one, and, in general, more when he does so to avoid pain than when
25 he does so to get enjoyment. For what is in one's power, on which the whole issue turns, is what one's nature is able to withstand. And what it is not able to withstand, and is not within the scope of one's natural inclination or reasoning, is not in one's power. That is why even with those who are possessed by divine inspiration, and utter prophecies, though they produce a work of thought, we say that it
30 was not under their control to say what they said or do what they did. Nor <is it done> as a result of desire. Hence certain thoughts and certain affections are not under our control, or the actions that occur in accordance with such thoughts and calculations; as Philolaos said, some reasonings are stronger than we are. So, if it was necessary to examine the voluntary and involuntary in relation to what is under
35 compulsion, let them be distinguished in this way. (For the arguments that are the greatest obstacle to the voluntary ... as acting under compulsion, but not voluntarily.)

CHAPTER 9

Now that that discussion is complete, and the voluntary has been
1225^b defined neither by inclination nor by choice, it remains to define what *in accordance with thought* is. The voluntary seems to be the opposite of the involuntary, and <acting> knowing either whom or with what or for what result — thus sometimes a man knows that it is his father, but not that he is aiming to kill him, but <instead thinks that he is acting> to save him, as in the case of the daughters of Pelias,
5 or he thinks that this is a drink, but in fact it was a love potion, or that it is wine when it was aconite — is opposed to <acting> in ignorance of whom and with what and what, because of ignorance, not incidentally; but what is <done> because of ignorance of what and with what and whom, is involuntary; so its opposite is voluntary.

So whatever a man does — not in ignorance, and through his own agency — when it is in his power not to do it, must be voluntary, and
10 that is what the voluntary is; but what <he does> in ignorance and because of ignorance, he does involuntarily. But since knowing and

understanding is of two kinds, one *having* and the other *using* knowledge, the man who has knowledge but does not use it could in a way
rightly be said to have acted in ignorance, but in another way not;
for example, if he failed to use his knowledge because of negligence.
Likewise, too, someone would be blamed even if he did not have it,
if it is what was easy or essential that he fails to have because of 15
negligence or pleasure or pain. So let these things be added to the
definition.

CHAPTER 10

Let this be enough on the distinction between the voluntary and the
involuntary; let us now say something about choice, after raising
problems in argument about it. For one might hesitate about the
genus in which it belongs and where to place it, and about whether 20
the chosen is or is not the same as the voluntary. In particular, some
people say — and on examination it would seem to be the case — that
choice is one of two things, either opinion or inclination; for both of
those things appear to accompany choice.

However, that it is not inclination is clear; for it would then be
wish or desire or spirit, since no one has an inclination without 25
experiencing one of those. Now spirit and desire belong even to
brutes, but choice does not. Further, even in the case of those to
whom both these things belong, they make many choices without
either spirit or desire; and when men are subject to affections they
are not choosing, they are resisting <the affections>. Again, desire 30
and spirit are always accompanied by pain, but we make many
choices without pain. Nor is wish the same thing as choice, either.
For men knowingly wish for some things that are impossible, such
as to rule over the whole of mankind and to be immortal, whereas
no one chooses them unless he is ignorant of their impossibility, 35
nor, in general, those things that are possible, but which he does not
believe are within his power to do or not to do. So one thing is clear,
that the chosen must be one of the things within the agent's power.

Similarly, it is evident that it is not opinion either, nor quite **1226ᵃ**
generally something that someone believes; the chosen was found to
be something in one's own power, but we opine many things that are
not in our power, for example that the diagonal is incommensurable.

1226ᵃ

Again, choice is not true or false. Nor therefore is it an opinion about
5 the things in one's own power, that whereby we in fact believe that
we should or should not do something.

This point holds alike of opinion and of wish: no one chooses an
end, only the things that contribute to the end. I mean, for example,
no one chooses to be healthy, rather he chooses to walk or to sit with
10 a view to health, nor again to be happy, but rather to engage in
commerce or take a risk with a view to being happy; and in general
a man evidently always chooses something, and chooses for the sake
of something; and the second is that for the sake of which he chooses
something else, and the first, what he chooses for the sake of another
thing. It is the end, above all, that he wishes for, and he judges that he
15 ought to be healthy and to act well. Thus it is clear from these considerations that choice is different both from opinion and from wish.
For wish and opinion are pre-eminently of the end, choice is not.

It is evident, then, that choice is not wish or judgement or opinion
of any kind. How does it differ from those, and how is it related to
20 the voluntary? It will then be evident also what choice is. Among the
things that can either be or not be, some are such that it is possible
to deliberate about them; about some it is not possible. For some
are capable either of being or not being, yet their coming to be is
not in our power, but, some come to be naturally, others on account
25 of other causes. About such things no one would attempt to deliberate unless in ignorance. Those things, however, which are such that
not only can they either be or not be, but also men can deliberate
about them, are those which are within our power to do or not do.

Thus we do not deliberate about affairs in India, nor how the
30 circle is to be squared; for the former of those is not in our power,
33 the latter not realizable by action at all, whereas things that are
31 chosen and realizable are among those that are in our power. But
nor do we deliberate about all the things that *are* in our power —
32 and that makes it evident also that choice is not any sort of opinion
33 either. This might lead someone to be puzzled about why doctors
deliberate about things that fall under the science that they possess,
35 but scribes do not. The reason is that errors occur in two ways (we
err either in calculation or in perception when actually doing the
thing); in medicine it is possible to make a mistake in both ways,

whereas in the case of a scribe's skill, it is possible only in perception **1226^b** and action, and if they reflect upon that, there will be no end to it.

Since, then, choice is not either opinion or wish, neither one of them nor both (no one chooses in a flash, but it seems that men act —and wish—in a flash), it must result from both of these; for both of them occur in one who chooses.

How should our discussion proceed from here? To some extent 5 the word 'choice' itself shows us. Choice (*prohairesis*) is a taking (*hairesis*), but not without qualification—a taking of one thing before (*pro*) another; that is not possible without examination and deliberation. So choice comes from deliberative belief.

No one deliberates about the end—that is there for everyone; 10 men deliberate about the things that lead towards it, whether this or that contributes to its attainment, or else, when that has been decided, how it will come about. We all continue deliberating until we carry the starting-point of the process of change back to ourselves. If, then, no one makes a choice without preliminary deliberation on 15 whether it would be better or worse to act thus, and one deliberates about the things, among those that are capable of being or not being, that are in our power and lead towards the end, it is evident that choice is deliberative inclination for that which is in our power. For we all deliberate about those things that we also choose, though we do not choose all the things that we deliberate about (by a 'deliberative' inclination, I mean one whose starting-point and cause is 20 deliberation), and our inclination results from deliberation.

So choice is not present in other animals, nor at every time of life, nor in a human being no matter what state he is in; for deliberation is not, either, nor an opinion about the why; an opinion about whether something should be done or not may well be present to many people, though not through reasoning. For that part of the 25 soul is deliberative which is capable of discerning a cause: the reason for the sake of which—which is one of the causes—'cause' being something because-of-which. And we say that that for the sake of which something is or comes to be is a cause—for instance, the carrying of goods is a cause of walking if it is for the sake of that that a man walks. That is why those who have no goal before them are not in a position to deliberate.

1226^b

30 So that, since a man voluntarily does or abstains from doing that which is in his power to do or not to do if it is through his own agency and not in ignorance that he acts or abstains from acting—we do many things of that sort not after deliberation and without premeditation—it follows that what is chosen is all voluntary, but 35 what is voluntary is not all chosen, and everything done from choice is voluntary, but what is voluntary is not all from choice. These considerations make this clear, and at the same time the fact that legislators are right to distinguish some deeds as voluntary and **1227^a** others as involuntary and others as premeditated; for even if they are not wholly correct, they are on to the truth in a way.

About this we shall be saying something in the examination of justice. But it is evident that choice is neither simply wish nor 5 opinion, but opinion *together with* wish, whenever as a result of deliberation they are brought to a conclusion.

Since one who deliberates always deliberates with something in view, and there is always some goal with reference to which he inquires what is useful, no one deliberates about the end, this being a starting-point and hypothesis, like hypotheses in the theoretical 10 sciences (a little was said about them at the start of our discussion, and they are treated in detail in the *Analytics*) but everyone's investigation, whether he is using some expertise or not, is about what contributes to the end—for example, those deliberating whether to go to war or not.

But before the process begins there will be that because of which, 15 i.e. *that for whose sake*—for example, wealth or pleasure or whatever else of that kind happens to be *that for whose sake*. For one who deliberates, if he has carried his inquiry back from the end, deliberates about what contributes to it, in order to bring the process back to himself, or what he can do himself towards the end.

The end is naturally always good, the good they deliberate about in a particular application: the doctor would deliberate whether to 20 administer a drug, and the general where to set up his camp, and to them the end, what is best without qualification, is good; what is against nature, on the other hand, and involves corruption is not the good, but the apparent good. The reason is that it is not possible to use some of the things that there are except for what they naturally

34

exist for—sight for example; it is not possible to see what is not an object of sight, nor hear what is not an object of hearing; but <it *is* 25 possible> to produce, by means of a science, that which is not what the science is a science of. For the same science is not a science of disease in the same way as it is the science of health; it is the science of one in accordance with nature, of the other against nature. Similarly, too, wish is naturally of the good, but also, against nature, of the bad, and one naturally wishes for the good, but, against nature, 30 and through corruption, also the bad.

However, the destruction and corruption of anything is not into any arbitrary state, but into the opposite ones and the intermediates on the way to them. For it is impossible to get outside these, as error also, when it occurs, takes place into the opposite state, where there is one, not into any arbitrary state, and to those opposite states that 35 are opposed with respect to the knowledge. So both the error and the choice must be from the mean towards the opposites (and more and less are opposed to the mean). The cause is the pleasant and the unpleasant; for the situation is that the pleasant appears good to the soul, and the pleasanter better, the unpleasant bad, and the more unpleasant worse. So from this, too, it is evident that virtue and vice 1227^b have to do with pleasures and pains. They are in fact concerned with things chosen, and choice has to do with the good and bad, and what appears thus, and such, naturally, are pleasure and pain.

So it follows, since virtue of character itself is a mean state and 5 always concerned with pleasures and pains, while vice lies in excess and deficiency, and has to do with the same things as virtue, that virtue is that state of character which chooses the mean, relative to us, in things pleasant and unpleasant, all those in respect of which a man is said to have a certain sort of character according as he enjoys 10 them or suffers pain from them. (For the man who is fond of sweet things, or the one fond of bitter ones, is not said to be a certain sort of person in regard to *character*.)

CHAPTER 11

Now that we have defined those things, we must say whether virtue makes choice free from error and the end correct, in such a way that one chooses with a view to the thing that one should, or whether, as

15 some people think, <it makes> reason <correct>. But *that* state
is continence, for continence does not corrupt reason. But virtue is
different from continence. We must speak about them later, as,
with those who do think that virtue renders reason correct, that is
why they do so. For continence is of that kind, and among the
things that are commended. Let us present our view after first
20 raising some puzzles. For it is possible for the goal to be right, but
for error to occur in what lies on the way to the goal; it is possible
also for the goal to be mistaken, but for the things leading towards
it to be correct, and also for neither to be correct. Does virtue make
the goal correct, or what lies on the way to it? We assert that it is the
goal, because of this there is no inference or reasoning. Let us, then,
accept this as a starting-point.

25 For neither does the doctor look into whether his patient should
be healthy or not, but rather whether he should walk about or not,
nor does the gymnast consider whether he should be fit or not, but
whether or not he should engage in wrestling. In the same way, no
other science is concerned with the end; as in the theoretical sciences,
30 the hypotheses are starting-points, so in the productive sciences, the
end is the starting-point and hypothesis. Given that this thing needs
to be healthy, if that is to come about, such-and-such must be the
case, as, in the other sphere, if a triangle contains two right angles,
so-and-so must be the case. Of *thought*, then, it is the end that is
the starting-point, but of *action* it is the terminus of thought.

So, if either reason or, if not that, virtue, is the cause of every
35 correctness, it must be because of virtue that the end is correct,
though not the things on the way to it. The thing-for-the-sake-of-
which is the end. For every choice is *of* something and for the sake
of something. The mean is the-thing-for-the-sake-of-which, of which
virtue is the cause, by choosing with a view to that. However, choice
is not of that, but of things with a view to it. It belongs to another
40 capacity to hit upon all that must be done for the sake of the end;
1228^a but that the end of the choice is correct—of this virtue is the cause.

And for this reason, it is from his choosing that we judge what
sort of person someone is; that is, what that for whose sake he does
something is, not *what* he does. Likewise, vice, too, makes choice a
5 choice with a view to the opposite things. So if someone, when it is

in his power to do fine things and abstain from reprehensible ones, does the opposite, it is evident that he is not a virtuous man. So vice and virtue must be voluntary, for there is no necessity to do vicious things. That is why vice is blamed and why virtue is commended; 10 for reprehensible and bad acts that are involuntary are not blamed, nor are good ones praised; only the voluntary ones are.

Moreover, we all offer praise and blame looking more at the choice than the actual deeds (though, even so, the actual exercise of the virtue is more worth having than the virtue itself), because men do bad acts when forced to do so, but no one chooses under 15 those conditions. Another thing is that it is because it is not easy to discern what sort of choice it is that we are forced to judge from the deeds what sort of person someone is. So the activity is more worth having, but the choice is commended more. All this follows from what was assumed, and also tallies with what appears to be ·he case.

BOOK EIGHT

CHAPTER 1

1246ª Someone might wonder if it is possible to use each thing both for its natural purpose and otherwise—and that either *as itself* or incidentally—for example eyes, to see or to mis-see, by twisting them, so that one thing appears as two. Now these were both uses of an eye

30 *as an eye*; but another <use of an eye is to use it> incidentally, for example for selling or eating.

Likewise also, knowledge: <it will be possible to use it> truly, and in order to err—for example, when someone voluntarily writes incorrectly, he will be using the capacity as ignorance, inverting its

35 use, as dancing girls use their foot as a hand and their hand as a foot. So if all virtues are forms of knowledge, it would be possible also to use justice as injustice. So the man who does unjust things will act unjustly from justice, just as he will be doing ignorant things from

1246ᵇ knowledge. But if that is impossible, it is clear that the virtues cannot be forms of knowledge. Nor, if it is impossible to be ignorant from knowledge but only to err and do the same things as <one would> from ignorance, will someone act from justice as <he would> from injustice.

But since wisdom is knowledge, and something true, it will do the

5 same thing also; for it would be possible <to act> foolishly from wisdom and to do the same erroneous things the foolish man does. If the use of each thing as itself were single, they would also be acting wisely in so acting. Now in the case of the other forms of knowledge, another superior form produces the distortion; but what is superior

10 to that which is superior to all of them? For it certainly cannot any longer be knowledge or intelligence. Nor <can it be> virtue, either, because it uses that; for the virtue of the governing element employs the virtue of what is governed.

What, then, is it? Or is it as incontinence is said to be a vice of the non-rational part of the soul, and it is said that the incontinent man, possessing intelligence, is intemperate? But, if it is the case that, if

15 desire is strong, it will distort, and the wisdom of the incontinent man, distorted by the non-rational part, will reach the opposite

38

conclusions, it is evident that, if there is virtue in this part, and ignorance in the rational part, the other will be reversed. So it will be possible to use justice not justly and virtue viciously and wisdom foolishly.

So there will be the opposite cases, also. For it would be strange if ever vice, when it comes to be present in the non-rational part of the 20 soul, *will* change the virtue in the rational part, and will cause it to be ignorant, yet virtue in the non-rational part of the soul, when ignorance is present in the rational part, will *not* change that and make it judge wisely and as it should, and again wisdom in the rational part of soul will not make intemperance in the non-rational act temperately, as continence seems to do. So it will be possible also <to act> wisely from ignorance.

These consequences are strange, especially using ignorance wisely; 25 for we never see that in other cases—just as intemperance changes knowledge of medicine or of writing, but not ignorance, if it is opposed, because the additional element is not there; rather, virtue 30 in general is related to vice in this way; for the just man can do all the things that the unjust man can do, and generally the incapacity is included in the capacity.

So it is clear that, at the same time, men are wise and their other states are good, and the view of Socrates is correct, that nothing is stronger than wisdom; but in saying that it is knowledge, he was not 35 correct; for it is a virtue, and not knowledge, but another form of understanding . . .

CHAPTER 2

Since not only does practical wisdom produce welfare and virtue, but we say also that the fortunate prosper, as if good fortune produces **1247ᵃ** welfare and the same things that knowledge does, we must inquire whether it is by nature that one man is fortunate, another unfortunate, and how the matter stands in regard to these men.

For, that some people are fortunate we see: though foolish, many people are successful in matters in which luck is decisive, others also 5 in matters in which skill is involved, but there is a large element of luck, for example in generalship and navigation. Is it then because of some state that these men are fortunate, or is it not through being

1247ª

themselves of a certain kind that they score successes? For, as things are, that is what people think—as if some are fortunate by nature,
10 and nature makes some people to be of a certain sort, and those are different right from birth and, just as some people are blue-eyed and others black-eyed through being necessarily thus because of being such-and-such a kind, so are people fortunate and unfortunate.

For that it is not by practical wisdom that they succeed, is evident. For practical wisdom is not irrational but has a principle on account
15 of which it acts thus and so, but these people would not be able to say why they succeed; for, <if they could>, it would be skill. For it is clear that, being foolish—not that they are so about other things —that would be not at all strange (Hippocrates, for example, was a geometer, but in other matters he seemed to be stupid and foolish, and when he sailed he was cheated of much money by the customs
20 men in Byzantium, as a result of unworldliness, as they say)—but that they are foolish even about those matters in which they enjoy good fortune. For in navigation, it is not the most skilful who are fortunate, but, as in dice-throwing, one man scores nothing, another throws a naturally fortunate man's throw. Or is it through being favoured, as they say, by a god and because the source of success is
25 external, in the way that a ship badly constructed often sails better, though not because of itself but because it has a good steersman? However, in that way the fortunate man has the divine being as a good steersman, but it is strange that a god or divine being should favour such a man, rather than the best and the wisest. So if success
30 must come about either by nature or intelligence or some guidance, and it is not two of these, the fortunate must be so by nature.

Nature, however, is the cause of what occurs in the same way always or for the most part, whereas luck is the opposite. So if to prosper contrary to expectation seems to belong to luck—but if <someone is fortunate>, he is so by luck—the cause would not
35 seem to be the sort of thing that is the cause of what is always, or usually, the same. Further, if it is because he is of such-and-such a sort that a man prospers or comes to grief, just as it is because a man is dark-eyed that he does not see clearly, then luck is not the cause, but nature; so he is not fortunate, but, as it were, naturally well endowed. Thus what we ought to say is that those whom we

call fortunate are not so by luck. They are *not*, therefore, fortunate; it is those for whom good luck is a cause of goods that are fortunate. **1247^b**

If that is so, will luck not exist at all, or will it exist, but not be a cause? In fact, it must both exist and be a cause. It will therefore also be a cause of good things, or bad, for some people. Whether we must eliminate it altogether, and say that nothing happens by luck, though we, when there is some other cause, because we do not see 5 it, say that luck is a cause – that is why, when they define luck, they lay down that luck is a cause not open to reasoning by human calculation as if it were some nature – that, however, would be another problem.

Since we see some people enjoying good fortune once, why should they not succeed again, for the same reason, and yet again? For the 10 same thing has the same cause. So this will not belong to luck. But when the same thing results from causes that are indefinite and indeterminate, it may be a good thing or a bad thing for someone, but there will be no knowledge of it, knowledge from experience, as otherwise some people could learn to be fortunate, or indeed all forms of knowledge would, as Socrates said, be forms of good 15 fortune. What, then, prevents such things from befalling someone many times in succession, not because he is of such-and-such a sort, but as it would be always to make lucky throws of the dice?

What follows then? Are there not impulses in the soul, some issuing from reasoning, others from non-rational calculation, and are not those, at least by nature, prior? For if by nature our desire is an 20 inclination for the pleasant, by nature, at any rate, all our desires proceed towards the good. So, if some people are naturally well endowed (as untaught singers, who lack knowledge of how to sing, are well endowed in that respect) and, without reason, are impelled in accordance with nature, and desire both what they ought and when they ought and as they ought – these people will succeed even 25 if they are actually foolish and unreasoning, as men may actually sing well who are not capable of teaching it; but certainly it is such men who are fortunate – men who succeed most of the time without reasoning. It is therefore by nature that the fortunate are fortunate.

Or is good fortune <so> called in several ways? For some things are done from impulse, and when people have chosen to do them, 30

41

1247ᵇ

some are not—the opposite holds. And in *those* cases, if they succeed in circumstances in which they seem to reason badly, we
say that they have had good fortune; and again in those cases, if
they wanted another good, or a smaller one, than they got. With
those people therefore, it is possible that they have good fortune as
a result of nature; for the impulse and the inclination, being for
35 what was required, prospered, though the reasoning was idle. And
these people, when reasoning appears not to be correct, but in fact
desire is the cause of it, are rescued because the desire is correct.
(And yet, on some occasions, from desire a man reasoned thus—
and came to grief.) But in the other cases, how can there be good
fortune in accordance with a good natural endowment of inclination
1248ᵃ and desire? But then either good fortune both in this case and in
that are the same, or there is more than one form of good fortune,
and luck is of two kinds.

Since we see some people having good fortune contrary to every
sort of knowledge and correct reasonings, it is evident that something
5 else is the cause of the good fortune. But is that good fortune? Or is
it not, if a man desires the things he should and when he should, a
man for whom human calculation, at any rate, is not the cause of
this? For that for which indeed the desire is natural is not altogether
without reason, but it is distorted by something; however, he seems
to have good fortune, because luck is a cause of things contrary to
10 reason, and that is contrary to reason, since it is contrary to knowledge and the universal. But, as it seems, it is not by luck, but appears
to be for this reason. So this argument does not demonstrate that
people have good fortune by nature, but that not all who seem to
have good fortune prosper by luck, and not through nature; nor that
luck is not a cause of anything, but that it is not a cause of all the
things it seems to be.
15 The question might be raised 'Is luck the cause of this very thing
—desiring what one should or when one should?' Or will luck in
that way be the cause of everything? For it will be the cause both
of thinking and deliberating; for a man who deliberates has not delib-
erated already before deliberating—there is a certain starting-point.
20 Nor did he think, after thinking already before thinking, and so on to
infinity. Intelligence, therefore, is not the starting-point of thinking,

nor is counsel the starting-point of deliberation. So what else is there save luck? Thus everything will be by luck. Or is there some starting-point beyond which there is no other, and this—because it is essentially of such a sort—can have such an effect? But what is being sought is this: What is the starting-point of change in the soul? It 25 is now evident: as it is a god that moves in the whole universe, so it is in the soul; for, in a sense, the divine element in us moves everything; but the starting-point of reason is not reason but something superior. What then could be superior to knowledge and intelligence but a god? For virtue is an instrument of intelligence.

And for that reason, as I was saying earlier, they are called fortu- 30 nate who succeed in what they initiate though they lack reason. And it is of no use for them to deliberate; for they possess such a starting-point as is superior to intelligence and deliberation (others have reason but do not have this), and a divine inspiration, but cannot do this; for, though unreasoning, they succeed ... that the power of prophecy of those who are wise and clever is swift, and, one should 35 suppose, not only what results from reasoning. But some through experience, others through familiarity with employing the god in inquiry ... sees well what is to be and what is the case, and those whose reason is thus disengaged; thus those of a melancholic temperament also have vivid dreams. For the starting-point seems to be stronger when reason is disengaged, just as blind people remember **1248^b** better, because the remembering element is better when that concerned with visible things is disengaged.

It is clear, then, that there are two sorts of good fortune, the one divine—hence it actually seems that the fortunate man owes his success to a god. This man is the one who is successful in accordance 5 with impulse; the other is so contrary to impulse; but both are non-rational. It is this one form of good fortune rather, that is continuous; the latter form is not continuous.

CHAPTER 3

We have spoken earlier about each virtue individually; but since we have distinguished and separated their capacity, we must also articulate the virtue that results from them, which we now call *nobility*. 10 Now it is clear that the man who is truly to meet this appellation

must have the individual virtues. For it cannot be otherwise in other cases, either. For no one is healthy in his body as a whole, yet not in
15 any part of it; rather, all parts, or most and the most important, must be in the same state as the whole.

Being good and being fine-and-good admit of distinction, not only in their names but also in themselves. For, of all goods, those are ends which are worth having for their own sake, while, of these, all
20 that are commended for themselves are fine. For of these things it is true that the actions from them are commended and they are themselves commended—justice, both itself and the actions from it, and those who are temperate; for temperance is also commended. But health is not something commended; for neither is its function. Nor is <acting> with strength, for strength is not, either. But, though they are not commended, they are goods.
25 Likewise, this is clear in other cases also, by induction. Now a good man is one for whom the natural goods are goods. For the things that are competed for and seem to be the greatest goods, honour and wealth and bodily excellences and good fortune and
30 capacities, are naturally good, but may be harmful for some because of their states of character. For neither a foolish nor an unjust or intemperate man would get any benefit from using them, just as neither will the sick man using the food of the healthy, nor would the weak and deformed using the adornments of the sound and whole
35 person. A person is fine-and-good because, among goods, those that are fine for themselves belong to him, and because he is a practiser of fine things, and for their own sake. Fine things are the virtues and the deeds resulting from virtue.

There is a certain state of a citizen such as the Spartans have, or other such people would have. This is a state of the following sort;
40 there are those who think that one should possess virtue, but for the
1249^a sake of the natural goods. They are therefore good men (for natural goods are so for them), but they do not have nobility. For they do not possess the things that are fine for themselves, but those who possess them, also choose things fine-and-good, and not only
5 those things, but also the things not fine by nature, but good by nature, are fine for them. For they are fine when the things for whose sake they act and choose are fine. So, for the fine-and-good

man, the natural goods are fine. For what is just is fine; and that is what is in accord with desert; and this man deserves these things. And what is fitting is fine; and these things befit this man, — wealth, noble birth, power. So, to the fine-and-good man, the beneficial 10 things themselves, too, are also fine; but for the many there is a divergence here. For the things good without qualification are not good also for them, but are good for the good man. But to the fine-and-good man they are also fine. For he does many fine actions because of them. But the man who thinks that the virtues should 15 be possessed for the sake of external goods, does the fine things incidentally. So nobility is complete virtue.

Concerning pleasure, too, it has been said what sort of thing it is and how it is a good, and that the things pleasant without qualification are also fine, and the things good without qualification are pleasant. But pleasure does not occur except in action; for that reason, the truly happy man will also live most pleasantly, and it is 20 not vainly that people believe this.

Now there is some limit also for the doctor, by reference to which he judges what is healthy for a body and what is not, and by reference to which each thing is to be done up to a certain amount, and is healthy, but is not so, if less or more is done. So too for the virtuous man, with respect to his actions and choices of the things 25 naturally good but not commended, there must be some limit both **1249^b** for the possession and the choice and avoidance of abundance and exiguousness of material goods and of successes. Now *as principle <prescribes>* is what was said earlier. But that is as if, in matters of nutrition, someone were to say, *as medicine and its principle <pre-* 5 *cribes>*. But that, though true, is not clear.

So it is needful, as in other cases, to live by reference to the governing thing, and by reference to the state and activity of what governs, as a slave to the rule of the master and each thing to its appropriate governing principle. But since a human being, also, is by nature composed of a thing that governs and a thing that is 10 governed, each too should live by reference to its own governing principle. But that is of two sorts; for medicine is a governing principle in one way, and health in another; for the first is for the sake of the second. Thus it is with the speculative <part>. For the

45

god is a governor not in a prescriptive fashion, but it is that *for*
15 which practical wisdom prescribes (but *that for which* is of two
sorts—they have been distinguished elsewhere—since the god is in
need of nothing.) So if some choice and possession of natural goods
—either goods of the body or money or of friends or the other goods—
will most produce the speculation of the god, that is the best, and
that is the finest limit; but whatever, whether through deficiency
20 or excess, hinders the service and speculation of the god, is bad.
Thus it is for the soul, and this is the best limit for the soul—to be
aware as little as possible of the non-rational part of the soul as such.
But let what has been said be enough on the limit of nobility, and
25 what the goal is of things good without qualification.

COMMENTARY

The sections of the Commentary correspond to paragraphs in the translation. In the case of references to other passages in Aristotle, where no work is mentioned, the reference is to another passage in the *Eudemian Ethics*, and where no book number is given, the reference is to a passage in the same book as the section of the Commentary in which the reference occurs. I have followed normal practice in referring to the three 'common' books (see Introduction) as *E.N.* V, VI, and VII, but have occasionally referred to them collectively as 'the disputed books'. I have used the following abbreviations:

E.E. : *Eudemian Ethics*
E.N. : *Nicomachean Ethics*
M.M. : *Magna Moralia*

Details of modern works cited in the Commentary, by author's name only, are given in the Bibliography.

BOOK ONE

CHAPTER 1
1214ª1-8

This couplet, quoted at the beginning of the *E.E.*, with which Aristotle expresses his agreement, is also quoted at *E.N.* I.8, 1099ª27-28, in a passage in which Aristotle is arguing that his account of happiness conforms to received opinions.

The word translated 'fine' (*kalos*) (alternative renderings would be 'noble' 'admirable'), is also applied in aesthetic contexts, roughly with the sense of 'beautiful', 'attractive'. Common to its various applications is that anything so characterized is represented as an appropriate object of admiration. It is sufficiently different in meaning from 'good' for it to be a serious question whether the finest life and the best life are the same. (Compare Plato, *Gorgias* 474 c f.). According to Aristotle, the fine supplies a motive for any fully virtuous action: the virtuous man acts in the way he does because by so acting he will be performing an action which merits this description. (Cf. III, 1229ª4: only the man who is fearless 'on account of the fine' is brave; 1230ª29, 32: the fine is the object of actions manifesting virtue, and the virtuous man acts with that in view, not with a view to pleasure. See, further, Commentary on VIII, 1248ᵇ 16-37, and cf. *E.N.* II, 1104ᵇ30-1105ª1, III, 1115ᵇ23-24; IV, 1122ᵇ6-7; IX, 1169ª18-1169ᵇ1).

Aristotle nowhere in our *E.E.*, and only perfunctorily in the *E.N.* (I, 1099ᵃ21–26), argues for the identity of the finest and the best life. In the discussion of the identity of the best life, the best life is always implicitly to be understood as the life which is best for the person living it; and so the actions which, according to Aristotle, are to be taken as constituting it are presumably to be thought of as best for the agent; but it is far from clear that a life which is the best possible from the point of view of the person living it will always be the finest from an impersonal point of view.

That happiness, as well as being best is also the most pleasant thing, is not argued in the *E.E.*, but is argued at *E.N.* I.8, 1099ᵃ7–28.

1214ᵃ7: 'Happiness'. I have translated the Greek word *eudaimonia* 'happiness', which is the traditional translation, and probably the least unsatisfactory. But it is clear that the concept expressed is different in a number of respects from that expressed by the English word 'happiness' as used in modern, non-philosophical English and in the writings of philosophers in the utilitarian tradition. If this fact is not borne in mind, Aristotle's position can easily appear closer to a utilitarian one than it is. The Greek word translated 'happy' etymologically has the sense of 'blessed with a good *daimōn* (divine guardian)' and this no doubt explains the tendency to associate *eudaimonia* with good fortune, and equate it with prosperity. (Compare VIII, c.2.) By the time of Plato and Aristotle, at any rate, the concept had come to possess a number of different strands, and it may be for that reason that the alternative views about the nature of happiness are extremely diverse.

Aristotle wrote as if it were tautological that the best possible human life is the life of *eudaimonia*. This appears from 1214ᵃ14 f., where, having introduced the question what living well consists in, he goes on to speak of *eudaimonia* in a way that would be unintelligible if he did not identify *eudaimonia* with the good life. In *E.N.* I, after introducing the notion of the good-for-man as the object of the inquiry in the first three chapters, he goes on in Chapter 4 to raise the question what the good-for-man is; but an answer is given almost immediately, at 1095ᵃ17–22: everyone is agreed that *eudaimonia* is the good for man, the highest human good, *eudaimonia* being equated with living and acting well (cf. 1219ᵇ1–2). The dispute, both in *E.E.* and in *E.N.*, is over what *eudaimonia* consists in.

It is thus not open to question, in Aristotle's thought, that the best life is the life of *eudaimonia*, and hence that an inquiry into the nature of the highest form of human life coincides with an inquiry into the nature of *eudaimonia*: one can no more intelligibly raise the question whether one should aim at *eudaimonia* than whether one should aim at having the best possible life. (Compare also Plato,

Republic 358-368.) Thus, whereas a utilitarian who proposes happiness as the sole standard of conduct is propounding a controversial ethical doctrine, one that will be objected to by those who insist that to single out happiness as the only thing of intrinsic value is too restrictive, and fails to harmonize with most people's intuitions, Aristotle's largely unargued assumption that happiness is the ultimate end seems fairly uncontentious, if his conception of happiness is properly understood. But see, further, Commentary on 1214^{b}6-14.

In elaboration of the discrepancy between the Aristotelian conception of *eudaimonia* and the notion of happiness more familiar to us the following points may be mentioned:

(i) Whereas some utilitarian writers, for example Bentham and Mill, identify *eudaimonia* with pleasure and the absence of pain, Aristotle regards it as a substantial question whether the happy life is pleasant, though he answers it in the affirmative. Compare *E.N.* I, 1099^{a}7 f, VII, 1153^{b}9 f, X, 1172^{b}35 f.

(ii) Not only does Aristotle regard it as uncontentious that *eudaimonia* is what a man *ought* to pursue, but he also holds that everyone does in fact pursue it, at least in the sense that each person represents to himself the life that he does pursue, or would pursue if he had the opportunity, as being *eudaimōn*. It is plausible to hold that, for Aristotle, this was not an empirical generalization but a consequence of his concept of happiness. This emerges from, e.g. 1215^{a}35–1215^{b}1, where Aristotle is ready to infer what a person's conception of happiness is from the start of life he would lead if he had the choice (cf. *E.N.* I, 1095^{b}15 f). Aristotle's idea of *eudaimonia* does not seem to leave room for someone who admitted that it was indeed an important ingredient in a satisfactory life, but held that other things were required in addition.

(iii) Whereas we should probably regard a person's own sincere statement about whether he was happy or not as carrying strong, if not decisive, weight in answering the question whether he was happy or not, Aristotle clearly thought that a man could quite erroneously think that he had achieved *eudaimonia*.

(iv) There is some indication that, for Aristotle, the term *eudaimōn* was applied primarily to lives, and only derivatively from that to the person leading the life. That would explain why the question what *eudaimonia* is leads immediately to a survey of different proposed ideal lives, and the identification, already mentioned, of *eudaimonia* and *living* well; it will also explain why Aristotle takes seriously the suggestion that no one should be called *eudaimōn* till the end of his life (cf. II, 1219^{b}6-8): if the primary use of *eudaimōn* is in the assessment of a life, one should perhaps wait until the whole of it is open to view before pronouncing, just as the cautious concert-goer will wait till the end of the performance before pronouncing on its merits.

(v)   Connected with (iii) and (iv) is the fact that a knowledge of the meaning of the term *eudaimonia* and the ability to use it correctly is not sufficient for a knowledge of the identity of the completely happy life.

For an excellent brief discussion of Aristotle's conception of happiness, see Austin, pp. 270–82, also Léonard. However, we must not immediately assume that what Aristotle says fits the concept of happiness of an ordinary Greek of Aristotle's day. For an alternative view on the relation between *eudaimonia* and happiness, see Kraut.

1214ª9-14

Aristotle here presupposes a division of sciences, inquiries, or branches of knowledge into theoretical and practical. It is assumed that the inquiry that he engages in in *E.E.* is practical: the aim is not to know what virtue, happiness, etc., are, but to acquire them. (Cf. 1216ᵇ16 f, and *E.N.* I, 1102ª23-26.) How does Aristotle distinguish these two sorts of inquiry? (i) From ª10-12 we might suppose that the distinction between practical and theoretical inquiries is that between those inquiries which yield knowledge only, and those which can be useful for action or production: the criterion will be whether or not the inquiry can or cannot be helpful towards answering a practical question – a question about what to do or how to bring something about. But ª12-14, which distinguish theoretical inquiries that are relevant to action from those that are not, suggest (ii) that the basis of the distinction is the aim of the person engaged in the inquiry – with a view to knowledge only or also to action or production. To try to answer the question what virtue is, is not to engage in a theoretical investigation if one does so with a view to acquiring virtue. Such a division between practical and theoretical inquiries is independent of the subject matter of the inquiry, since precisely the same inquiry may be undertaken either with a practical or with a theoretical aim. However, (iii) there seems to be implicit in this passage a further basis for distinguishing the practical from the theoretical. As already mentioned, at ª12-14, he implies that some of the findings of theoretical science will be relevant to the purposes of the *E.E.* and others will not, which suggests a distinction by subject matter, and not by the motive for engaging in the inquiry. If so, the distinction between the practical and theoretical is perhaps that found at *Metaphysics* E 1025ᵇ18-28 (see Kirwan's note *ad locum*) where there is a threefold distinction between theoretical, practical, and productive sciences, according to whether or not the originating principle is within the person who has the science.

Since the aim of the inquiry is practical, the question what happiness is is relevant only because it contributes to its attainment. It is natural to relate this section to the distinction in the next section between the question of what happiness is and the question of how it is to be achieved (see Rowe, p. 15, note 4), and regard the former question as theoretical and the latter as practical; but it is doubtful if Aristotle would ever have regarded the former as a theoretical question. However, it is true that the answering of it requires the use of some results of theoretical philosophy — for example, the distinction between states, capacities, and dispositions (cf. II, 1218^{b}35-36). For a different view, see Kenny, pp. 191-2.

1214^{a}14-25

Compare E.N. I, 1099^{b}9-11, X, 1179^{b}20-26. The alternative possible explanations of the possession of happiness by human beings are reminiscent of the question about the source of virtue discussed in Plato's Meno (70A1f). Although the questions in what living well consists, and how it is to be achieved, are presented as distinct, in fact the answer to the first given by Aristotle determines the answer to the second; at any rate, we do not find the two questions discussed separately.

The five alternative possible answers proposed by Aristotle divide into two groups, the first of three (^{a}15-21) and the second of two (^{a}21-25). The plausibility of the view that happiness is attributable solely to luck is no doubt a reflection of the two strands in the Greek concept of eudaimonia that are apparent from its etymology. (See Commentary on 1214^{a}7, and also VIII, c.2.) Aristotle's answer is that it is, in part, a matter of training: a man acquires the relevant dispositions by habituation, i.e. by performing the appropriate actions (cf. Book II). But complete virtue would also require practical wisdom, an intellectual virtue not acquired by habituation. Aristotle's view seems to be that nature (phusis) plays a part because a natural capacity is required — one which animals lack (cf. 1217^{a}24f) — but this natural endowment is possessed by all normal human beings, though whether this natural endowment is so developed that a man leads a happy life depends on other factors. Aristotle's account of what the happy life consists in supplies an answer to the question how happiness is acquired.

1214^{a}26-30

Aristotle recognizes that happiness may be attributed to all of these things: though they are, he argues, exhaustive alternatives, (27-30), they are not exclusive of one another. None the less, he does not seem to have recognized that to hold that whether the happy life is achieved depends crucially on 'training' (or again learning what happiness is) will still leave a large role to luck; for whether a person is trained in the right manner or acquires the appropriate knowledge will presumably depend on a large number of chance factors, such as the sort of community he grows up in.

1214^{a}30-^{b}5

These candidates are mentioned in *E.N.* I, c.5.

1214^{a}32: The word *phronesis* has here been translated simply 'wisdom'. The word in ordinary Greek meant, in different contexts, 'intelligence', 'good sense', 'prudence', but it was used by both Plato and Aristotle in specialized, semi-technical, ways. In *E.N.* VI, the word is used as the name of the main intellectual virtue in the practical sphere, and hence must be translated 'practical wisdom' or something of the sort, and I have so translated it where it seems appropriate; a different word (*sophia*) is used for the intellectual virtue involved in theoretical speculation. The use of the word *phronēsis* in the same way as in *E.N.* VI is found in *E.E.* outside the disputed books at III, 1234^{a}29. In *E.N.* VI, at least, there is a discontinuity between the theoretical and the practical.

1214^{a}33: The Greek word *aretē*, is here, as in many other places, translated 'virtue'; but the word is in fact the normal abstract noun corresponding to the adjective 'good': any respect in which something may be called 'good' counts as an *aretē*, and hence in some passages a translation like 'excellence' is more appropriate. However, it is probable that in this passage, when he speaks of *aretē* as one of the things in which the good life has been thought to consist, he has in mind what we might think of as the virtuous life. 1215^{a}33 refers back to the three proposed highest goods, and associates them explicitly with three lives. See, further, Commentary on that passage.

1214^{a}31: 'Divinely happy': see Commentary on 1215^{a}10.

CHAPTER 2
1214^{b}6-14

Aristotle assumes not merely that the sensible man will reflect on how he should act, but also that the result of such reflection must lead to the adoption of some specifiable ends or goals to which he will orient his actions. Although the first may be thought to need no justification, the second surely does: a teleological view is not the only ethical view possible, as the subsequent history of ethics has shown. Further, why should reflection on matters of conduct lead one to have a single aim which one will have in view in *all* one's actions (^{b}9)? It may be that a man's reflections on matters of conduct will lead him to hold that there are a number of independently valuable things, all of which deserve, on occasion, to be pursued.

1214^{b}8: 'Cultivation': The possible conception of the good life suggested by this word drops out of consideration in what follows.

1214^{b}14-27

A distinction is drawn between what the good life consists in, and those things without which it is impossible to live the good life (we might say 'its necessary conditions'). Presumably only the first should be mentioned in a proper definition. In outline at least, the distinction is fairly clear: among those things that qualify merely as necessary conditions, we might include those things that are causally necessary for happiness, whose desirability has to be shown by what they produce. The nearest parallel to the distinction in *E.N.* is perhaps the distinction between internal and external goods (*E.N.* I, 1099^{a}31-33, and elsewhere); at any rate external goods, such as wealth and friends, will presumably count as necessary conditions of happiness, rather than constituents of happiness, though not all internal goods need be regarded as constituents. But on any reasonable view some things will qualify both as necessary conditions and as parts of happiness. Is not health both a necessary condition and a constituent?

The importance of this distinction is explained in the last sentence: confusion about what happiness is is caused by the fact that some people wrongly take necessary conditions for happiness to be parts of it. Someone who took happiness to consist in material prosperity might be wrongly taking what is indeed a necessary condition of happiness to be a constituent of it. Hence the need to scrutinize any proposal and see that the distinction between constituents and necessary conditions of happiness is properly observed. Aristotle no doubt exaggerates the extent to which a proper regard for this distinction will help one to avoid erroneous views. The alleged view of the generality of mankind, which he rejects, that happiness consists simply in pleasure is surely not to be disposed of by insisting on the distinction.

I have taken ^{b}17-24 as parenthetical, and introducing a further distinction *within* the class of necessary conditions of the good life; some such conditions are conditions of a quite general kind, being conditions of living at all; only some are conditions specifically of the *good* life. The eating of food is a necessary condition of health specifically; some necessary conditions of health are quite general, such as those mentioned earlier as being necessary conditions of being alive at all. They are necessary conditions of health because only a living thing can be truly described as either healthy or not. With these lines enclosed in parentheses, 'these' in ^{b}24 has to be taken as referring back to the material *before* the parenthesis. The point of making this distinction among necessary conditions is perhaps that the dichotomy between general and specific conditions of something may be confused with the other distinction between constituents and (mere) necessary conditions; or that, although some things are clearly no more than necessary conditions, others are less clearly so. I see no reason to hold that ^{b}26-27 refer to a philosophical view held by some people explicitly in those terms: it seems more natural to suppose that some people's views about what happiness is *in fact* involve treating necessary conditions as if they were parts of happiness.

The use of the concepts of part and whole in connection with happiness indicate that Aristotle envisaged that a proper answer to the question what happiness consisted in would involve an enumeration of the items that the good life would possess (cf. *E.N.* V, 1129^b 18). This suggests, at least, that Aristotle is leaving open the possibility that quite a number of goods will need to be enumerated as parts of happiness.

CHAPTER 3
1214^{b}28-1215^{a}7

Compare *E.N.* I, 1095^{a}28-30. In the *E.N.* Aristotle says that ethics is not an appropriate subject of study for the young, on the grounds that experience is required. The need for experience seems to be due to the facts, firstly that ethical precepts require judgement in order to be applied in actual situations, and hence some degree of maturity, and secondly that the purpose of ethics is to help us to live well, and for this more is required than assent to certain propositions: a person's inclinations need to be directed, in a settled fashion, in the right direction, which requires a lengthy process of habituation (cf. *E.N.* I, 1095^{a}2-12; VI, 1142^{a}11-18).

1214^{b}33:   On Aristotle's conception of the *politikos*, see Commentary on 1215^{b}1-14. Whereas Plato, notably in the *Gorgias*, had assimilated punishment to medical treatment, punishment being curative of the soul as medicine is of the body, Aristotle here facetiously makes the opposite assimilation.

1215^{a}5-6:   Aristotle insists that there are some issues that properly belong to ethics and need to be discussed in an ethical treatise; when he says that it is *these* opinions that must be investigated, by 'these' he means the opinions of reasonable men referred to in ^{a}2, if the text adopted for the translation is correct. (See, further, Notes).

54

1215ª8-19

Compare *E.N.* I, 1099ᵇ13-25. This section and the next may be regarded as carrying further the inquiry started at 1214ª14-25. Aristotle seems to exaggerate the extent to which the issue of whether happiness is a gift of nature or achieved by one's own action is tied up with the attainability of happiness by the generality of mankind: if happiness is a natural endowment, it will depend on how widely distributed it is, and conversely, if it depends on one's own actions, it will again depend on the extent to which one's own actions are under one's control.

1215ª10: The single Greek word translated 'divinely-happy' means much the same as that translated 'happy' but is rather stronger (cf. English 'bliss'). Aristotle here, and at 1215ᵇ13-14, is squeamish about using it in relation to human happiness because the work is most appropriately used of the life ascribed to the gods (contrast *E.N.*, I 1099ᵇ17-18).

1215ª11: 'with each alternative'. He presumably means that the prospect of attaining it will vary according to what view is taken of the character of the happy life.

CHAPTER 4
1215ª20-25

Aristotle's own view on this is, briefly, that the happy life consists in activities of a certain kind; hence he opts for the second alternative mentioned here. The allusion to 'older philosophers' may be a reference to Socrates or Plato, though it need not be exclusively to them. On the Socratic view that virtue consists in knowledge, compare 1216ᵇ3-25, with Commentary.

In fact Aristotle holds that a certain state of the soul is sufficient for happiness, though not constitutive of it, as he holds that the activities of the man living the good life must result from a settled disposition. Hence the opposition between the alternatives mentioned seems a little artificial. Aristotle here draws a contrast between one's soul's having a certain character and the man himself's having such a character, but elsewhere he sometimes identifies the man himself with his soul.

1215ª26-ᵇ1

Aristotle here simply assumes that the lives he dismisses rather scornfully could never be pursued by someone who had a completely free choice about what sort of life he should lead. The argument that a life dominated by activities by which one earns one's living could not be the best life since the activities were not pursued for some further end is inconclusive, since the same activity may be pursued both for its own sake and for the sake of a further end, a fact of which Aristotle shows more awareness in the *E.N.* than in the *E.E.* (cf. *E.N.* I 1097ᵃ30-33). Even the political and theoretical lives, which he regards as deserving serious consideration, could presumably be engaged in to provide for the necessities of life. If Aristotle was restricting his attention to those occupations which could have no attraction except as a means of earning one's living, Aristotle's survey of alternatives is grossly inadequate. What should one say about the life of a poet or composer?

1215ᵃ34: 'wisdom': on the meaning of *phronēsis*, see Commentary on 1214ᵃ32.

1215ᵇ1-14

These three lives are associated with the three ultimate ends of human action that have already been mentioned as being the ones proposed (1214ᵃ30-ᵇ5). Earlier, it had been allowed that the good life might consist in more than one of these goods, and they might contribute in different ways and in different degrees to it; Aristotle now seems to think that there are just three lives to be considered, each associated with one of the three goods mentioned earlier. The three lives are a traditional trio.

By the 'philosophical life', Aristotle does not, of course, mean a life devoted to philosophy in a narrow sense: the philosophical life is here explained as being devoted to speculation concerning truth, a life devoted to theoretical inquiry, pursued for its own sake and with no further aim in view apart from the knowledge attained. As characterized here, the theoretical life could include investigation of the natural world, the province of physics, but later Aristotle claims that the proper concern of the man living this life should be the superior beings lying beyond the physical universe. On this, see further VIII, c. 3.

The description of the life associated with the pursuit of virtue as the 'political' life may strike us as surprising; and Aristotle later admits that his description does not fit those who actually tend to be described as 'politicians' (1216ᵃ23-27). In fact, the description of the life in which virtue is the dominant end as the political life, and the characterization of that as being devoted to 'fine actions' resulting from virtue, and the description of the inquiry that Aristotle is engaged in in the *E.E.* as 'political science' (1216ᵇ19), reflect doctrines which may be schematically stated as follows:
(i) In the case of each man, the question what the best life for him

to lead would be has a definite, decidable answer: doubts about the end to which one's actions ought to lead are capable of resolution. (ii)   With each person, the question what the good life consists in *for him* is to be settled by determining what the best life is *for a human being*: the character of the good life, both in *E.E.* and *E.N.* is established by reflection on the nature of man, and the result of this consideration of human nature is a conception of the highest possible human life, to be aspired to by every human being endowed with normal human capacities.

(iii)   Hence, in giving an adequate conception of what the good life consists in for himself, each person at the same time will necessarily be acquiring knowledge of how others should live. (Compare *E.N.* I, 1094^{b}7-8, with *E.N.* VI, 1141^{b}23-33, where the identity of the practical knowledge used in organizing one's own life with that used in dealing with affairs of a city is asserted.)

(iv)   In order to live the best possible human life a man needs not merely to have an adequate conception of what the good life is, but also to have his desires and inclinations rightly directed, which depends upon education and habituation; these two requirements, the interplay between which is subtly described in *E.N.* VI, cc. 12 and 13, involve the development of different parts of the soul, one rational and one non-rational (cf. II, 1219^{b}26-1220^{a}12).

(v)   The conditions in which proper development can take place are realized in a city (*polis*) which provides the appropriate institutional framework, by providing education and a legal system backed by sanctions. (Cf. *E.N.* X, c. 9, the last chapter of that work, which leads up to the inquiry into the institutional arrangements that are required, to which the *Politics* is devoted.)

(vi)   In so far as, in having an adequate conception of the good life I am in a position to secure it not merely for myself but also for others, to work towards securing it for others is a finer and more noble task than simply seeking it for myself (cf. *E.N.* I, 1094^{b}8-10).

(vii)   Hence the highest fulfilment of the capacities of the virtuous and practically wise man will be in its application at a political level, in regulating the affairs of a city with the aim of the good life for all the citizens in view; and so the man whose highest good is virtue will naturally wish to devote himself to political activities. Thus the political life and the life of virtue are here associated with one another. (On this, see further 1216^{b}17-19, and Commentary.)

(i) and (ii) are assumptions of the *E.E.* throughout Book I. In regard to (iii), the view that the knowledge of the good for man may be applied to secure the good life for oneself alone or for other members of the community also is implied by 1218^{b}11-14, which may be compared with the passage from *E.N.* VI cited above.

Aristotle's view in *E.N.* X is that the highest possible life is the
life of speculation, the third life mentioned in this passage. That this
is the view of *E.E.* has been disputed: on this see Commentary on
VIII, c. 3 and also Monan, Cooper, and Kenny. However, the conception of political science here discussed does not depend essentially on a particular view of what the best life is.

Aristotle appears to think the three kinds of life here distinguished
exhaust the field of possible candidates for being the best life, on
the grounds that these are the lives that have been proposed by
previous thinkers. No doubt the three descriptions are intended each
to cover a number of different alternatives; but would any proposed
ideal human life necessarily fall under one of the descriptions given?
It may seem plausible that that should be so in so far as the life of
enjoyment is perhaps something of a catch-all, intended to cover a
variety of pursuits that might dominate a man's life. But if so, there
is no justification for characterizing the life of enjoyment as he does
at 1215^{b}4-5, as concerned specifically with bodily pleasures. On this
see further Commentary on 1216^{a}28-36.

1215^{b}2:   On the meaning of 'wisdom' (*phronēsis*) in this passage,
see Commentary on 1214^{a}32.

1215^{b}11-14:   Cf *E.N.* X, 1179^{a}13f.

CHAPTER 5
1215^{b}15-1216^{a}10

The passage purports to show how difficult it is to determine what a
desirable life consists in, as appears from the remarks both at the
beginning and at the end of the section; but in fact it is devoted to
showing that there are certain actual or conceivable forms of life
which would be agreed not to be worth living. Yet the existence of
such lives seems to have little bearing on the difficulty of deciding
what the good life is; nor, of course, is a life which is satisfactory
enough not to warrant suicide, or the thought that it would have
been better if the person living it had not been born in the first
place, the same as the good life. Perhaps the point is that there is
a discrepancy between the unreflective judgements that people make
about specified lives and the view that they would take of such lives
if they had to live them. The question is not merely difficult, but
harder than most people think. Alternatively, the point may be that
the considerations mentioned in ^{b}15-30 show that life itself is not
in all cases desirable, and then ^{b}30-1216^{a}7 show that pleasure is not
always a good; hence the question what life's intrinsic goods are is a
pressing one. On the relevance of this section to its context, see Rowe,
pp. 16-17, 76.

1216ª2-3:   On the rather strange notion of the pleasures of sleep, cf. *Politics* VIII, 1339ª17f.

1216ª11-27

1216ª16:   Sardanapallus: cf. *E.N.* I, 1095ᵇ22. A proverbial example of luxurious and hedonistic living.

1216ª19:   'Wisdom': see Commentary on 1215ª32.

1216ª23-27:   See Commentary on 1215ᵇ1-14.

1216ª28-36

The questions raised are (i) how, if at all, physical pleasures contribute to happiness, and if so, (ii) whether they should be ascribed to the good life, or whether other pleasures should be regarded as responsible for its being the case that the happy life is a pleasurable one. Aristotle does not answer these questions in the *E.E.* (outside the 'disputed books'), but there is a reference forward to a future discussion of the different kinds of pleasure in III, 1231ᵇ2-4 (compare VIII, 1249ª17-20). There are discussions of pleasure in *E.N.* VII and X. In both passages, different sorts of pleasure are distinguished, and evaluated differently, though without much explicit discussion of the role they play in the good life. On the significance of the forward reference, see Kenny, pp.52-3. However, although Aristotle does not answer the question raised here in the *E.E.* as we have it, he probably thought the physical pleasures contributed to happiness *not* by being parts of it, whereas the other pleasures are properly to be regarded as parts of happiness. It is natural to relate the implied contrast between the ways in which something may contribute to happiness to the distinctions made in 1214ᵇ14-27. If so, to ascribe certain pleasures to happiness will be to treat them as parts of it, and not merely necessary conditions in a causal or instrumental sense. The contrast hinted at here, between the pleasures that are properly parts of happiness and those which are merely necessary conditions of it, will then perhaps correspond to that drawn in 1215ᵇ30-34, between the pleasures of sex and nutrition, and those of sight and the intellect, which are regarded as involving higher human faculties. (Sight is mentioned at *E.N.* I, 1096ᵇ17f, along with 'certain pleasures' as pursued both for their own sake and with a view to happiness, and it may be argued that as such they must qualify as parts of happiness.) But there is a difficulty in seeing how those not qualifying as parts of happiness may yet contribute to it in an instrumental way; pleasures are not pursued in *that* way, with something else in view. Perhaps the best that can be suggested is that the 'lower' pleasures accompany activities which are necessary to life, and therefore the good life; the man living the best sort of human life will therefore not be able to dispense with them, even though they do not essentially form part of the good life. The view implied here of what should strictly be treated as belonging to the good life is somewhat restrictive.

1216ᵃ37-1216ᵇ2

After discussing pleasure, in ᵃ30-36, the topic is now the final ends of the two remaining of the three lives distinguished at ᵃ15-21, 28-29. Rowe (p. 65), conceding that this is a natural reading, argues that it cannot be correct because (a) 'actions' (*praxeis*) would then have to be taken in an uncharacteristically wide sense, covering activities of speculation as well as virtuous actions, and (b) the following passage, about Socrates, is more intelligible if *phronēsis* here means practical wisdom. But (a) is inconclusive in view of the admitted parallels for a wide use of *phronēsis*; and, against (b), it may be said that this passage need not be taken closely with what immediately follows.

On this passage, see Kenny, pp. 53-4. It has been held that this passage constitutes an announcement of the plan actually followed in *E.E.*, including the 'disputed books', II and III, then IV and V (= *E.N.* V and VI) being devoted to virtue, followed by a treatment of pleasure in VI (*E.N.* VII). This is connected with the issue of the meaning of *phronēsis* in this passage (see Walzer, pp. 274 f, Rowe, op. cit., Kenny, p. 196, and Commentary on 1214ᵃ32): if *phronēsis* here denotes the practical wisdom of *E.N.* VI, an examination of virtue will include an examination of the intellectual virtue *phronēsis*. But it is natural to suppose that 'wisdom' (*phronēsis*) is here used not in the manner of *E.N.* VI, but as it is used at 1214ᵃ32, ᵇ2, 1215ᵃ34.

1216ᵃ39:   'Parts': on the application of this notion to the good life, see Commentary on 1214ᵇ14-27.

1216ᵃ40:   on the contrast, compare 1215ᵃ20-25.

1216ᵇ3-16

Aristotle here discusses the Socratic position, summed up in the phrase 'virtue is knowledge'. The view, advanced in various Platonic dialogues, notably in the *Protagoras*, *Gorgias*, and *Meno*, is that knowing what courage and prudence are is sufficient (and also necessary) for being courageous or prudent, and similarly with the other virtues. Thus, Aristotle argues, Socrates regarded the purpose of ethical inquiry as being to discover what individual virtues, and virtue in general, are; hence the Socratic search for definitions. In fact, Socrates might well have conceded that the purpose of ethical speculation was a practical one, and differed from Aristotle only in holding that knowledge of the sort he was after was sufficient. Aristotle's position is that to acquire a virtue in the fullest sense involves not merely the intellectual virtue possessed by the practically wise man, but also the development of virtue of character, which is a matter not of knowledge but habituation. What Socrates regarded as sufficient corresponds only to the first of these (cf. *E.N.* VI, 1144^{b}28-32). On the distinction between virtue of character and intellectual virtue, see further, Commentary on II, 1220^{a}5-12.

1216^{b}8-9: Aristotle here suggests that Socrates' position was arrived at by mistaken analogy between the learning of virtue and the learning of skills like astronomy or building. In fact, though something like this occurs in *Gorgias* 460A 5-C 6, the main Socratic argument we find for the 'virtue is knowledge' thesis turns on the plausibility of the principle that each person always chooses what he believes to be the best course of action, hence a failure to choose the best course must always be due to ignorance. On the subject generally, see Irwin.

1216^{b}11-16: On the concept of the theoretical sciences, and their relevance to action, see 1214^{a}9-14, with Commentary, and the Commentary on the next section.

1216^{b}16-25

The purpose of this section and the last is presumably to make a methodological point: the purpose of ethics is practical—to acquire the virtues and lead a good life. Compare *E.N.* 1103^{b}26-29, and elsewhere. In fact the reasons mentioned in the Commentary on the last section for holding that knowing what courage is is not sufficient to make someone courageous are equally reasons for holding that the knowledge obtained from the sort of investigation carried on in the *E.E.* is not sufficient for making men virtuous, as Aristotle himself recognizes (see 1214^{b}28-1215^{a}7 with Commentary). Hence, nothing in the argument of the present passage tends to show that the method to be employed is totally different in kind from that directed towards Socratic definitions. At 1216^{b}20-21, Socrates is criticized for asking what virtue is, instead of trying to see how it is achieved. But Aristotle's own answer to the latter question is arrived at, in II, by way of an investigation into the question what virtue is. Throughout the *E.E.* and *E.N.* Aristotle poses, and attempts to answer, questions of the 'what is X?' form. It is difficult to see how ethics can contribute to the practical aim which is here insisted on except by answering theoretical questions of this kind.

Aristotle here seems to argue for his view of the aim of ethics by appealing to the fact that, where knowledge is sought after with some further end in view, a higher value is always to be placed on that end than on the knowledge needed for achieving it. It may be disputed whether this need always be so. Some inquiries may be engaged in primarily for the sake of the knowledge they yield, but secondarily for some further aim. Aristotle, it is true, at 1216^b15-16 concedes the possibility that theoretical science may, incidentally, serve a practical purpose; but then, in classifying ethics as a practical science, Aristotle is in danger of begging the question.

1216^b17-19: 'Productive sciences'. This phrase is here clearly intended in a broad sense, and is intended to cover all kinds of knowledge of a practical kind (and therefore the translation 'sciences' may give a misleading impression). In the *E.N.* a distinction is drawn among activities (and therefore presumably also types of knowledge) that have a practical aim, between those that have as their ultimate objective the production of something beyond the activity itself, and those whose aim is simply the activitiy itself. The knowledge that is used in specific acts or skills like medicine, shoe-making, or generalship is used to produce a result distinct from the various activities that practice of these skills involves; whereas the actions of the practically wise man are engaged in for their own sake: acting well is itself the end (*E.N.* VI, 1139^b3-4, 1140^b7). In the *E.E.*, on the other hand, no such division of practical knowledge is explicitly made, and the term here translated 'productive', which is derived from a verb which can be used of either making or doing, both here and in the other passages in which it is used in the *E.E.* (II, 1221^b5, 1227^b29) is used in a quite general sense. It is perhaps significant that the word is used in a similar broad sense in a 'disputed book' at *E.N.* VII, 1147^a28.

At 1216^a25-26 the 'political man', in the true sense, is said to have as his aim the performing of fine actions for their own sake, yet here ($^b18$) the end of the political man is said to be the good ordering of a community, and compared with health, an end which lies beyond the practice of medicine.

The word *eunomia* which has been translated 'good social order' is used to describe that state of a community in which activities are satisfactorily regulated by a good system of legal and other normative principles, which are generally accepted and conformed to. Presumably, this good ordering is not the ultimate aim of the political man: his ultimate aim will be the providing of the opportunity for living a good life which political institutions make possible. See Commentary on 1215^b1-14.

CHAPTER 6

1216^b26-35

It is an established part of Aristotle's procedure to begin an inquiry by setting out what appears to be the case, on the grounds that the final solution to the problem under discussion ought to be either consistent with what appears to be the case, or, if not, to explain how these appearances are created. (Cf. *E.N.* VII, 1154^a24-25). On this feature of Aristotle's method, see Owen (1961). The justification for attaching weight to what appears to be the case is that, according to Aristotle, no philosophical doctrine can be correct which conflicts completely with such appearances. (Compare *E.N.* X, $1172^b35-1173^a2$, when the Speusippan view that pleasure is not a good at all is rejected on the gounds that it conflicts with a universally held view; cf. also VII, 1153^b27-28); hence the clarification and refinement of such intuitively held opinions must lead in the right direction. Here, the reason given for starting with appearances is that we wish to win acceptance for the conclusions, which can be hoped for if the conclusions can be represented as the result of a systematic development of ordinary intuitions. Although it is impossible to bring this out in translation, in $^b32-35$ Aristotle, in speaking of the unclarity and imprecision of ordinary opinions has in mind not merely the inaccuracies and other defects in their formulation, but also the lack of certainty attaching to them in their unreflective, pre-philosophical form. With this passage may be connected the distinction between those things which are intelligible in themselves and those which are intelligible to us (with which inquiry must start, cf. e.g., *Posterior Analytics* I, 71^b33 f). Compare also *E.N.* I, 1095^b2-9.

$1216^b35-1217^a10$

The political man is encouraged to regard it as worth his while to take note of philosophical arguments which will show not merely *that* something is the case, but also *why* it is, but he is then warned to arrive at his opinion not exclusively on the basis of such arguments. The contrast between philosophical and non-philosophical statements is explained as that between discourse which does, and that which does not, reveal why something is so (taken up at $1217^a 10-11$ with 'account of the reason'). In the sphere which the political man is concerned with, the contrast in question would presumably be that between statements about which things are human goods, and arguments that show what they are, no doubt by reference to a systematically worked-out conception of the good life. Perhaps we should regard the full justification for the political man's taking an interest in philosophy as given only in the sentence 1217^a3-7, where the example of experienced practical men who fall victims of spurious philosophical argument is intended to show the penalty, for the political man, of neglecting philosophical arguments altogether. The form of erroneous philosophizing, which practical men who are innocent of philosophy are said to be taken in by, is said to lie in using arguments that are alien to the discipline and 'idle'; and the reason that this error may fail to be detected is that it is thought to be the mark of the philosopher not to say anything without the support of an argument. This last idea is presumably intended to be recognized as mistaken: any discipline must have some starting-point – propositions which are not open to proof; hence any attempt to prove them must involve the use of arguments of an inappropriate kind. Aristotle refers to the error of asking for a reason for everything in the ethical field at *E.N.* I 1098^a34-^b3.

1217^a10-17

Two reasons are given for the importance (sc. for the political man) of distinguishing properly between the 'account of the reason' and 'what is being demonstrated': (*a*) that sometimes more attention should be paid to appearances than to arguments; that there may be good reason for accepting a proposition as true, on the basis of what appears to be the case, even if a valid argument appears to show the contrary (as may happen if the premisses are false). That is suggested by 1217^a13-14; 'as things are', i.e. not paying attention to what appears to be the case; (*b*) that often what appears to have been demonstrated is true, but not for the reason which the argument gives. Aristotle is here appealing to his theory that a proper account of the reasons for something should be presented in deductive, syllogistic, form. The possibility alluded to here is not, I think (or not solely), the possibility that a valid argument with a true conclusion may have a false premiss, but that even a valid argument with true premisses may not give the correct reason. In the *Posterior Analytics* this is regarded as a matter of finding the correct middle term; though in that work he is not concerned with the sort of demonstrations that this work is concerned with. Here we must suppose that he is interested in reasoning from general principles of an evaluative kind to their application in specific cases. Admittedly, ^a16-17 literally mean 'it is possible to demonstrate something true by means of something false', which might naturally be taken to be referring to the possibility of valid reasoning from falsehood to truth, but it is doubtful if such reasoning could properly be called demonstrative. He may have the same possibility in mind at *E.N.* VI, 1142ᵇ22–24, but the exact interpretation of that passage is disputed.

1217ª11: 'What has just been said'. This has not been explicitly stated, but emerges from the argument of the chapter up to this point: what appears to be the case should be given special weight and arguments should be used with caution.

1217ª17: It is not possible to determine the reference to *Analytics* with any certainty. Possible passages are *Prior Analytics* II, 53ᵇ8–10, 57ª37–40.

CHAPTER 7
1217ª18-29

The theme taken up is that the character of happiness must be investigated. On the idea that there are creatures superior to human beings, compare *E.N.* VI, 1141ª34 f.

1217ª24–26: In this sentence a reason is given for the observation in the previous sentence: the need for the qualification 'human' is not created by the existence of happiness among the lower animals. Aristotle seems to regard it as a plain fact, that will not be disputed, that lower animals are not said to be happy or unhappy. If the Greeks were indeed not willing to call horses happy or unhappy, the explanation may be that they thought they lacked a divine element possessed by human beings (and this may reflect the etymology of the word—see on 1214ª1–8). None the less, if, as implied here, human beings are described as happy or unhappy on the strength of their possession of human goods it is not clear why a horse should not be so called, by analogy, on the strength of its possession of the appropriate equine goods. (On the thought, compare *E.N.* I, 1099ᵇ 32–1100ª3, where a somewhat different reason is given for restricting the attribution of happiness.)

1217ª30-40

On the distinction between things realizable by action, and those not, see further 1218ª38–ᵇ6, with Commentary.

The translation 'realizable by action' of the Greek word *prakton* in fact corresponds only to the first of the senses of the Greek word here distinguished. There seems to be no natural equivalent in English to the word, which is formed from a verb meaning 'do' using a suffix similar to the English '-able'. Aristotle uses it not only of the kind of thing which can be properly described as done (i.e. actions) but also to the results of those actions, though recognizing that this

65

involves two senses. Thus the term is applied, in a different sense, both to money-making activities and to the wealth they produce.

1217ª30:   The reference might be to *E.N.* VII, 1148ᵇ15 f, where Aristotle distinguishes the different manner in which lower animals can experience pleasure, if we connect this with the immediately preceding sentence at the end of the last section.

CHAPTER 8

This chapter and the parallel chapter in *E.N.* I, c. 6 have been the subject of considerable discussion. They raise problems concerning the relation of the *E.N.* and *E.E.* to one another, and the attitudes of Aristotle towards Plato's theory of Forms.

1217ᵇ1-15

Aristotle's opening remark, that the question what the best is must be examined, is intelligible in the light of what has preceded; what is less clear is why it must be asked in how many senses it is used. This inquiry is said at the end of the chapter (1218ᵇ26) to be yet to come, though in fact it is not discussed later in the *E.E.* Berti argues that the final good, happiness, must be the best in a plurality of senses corresponding to the various ways in which other things called 'good' by reference to it are related to it. Berti's suggestion might perhaps be developed as follows: in taking happiness to be the best of human goods, a comparison is implied between the goodness of the final end, and that of the various other human goods; but these other goods are so called in different senses, though these senses will be related focally to the sense in which the final good is so described; hence the final good will have to be regarded as best in a corresponding plurality of senses. But this does not correspond to any argument that we find in Aristotle; nor is it clear that Aristotle would have accepted the principle implied in the argument, that where *A* is correctly described as better than *B*, they must both be called good in the same sense. (On this see Robinson, pp. 188-9.) It may be better to interpret Aristotle as not concerned with different senses in which one thing (sc. the final good) may be described as the best, but with those in which different things (e.g. states, activities, and lives) may all be described as the best in the human sphere. This will then relate to II, 1218ᵇ37-1219ª39.

Aristotle proceeds to a discussion of the Platonic theory of Forms in its application to goodness. Plato is not mentioned by name, and it has been disputed how far the criticism should be regarded as aimed at the theory that we find in some of Plato's dialogues. It is impossible here to discuss fully the evidence about how the theory was developed in the Academy; but with the exception of 1218^{a}15–32 (see Commentary), the chapter does seem to be dealing with a theory that is recognizably the same as that to be found in such Platonic dialogues as the *Phaedo*, *Republic*, *Symposium*, and *Timaeus*.

The character of the theory, as found in Plato can here only be sketched. According to the theory, whenever a plurality of objects are all F (for a wide range of values of F, at least), there is a common character they all have; this common character, whose existence is a condition of Fs having the sense it does, and which determines Fs application to sensibles, is an eternal object, a Form or Idea, not perceptible by the senses and not subject to change; these objects are regarded as the proper realm of knowledge, which according to the theory was strictly only of Forms. In various places where the doctrine is presented it is said or implied that the general term is applicable, primarily and in the strictest and fullest sense, to the Form and only derivatively and in a qualified way to sensible objects. The relation between Forms and corresponding particulars is described by Plato in various metaphorical ways, but most commonly particulars are said either to participate in (or have a share in) the Form, or to be imperfect copies or likenesses of it. Besides serving to explain how a set of objects can have a single general term applied to them, the Forms were sometimes regarded as explaining the actual possession of properties by sensible objects; being thus assigned a causal role, they were thought of as figuring in explanations of physical phenomena (cf. the *Phaedo*). Although there is considerable dispute over precisely which general predicates were held by Plato to have a Form corresponding to them, it is reasonable to hold that, so long as he held anything at all approximating to the theory I have described, he would have recognized the existence of a Form of goodness. In the *Republic* it is assigned a special role *vis-à-vis* the other Forms.

Forms were designated by Plato in a number of different ways. Where F is a general predicate with a corresponding Form, the Form in question was sometimes designated simply by the abstract noun derived from the predicate (e.g. Fness), sometimes by the phrase 'the F' or 'the F-itself'. Aristotle strikingly makes use of the phrase 'the good itself' in this chapter. It seems to reflect the fact that Plato usually held that the Form was the only object to which the associated general term was applicable in the full sense: particulars were *called F* only derivatively from the primary application of F to the Form; only the Form is F, strictly speaking. This seems to have made it natural to contrast the Form, as being the only thing that is *itself F* (strictly), with other things which were *called F*, but were so called only on the strength of participation in, or likeness to, something else which is properly so called.

67

In view of this, we might expect to find Aristotle using the phrase 'the good itself' as simply an alternative designation of the Platonic Form of goodness, an alternative to the phrase 'the Idea of the good' which he also uses. In fact, however, in this chapter the phrase 'the good-itself' is clearly not simply a label for the Form of the good. The phrase is introduced in the present section before Aristotle begins to discuss the Platonic theory. He then points out that the Form of the good would be held by the proponents of the theory to qualify as the good itself, in the sense in which he has defined it. Towards the end of the chapter, after his criticisms of various theories, he expresses his conclusion not as a denial that a good itself exists, but a refusal to identify the good-itself with any of the candidates he has criticized. None of them is the good-itself that he is in search of (1218^b7). Soon afterwards, 1218^b11, something else is identified with the good-itself. He repeats, at $1218^b9–11$, the criteria mentioned for something's being the good-itself.

In his description of the reasons for identifying the good-itself with the Form of the good, Aristotle says (i) that it will indeed be first among the goods; the reason given is that it could exist without the other goods, but not the other goods without it, and that defines the relation of priority; (ii) that it is a cause, by its presence in other things, of their being goods; for this the reason must be that given in $^b9$, that 'good' is most truly predicated of it alone, which in turn is explained by the remark that other things are good in virtue of similarity to, and participation in, the Form of the good. The thought seems to be as follows: participation in a Form will only explain how something comes to be called F if the Form is F in a non-derivative, and hence stricter, sense; conversely, if the Form alone is really F, then, if other things are properly called F, that must be on the strength of some relation (e.g. participation) between it and the Form; and if it is after this fashion that goods other than the Form are so called, the Form is, in some sense a reason for their being goods.

What is the relation between (ii) and (i)? It seems that if the Form is a reason for the goodness of the other good things, there will certainly be a sense in which the Form is prior to other goods: moreover the priority involved will be one which will satisfy the criterion of priority mentioned: goods could not exist without the Form if they owe the fact that they are goods to the Form. But the principle that A is prior to B when A could exist without B but not conversely, will cover a variety of different sorts of priority. (On this see *Categories* and *Metaphysics* Δ, c. 11.) So it is not clear whether (i) says something over and above (ii).

$1217^b14–15$:   On the meaning of 'separate' in application to Forms, see Commentary on $1218^a1–15$.

1217^b16–23

The tone of his initial remarks about the Platonic theory is trenchant, almost hostile, and contrasts with the observation at *E.N.* I, 1096^a11–17, that the fact that the doctrine was introduced by friends makes the task of criticizing it a disagreeable one. This has been taken as indicating that the *E.E.* is earlier than the *E.N.*, on the grounds that the polemical tone is what one might expect from a younger man criticizing a theory of which he had been an adherent not long before. (This argument, of course, assumes an earlier, 'Platonic', phase in Aristotle's thought; see Jaeger.) But the argument seems to have little strength on its own; a number of different explanations are possible of the difference in tone between the two works.

When he says that a thorough investigation of the matter belongs to another, more accurate discipline, the reference is to dialectic in the sense in which that term is used in the *Topics* (cf. *Topics* I, 101^b2, *Sophistici Elenchi*, 183^a39). Although Aristotle thought of the sciences as autonomous, each having its own principles and methods, dialectic was conceived as having a role in other disciplines; its arguments are in this sense 'common' to all. A large part of the task of dialectic consisted in the exposure of fallacies, ambiguities, and the like. Since the theory of Forms has a bearing on a number of sciences that Aristotle distinguished, a thorough and general discussion of it cannot be regarded as belonging to any one science. It is not necessary to suppose that he regarded the examination of the Form of the good that we find in this chapter as belonging to dialectic and not to ethics; what he seems to be saying is that a *full* examination of the theory (i.e. one that looked at the theory as a whole and did not restrict its attention to the Form of the good) would involve going outside ethics into dialectic; hence for the general criticisms, he is content to summarize his opinion and refer to other discussions. All the criticism that follows concerns itself directly with the claim that the good-itself is the Platonic Form of the good.

What is meant by the remark that to say any Form exists at all is to say something 'verbal and vacuous'? At *Metaphysics* A 991^a20–22, Aristotle says that to say that Forms are exemplars and other things participate in them is 'to speak vacuously and use poetical metaphors'. The objection that talk of exemplars and participation is metaphorical would be cogent if the metaphorical language used by Plato was incapable of being replaced by an intelligible non-metaphorical exposition of the theory. This suggests that the objection is that the theory is in fact unintelligible. No such objection seems to be found in what have been held to be fragments of lost works of Aristotle in which he criticizes the theory; but the argument of 1218^a24–28 seems to be not dissimilar.

The statement that to assert the existence of Forms is to speak 'verbally' is less easy to interpret; at *de Anima* 403ª2 we find the same combination, with 'verbally' replaced by 'dialectically' (though not in the context of a discussion of the theory of Forms). The point of the criticism may be that the theory involves a misconstrual of what is perfectly acceptable in a dialectical discussion; in a modern idiom it involves ascribing unwarranted ontological implications to features of ordinary discourse.

1217^b22: 'external discussions': The significance of such references, which are fairly frequent in Aristotle, has been much disputed. They may contain works of Aristotle now lost, intended for a wider circle than treatises like *E.E.*

1217^b23–25

This is the *second* summary remark that Aristotle makes and I think it is best taken as summarizing the main burden of his criticism of the theory of Forms in this chapter. (Note 'for' in ^b25, suggesting that what follows is going to justify the remark about the irrelevance to practice of the Form of the good). This theme is taken up at 1218ª33 f.

1217^b25–35

In this passage Aristotle introduces his doctrine that the verb 'to be' is used in a plurality of senses, corresponding to the various categories, and argues that something similar is true of 'good'. In the translation I have adopted the rendering: 'is so called in many ways', as it is anachronistic to suppose that Aristotle had in mind a plurality of senses, as we should understand that term now. But it is convenient, none the less, to think of the doctrine in that way, because the ground for saying that a term was 'said in many ways' was that different uses could be associated with different 'accounts' (*logoi*) or specifications of the conditions for its application. From this he concludes that there is no single science of good, just as there is no single science of being. The central questions of interpretation are: I: How does Aristotle try to establish the plurality of senses of 'good'? II: How is the conclusion derived, that there is no single science of good, and what is the bearing of this on the Platonic theory?
I: It is impossible here to go into the doctrine of categories fully, or the associated doctrine of the multivocity of 'be'. (For fuller discussions of this, see Ackrill's commentary on *Categories*, c. 4 and Kirwan's on *Metaphysics* Γ, c. 1.) The theory of categories underwent development in Aristotle's writings (in the *Categories* it was

not related to any ambiguity in the meaning of the verb 'to be'), but it is probably true that at all times, the theory involved treating all the things that are said to be (or, as we should say, exist) as belonging to one or another of a listable set of ultimate classes or *summa genera*. This classification of existents into *summa genera* or highest kinds is an ultimate one in the sense that the *summa genera* are not to be regarded as themselves subordinate to a still more comprehensive genus embracing everything that there is. Hence Aristotle denies that being is a genus (cf. *Metaphysics* B 998^{b}22, *Posterior Analytics* II, 92^{b}14). The list of categories which Aristotle gives varies a good deal, and is seldom as long as it is in this passage. In the *Categories* ten are listed, but most commonly only substance, quality, relation, and perhaps quantity are mentioned. According to Aristotle, though both an individual substance (e.g. Socrates) and a quality (e.g. courage) may be said to exist, we must not suppose that the possibility of making this assertion about each of them implies that there is a genus, or kind, containing all existents, to which they both belong. The doctrine of the plurality of senses of 'to be' might then follow from this doctrine in the following way: since in saying of courage that it exists, we are not assigning it to a genus of existents (there is none) we must be assigning it to one of the several ultimate genera, to one of which everything that exists belongs—in this case, the *summum genus*, or category, of quality. But when an existential assertion is made about an item in another category, the assignment will of course be to a different category; and this might be thought to have the consequence that 'to be' is systematically ambiguous, having a different sense according to the category of item involved: for one thing, to exist will be to be a quality, for another, to be a substance, and so on. This interpretation goes beyond anything explicit in Aristotle's works, but is in line with his general views on the sources of ambiguity, though it requires us to hold that the ambiguity of 'to be' associated with the theory of categories is exhibited solely in existential assertions.

What are the features of the use of 'good' which he takes to show that 'good' has as many senses as 'be'? This passage is closely parallel to *E.N.* I, 1096^{a}23-29, and it seems reasonable to make use of what he says there for interpreting it. Here he says simply that the good is in each of these 'categories' (for the translation of ^{b}30, see Notes). In the *E.N.*, he says, more explicitly, that the good (or perhaps the word 'good') is said in the category of substance (literally 'in the what-is') or of quality or ... and later implies that it is 'said in all the categories'. Assuming that the same point is being made here, the problem is to determine what is meant by saying that the good is said (i.e. predicated) in all categories. Both here and in the *E.N.*, examples are given of goods in the various categories; the list is almost the same in both passages.

The simplest interpretation is that Aristotle means that the term 'good' can be predicated of things in any of the categories; in favour of this is the fact that it can hardly be disputed that something properly described as good may belong to any of the categories he distinguishes, as Aristotle's examples show. This straightforward view is open to the following objections. (i) Aristotle seems to think that it follows immediately from the feature of the use of 'good' that he refers to, that 'good' is used in as many senses as 'be'. We are not told why that should follow, but presumably it does so in virtue of some general principle which Aristotle accepted. Now if, when he says that the good is predicated in all the categories, he means simply that goods are distributed among all the categories, it is difficult to see what the principle used is, if not some principle that no word may be used, in the same sense, of items in different categories. Such a principle might appear initially plausible if certain kinds of example are considered. It seems natural to suppose that 'pale' cannot be applied in the same sense both to Socrates and to the colour of his complexion; or again that a field and the distance across it cannot in the same sense be described as small. But if applied quite generally, the principle seems to be quite unacceptable. There seems little to be said for the view that 'visible' is not applied in the same sense to substances, qualities, quantities, and relations. Aristotle nowhere enunciates such a principle, nor does he seem to employ it explicitly elsewhere. There is no mention of such a principle in the *Topics* in the discussion of the ways of detecting ambiguities. As interpreted above, the thesis that the different categories generate corresponding different senses of 'be' does not imply that items in different categories cannot have the same term applied to them in the same sense: that items do not belong to a common genus does not imply that a term may not be predicated univocally of them, since such predications need not be construed as involving the assignment of the categorially different items to a single genus. For further discussion, see Ackrill (1972).

(ii) The interpretation under discussion is not very easy to reconcile with the language of Aristotle, both here and in the *E.N.* To say that the good is 'said in all the categories' is at least not a very natural way of expressing the thought that goods may belong to any of the categories, and this thought is one which could easily have expressed succinctly and unambiguously if that had been what he had in mind here.

It seems to me that the correct interpretation must take proper account, firstly of the fact that Aristotle seems to regard the ambiguity of 'good' as in some way parallel to the ambiguity of 'be', and secondly of the fact that the examples given are all of things which are necessarily and essentially good, not of things that may be intelligibly described as good, but are so or not depending on the individual case. This may suggest that Aristotle's thought was that for some things, to be good *is* to be (a case of) justice, for others to be good is to be the right amount, and similarly in the other cases. This line of approach is perhaps more plausible if we suppose that Aristotle has in mind, at least primarily, judgements of the form 'X. is a good' rather than 'X is good'; these are distinguishable in many cases in Greek by the inflexion of the adjective, and Aristotle at several places certainly does allude to identifications of an item as a good (1218^{a}10, 18-19, 1218^{b}22). The point will then be that to be a good consists sometimes in being a certain sort of substance, sometimes a certain sort of quality, sometimes a certain sort of quantity; it follows from this that there can be no abstractable generic feature common to all goods: giving a *logos* or specification of what it is which constitutes an item as a good will be essentially different in different cases: sometimes the specification will be 'to be a substance which . . .' sometimes 'to be a quality which . . .'

This may be a correct account of Aristotle's doctrine here, but as a doctrine it is open to fairly obvious objections. In the first place, the narrowing of attention to identificatory judgements of goodness, of the form '—is a good' may seem unduly restrictive, and to treat as primary what seems to be secondary, since judgements of the form 'x is a good' are most plausibly regarded as analysable into statements of the form 'x is a thing which is good', where the relative clause contains an adjectival, non-identificatory predication of 'good'. Nothing in the argument attributed to Aristotle rules out the possibility that some single character whose presence in items in any of the categories leads to their being described as goods: to be a good will be to be a substance which is ϕ or a quality which is ϕ, etc. If so, it will be natural to identify goodness with ϕness, a single character possessed by all goods, even though to be a good will vary according to the category of item involved. If an objection is raised to the suggestion that there could be a common character shared by substances, qualities, quantities, etc., the objection would have to appeal to some general principle of a kind we have already rejected. An alternative way of meeting the objection that no argument is offered to rule out a common character, ascribed to things in attributive, non-identificatory judgements of goodness would be to argue that *being good* needed to be explained in terms of *being a good* and not vice versa; but no such argument is offered.

Whatever may be the correct interpretation of this extremely puzzling passage, it is doubtful if a satisfactory argument for the multivocity of 'good' can be extracted: for Aristotle is plainly trying to show that 'good' cannot be univocal by an entirely general argument which appeals only to the locutions in which 'good' occurs. But such linguistic phenomena are hardly by themselves inconsistent with the word's having a constant meaning. If someone wishes to define good as meaning 'conducive to happiness', this view can hardly be rejected on the basis of the sort of considerations that Aristotle seems to be alluding to here.

II: The wider problem raised by this passage is how it fits into the criticisms of the Platonic theory. Aristotle says that, just as the good is not a single thing embracing the things mentioned, neither is there a single science of the good. In the next section he argues that even in the case of goods so called within a single category, there is no single science that investigates them. It is Aristotle's view that where a class of things belong to a single genus, they are all objects of a single science. He has argued that goods do not belong to a single genus or kind; hence there is no single science of the good; but what is the relevance of establishing that goodness is the object of numerous distinct sciences? It has been suggested that Aristotle is implicitly arguing against the existence of the Form of the Good by showing that at least its existence cannot be established by one of the standard arguments for the existence of forms—the 'argument from the sciences' (cf. Berti). The argument from the sciences is referred to by Aristotle at *Metaphysics* A 990^b12, M 1079^a8-9, and an exposition of the argument is to be found in what appears to be a fragment of the lost work *On the Ideas* (Ross fr. 3, Oxford Translation, XII, p. 125). According to that passage, the Platonists argued that a single unified science required correlative, unitary items to form its subject-matter, and this was one of the arguments used in the Academy for the existence of Forms. But it is difficult to believe that Aristotle is here arguing against the existence of the Form of the good, in this manner, by arguing against the existence of a single science. In the first place, the conclusion that goodness is not a single genus containing all goods surely would have enabled Aristotle to draw the conclusion that there is no Form of the good directly. Indeed, the statement here that there is no single science either of being or of the good appears to be a *conclusion* from the doctrine, stated at ^b33-35, that neither being nor good is a single thing embracing what he has mentioned, and it therefore seems impossible to treat it as an attempt to undermine the 'argument from the sciences' without making it into a *petitio principii*. The remark that there is not a single science either of being or of good is, as I interpret it, an *obiter dictum*, interesting because it shows that Aristotle at the time that he wrote the *E.E.*, regarded the absence of a single genus as precluding the possibility of a single science, and there is no sign of his later doctrine that things that are focally related may form the subject-matter of a single science. On this see, further, Owen (1960).

1217^{b}35-1218^{a}1

Aristotle now says that it does not fall to a single science to investigate all goods even of a *single* category. The examples given are of the moderate and right occasion, i.e. the goods in the categories of time and quantity (cf. ^{b}31-32). This passage is paralleled by *E.N.* 1096^{a}29-34. Different sciences concern themselves with each in diverse spheres of human interest. In this section he is willing to allow that a single science might investigate goods both in the category of time and of quantity, as in the examples of generalship and medicine; so the argument of ^{b}25-35 from the categorial diversity of good to the non-existence of a general science of good is not thought to rule out sciences whose objects belong to more than one category; but it is difficult to see, in view of the concession that the objects of a single science may be categorially diverse, how there can be any immediate step from the thesis that the good does not constitute a genus to the conclusion that there is no single science of the good. The difficulty seems to be that Aristotle's view of the way that sciences ought to be unified and differentiated assigns to each science a single genus, whose members are objects with which the science deals (cf. *Posterior Analytics*). That would indeed preclude the existence of a single science with a categorially variegated subject-matter. But this picture is certainly something of an idealization, as shown by his examples here, of medicine and generalship.

This section appears to argue directly against the Platonic theory, by claiming that the existence of different sciences that study the good precludes the existence of a general science of good; whereas the Platonic theory presupposes the existence of such a science, with the Form as its object. So, while ^{b}25-35, as I have interpreted it, starts from the doctrine of categories, derives from that the conclusion that there is no single genus of good, and then mentions in passing that it follows that there is no single science for the good, this section moves from the observed phenomenon of a plurality of sciences to the denial of a general science, of which the (unstated) conclusion is that there is no Form of the good. That this is the point of this section is corroborated by the parallel passage in *E.N.* (I, 1096^{a}29-34), where it is presented explicitly as a *reductio ad absurdum* of the Platonic hypothesis.

As an argument it is open to serious objection. Although there are

indeed the different sciences that Aristotle mentions, that will certainly not rule out the possibility of a 'higher', superordinate science,
set over such sciences (see, later in this chapter, 1218ᵇ12 f., with
Commentary). The science of the good for man is that to which
more special sciences, concerned with specific human goods, are
subordinate. It is, of course, perfectly consistent to allow that there
is a single, architectonic science of human good, and deny that there
is a wholly general science of good in general (and not merely *human*
good). But the *argument* from the existence of distinct sciences,
dealing with specific human goods, to the impossibility of a completely general science of the good, such as Plato accepted, is invalid;
and if it were accepted as valid, it is difficult to see how the inference
from the same premises to a denial of a single science of human
good could be disallowed.

1218ᵃ1-15

This passage must be considered as a whole, because the text is in an
extremely poor state, and it looks as if we have lacunae in at least
two places. There is a general correspondence between the first part
and *E.N.* 1096ᵃ19-23, and between the second part and *E.N.* 1096ᵃ
34-35. But there are two striking differences: in the *E.E.* Aristotle
says that there is no Form corresponding to a set of things serially
ordered as if it were his view, with no hint that it was also held, and
actually argued for, by Plato. He says that in the case of everything
in which the earlier and later is present, there is no common thing
over and above them, that is separate from them. If there were it
would be prior to the first member of the series. The argument is
then illustrated for the case of the double, which is the first of the
manifolds. In the *E.N.*, on the other hand, the argument is presented
purely as an *argumentum ad hominem*. The introducers of the
doctrines of Forms are said to have denied that there was any single
form of things that are serially ordered; they therefore ought, in
consistency, to have denied that there was a single form of goodness
either, since, as Aristotle argues, goods fall into a serial order.

The argument has often been attacked as extremely weak (cf.
Cherniss, Appendix VI). In a series like the sequence of natural
numbers, the number two (according to the Greeks) is prior to all
the others; and the argument is that the Form of number, like the
other Forms, is prior to the particulars falling under it, which would
mean that it was prior to the first number, which it cannot be if two
is the first number. But the contradiction thus generated is only the
apparent one, and arises from a failure to distinguish different senses
in which one thing may be said to be prior to another. Aristotle
himself is at pains, elsewhere, to make just this sort of distinction

between senses in which one thing may be said to be prior to another. In this passage in the *E.E.*, Aristotle does offer some explanation of the sense in which the form is prior to its particulars – the first member of the series depends on the common element for its existence (whereas the converse relation does not hold, as we have to add); and one might attempt to rehabilitate the argument by claiming that the same ontological dependence holds between each member in the series, so that the argument does not exploit an ambiguity in the sense of 'prior'. But the relation between a Form and its particulars, as conceived by holders of the theory, is different from the relation between an earlier and a later member of the number series: the formula '*A* could exist without *B* but not *B* without *A*' covers a number of specific differences. In any case, there seems no good reason why a holder of the theory of forms should retain the premiss that the number two is, without qualification, the first number. It may be the first number *in the number series*, but there seems no reason why a holder of the theory of Forms should continue to hold that it is the first number in every sense, if he holds that each Form is prior to its particulars and itself a possessor of the character it represents. The Form of number will itself be a number, and in an appropriate sense prior to any member of the number series.

Why then do we have in the *E.N.*, the same thesis about the existence of a Form of things serially ordered presented without argument, and as a view accepted by Platonists? The most natural explanation seems to be one which would place the *E.N.* after the *E.E.*: that Aristotle had had doubts about the argument's validity, but it was one which had been used by some members of the Academy. It seems difficult to see otherwise why Aristotle should have presented the argument in the *E.N.* as an *argumentum ad hominem*.

Another difference between the *E.N.* and *E.E.* is, of course, that in the text of the *E.E.* as we have it, there is no argument for the serial ordering of goods. Assuming the argument is the same in both we have to choose between saying that Aristotle expected the essential premiss that goods are serially ordered to be gathered from the context, and supposing that there is a lacuna in ª8.

This passage stresses that there is no common Form which is, in addition, *separate* from things that are serially ordered. There is no suggestion that all things serially ordered lack a common character. What is denied is that such a common element is a Platonic Form. In the *E.N.*, on the other hand, it is simply said that there cannot be a 'common idea over and above these things'. I take it that the reason why the separate character of the Form is emphasized in the *E.E.* is that only if it is separate will the premiss of the argument be true, that the Form is prior to its instances. In the *E.N.*, on the other hand, the argument occurs in a passage all of which, at least up to 1096ᵇ32, is directed against the thesis that the Form is something common which all goods share. What is found objectionable, there, is that the theory of Forms involves the view that goodness is a common character. Thus, in the *E.N.*, we have the argument presented as an *argumentum ad hominem* with no mention of the crucial assumption which was thought to cause difficulty. That suggests a later date for the *E.N.*

Keeping the manuscript reading at ª8 f, which gives us '*if* it results that the common character is the Form', and postulating no lacuna before the conditional clause, the text is extremely difficult to make sense of. For we have to suppose that the conditional clause has as its consequent the sentence 'it will be prior to the double', so the conditional will be saying that the Form *many-fold* will have to be prior to the double *if* the common character is construed as a Platonic Form by being treated as separate. But although it is certainly correct to say that the supposedly absurd conclusion that the many-fold would be prior to the double follows only if the Form is treated as separate, it would be superfluous to add such a condition there, since it has already been said at ª6–7 that the conclusion is that the many-fold cannot be predicated in common *and as a separate entity*. ª7–8 will then give as a reason for this that (if such a common predicate is separate) it will be prior to the double, and the assumption that the common character is separate would not need to be mentioned again.

I conclude that either emendation, or the postulation of a lacuna, is necessary. D. J. Allan (1963–4), proposes emending the text so that 'if' is replaced by 'or' ('or else the consequence follows . . .'). This gives the whole passage the form of a dilemma.

The suggestion is ingenious, and involves a minimum of alteration to the text. The difficulty is that it seems to require that we interpret as having the form of a dilemma an argument in which only one horn of the dilemma is stated. Already, at ª1–3, Aristotle has indicated the possibility he wishes to argue against as the possibility of a separate Form common to all members of an ordered sequence. It seems very difficult to take the strikingly similar language of ª9 as referring, instead, to the supposition that there is a separate Form corresponding to all goods, conceived as being on the same level and not serially ordered. Allan does, however, seem to be right in holding that the section from ª8 onward represents a more general argument against the Platonic theory, which does not exploit the serial ordering of goods.

In the absence of any satisfactory emendation I assume that a sentence or two has dropped out in ª8. As mentioned earlier, the argument as presented in *E.E.* lacks an explicit statement of the crucial premiss that goods constitute an ordered series, and it may well have been enunciated in the section that has dropped out. As consequent for the conditional at ª8–9 we might supply a sentence like 'There are other problems if . . .'; an advantage of the view that there is a lacuna in ª8 is that the conditional seems to belong with what follows rather than with what precedes, and what follows is a new argument closely parallel to *E.N.* I, 1096ª34–ᵇ5.

The argument is that the Platonists inferred from the fact that distinct things could be correctly described as goods, that there is a good-itself. Aristotle then argues that the word 'itself' occurs as an extra element in the specification of the Form, over and above the general definition of goodness which the other goods satisfy. But what can be the significance of this 'itself', except to signify that the Form is eternal, and separate? But, Aristotle argues, the mere fact of eternity will not make the Form of the good any better than any ordinary good thing. So, the common character, goodness, will not be the same as the Form.

There are a number of puzzling features in the argument. (i) If we postulate a lacuna in ª14 and fill the text out in the way suggested, the argument will be an argument against the identification of the Form of the good with the highest good. The point of the assertion that being eternal does not necessarily make a thing any better must be that, on the view being attacked, the only difference between the Form of the good and any other good thing will be that the Form is eternal and that therefore the fact that it is eternal is the only ground for regarding it as the highest good. Neither here nor in the *E.N.* is there an argument against the *existence* of the Form of the good, only against its identification with the highest good. It is then surprising that Aristotle, at ª14–15, concludes that the Form of the good is not identical with the common character, goodness, as though an argument to show that the character common to all goods cannot be a separate Form had preceded.

(ii) Aristotle seems to introduce the notion of a good-itself here in ª10–11 as if it were an entirely new conception, not something already mentioned at the beginning of the chapter.

(iii) His argument seems to involve a misunderstanding of Plato's reason for using phrases like 'the *X* itself', which is that the Form is conceived as being that which is *itself* good, not good only through the presence of something else that is good in its own right. If so, 'itself' does not introduce a further specification of the definition of the Form. The same argument occurs at *E.N.* I, 1096ª34–ᵇ5. Compare also *Metaphysics* A 991ª2–8 and M 1079ª33–ᵇ11. At ª15, it is said that the common character must belong to every member of the

class (presumably every member of the class in question), and that is
given as a reason for denying the identity of the Form with the common character. The argument appears to be that if one introduces a
good-itself, the qualification 'itself' disqualifies the Form from being
a common character shared by every good thing, presumably because
it represents a different form of goodness from that possessed by
any ordinary good thing. But if so, Aristotle is simply misunderstanding the sense of 'itself'.

(iv) In the *E.N.*, unlike the *E.E.*, it is implied that the addition of
'itself' must signify solely, in each case, that the Form is eternal;
whereas here there is mention also of the status of the Form as
something separate. Does that mean that it does not depend for its
existence on particulars? Or is it rather that it has to be conceived of
as a distinct *good*? The argument does seem to assume that the
Form of the Good is itself a good, and argue from that that it will
be a good after a different fashion from other goods, and hence not
the common character.

(v) The argument appears to assume that there is such a thing as
the common character goodness, despite the fact that the earlier
arguments about 'good' and the categories, have tended to undermine that assumption.

(vi) Why does Aristotle adopt here such an ambivalent attitude
towards the acceptability of the notion of good-itself? Perhaps because he regarded himself as offering an alternative theory to Plato's,
and a better one, hence he sometimes expressed his view as a view
about what could be identified with the Form of the good. However,
given his theory, the phrase is inappropriate, since it goes with the
view that other goods are not really goods at all. If we suppose that
the *E.N.* is later, it will be easy to see why he should have abandoned
it in the *E.N.*

The alternative, of not postulating a lacuna at ^a14, will give a
perfectly translatable text, but it is open to the objection that it is
quite unclear why the point that an eternal *F* is not *more F* than one
that is not should establish the non-identity of the common character
with the form.

Neither here nor in *E.N.* is it made clear precisely *what* sort of
argument against Plato is to be obtained from the consideration that
the good-itself is no better than any other good, but, in both cases it
is plausible to suppose that it is an argument against the identification
of the Form of the good with the best. Perhaps we should suppose
that there is a rather *longer* lacuna than has been supposed, in which
Aristotle *first* draws his conclusion that the common character (conceived as being separate) cannot be highest good and then adds
that the Form was said to be the highest good, and then concludes

(ᵃ14–15) that the common character cannot be identified with the Form. The reason is given that the common character is common to all the things that possess it. This is presumably intended to point out the inconsistency of treating the common character shared by all goods as itself a further good.

1218ᵃ15-32

This passage divides into three sections (ᵃ15–24, ᵃ24–30, ᵃ30–32) the internal argument of which is reasonably clear; what is obscure is the connection between them, and whose views are being attacked by Aristotle here. An admirable analysis of the argument, and discussion of the identity of Aristotle's opponents is given by Brunschwig, and my discussion of both issues owes a good deal to his article.

This passage is almost entirely without parallel in *E.N.*: I, 1096ᵇ5–7 is no more than a passing reference to the Pythagorean doctrine, and a different one from that under attack here. Likewise, *M.M.* 1183ᵃ24–28 is parallel only in a general way.

In the first section, Aristotle objects to his unnamed opponents that the procedure they follow is the reverse of the correct one: they seek to demonstrate the goodness of things agreed to be good, like justice and health, from propositions that are far more dubious. The argument seems to be as follows: (i) Numbers are goods. (ii) Virtues are numbers. (iii) Virtues (e.g. justice) are goods. To this he objects that it requires demonstration that 'the fine' has application in the sphere of unchanging objects; that is, (i) (or rather, a presupposition of it) needs demonstration. The procedure ought to be reversed, and propositions like (iii) should be the premises of the argument. Aristotle's view seems to be that, although, strictly, goodness has application only within the sphere of the changeable, since only there are there things that can be brought into existence, the fine is to be found in both fields (compare *Metaphysics* M 1078ᵃ31: 'Since the good and the fine are different (for the one is always in action, but the fine occurs also in unchanging things . . .)' See also 1218ᵇ4–6, with Commentary). So the conclusion of the quasi-inductive argument that he thinks would have been acceptable is not precisely the inverse of the argument criticized.

Although the methodological criticism is levelled against the argument just mentioned, ᵃ19–21 suggest a second syllogism, to establish I (i), as follows: II (i) Good-itself is the One. (ii) The One belongs to numbers. Therefore (iii) Good belongs to numbers. Only (i) is stated, at ᵃ20–21, but (ii) seems to be required if (i) is to support (iii), which in its turn differs only verbally from (i) in the first argument.

At ᵃ16, he says that they ought to demonstrate the good-itself in the opposite way to that in which they do now, but the argument

(I) that is directly criticized does not mention the good-itself. Such a mention occurs in II, but in a premiss ((i)): II is not a demonstration of what good-itself is. Such a demonstration, as Brunschwig points out, occurs in the second section (^{a}24–32), as appears from ^{a}26, and it may be reconstructed as follows: III (i) Numbers seek the One. (ii) That which numbers seek is the good-itself. Therefore (iii) Good-itself is the One. (ii) needs to be supplied in order to make ^{a}24–26 intelligible. Since I(i) = II(iii), and III(iii) = II(i), II forms a bridge between the first two sections of this passage, supplying a premiss to the argument of the first section, and using the conclusion of the second. In III, the main burden of his criticism falls on (i), which he criticizes as being unintelligible and metaphorical, and requiring support that is not forthcoming. III(ii), however, though unstated, seems to require support. We might reconstruct the following argument: IV(i) What numbers seek is what all beings essentially seek. (ii) What all beings essentially seek is the good-itself. Therefore, (iii) What all numbers seek is the good-itself. IV(ii) would then be undermined by Aristotle's observation that there is no single good which everything seeks, as each sort of thing seeks its own specific good, and IV(i) would rest on an ontology that reduced everything to numbers. If this reconstruction is correct, 1218ᵃ15-32 forms a passage that needs to be examined as a whole, in which a single metaphysical theory, relating goodness to a mathematical ontology, is subjected to criticisms at several points. The passage is marked off by the summary of the chapter which follows it, and the criticism of the classical Platonic Ideal Theory that precedes it.

What argument, of a more acceptable kind, does Aristotle gesture towards at ^{a}21–24? The argument seems to be that agreed goods like health and strength are so regarded because they exhibit order and stability (equilibrium, balance); but such characteristics are to be found in a higher degree in unchanging objects, so the good, (or rather, Aristotle qualifies, the fine) is to be discerned there still more. The argument is an inductive one in a loose sense. For the claim that virtues are goods because they possess order and structure, compare II, 1222ᵃ3. The idea that health consists in a certain structure of bodily elements is to be found in *Physics* VII, 246ᵇ3–8, *Topics* 145ᵇ7–8. A generalization of such propositions about agreed goods would yield the doctrine of *Metaphysics* M 1078ᵃ36: 'The most general forms of the fine are order and proportion and definition, which characteristics are established pre-eminently by the mathematical sciences.'

The object of Aristotle's attack has been identified as Plato, as the Pythagoreans, or as Xenocrates.

In favour of the hypothesis that the Pythagoreans were the object of Aristotle's attack is the apparent attempt, in the theory being criticized, to reduce health and justice to numbers, or to a mathematically expressible structure. (Compare Aristotle's remarks about the Pythagoreans at *Metaphysics* A 985^{b}26-32, 1078^{b}21-22.)

In favour of the identification of Xenocrates as the holder of the doctrine here criticized is the fact that the reference to 'now' at 1218ª16 suggests a certain topicality, and the fact that in the passage under discussion no distinction is drawn between 'ideal' and 'mathematical' numbers. Xenocrates appears to have rejected such a distinction (for the evidence, see Ross (1951), pp. 151-2), and in that respect satisfies the specification found in this passage.

How strong is the evidence that Plato ever held such a theory? There are a number of passages in which Aristotle appears to claim that Plato identified all Forms with numbers, at some stage (Compare *Metaphysics* A 991^{b}9-10, 992^{b}16, M 1073ª18-19, 1081ª5-17, 1082^{b}23-24, 1083ª17-18, 1086ª11-13, N 1090ª16-17, 1091^{b}26). That Plato ever held such a doctrine has been disputed (see Cherniss and Ross (1951)), but for present purposes it is sufficient that such a doctrine was attributed to Plato by Aristotle. There is similar evidence that Plato was credited by Aristotle with having treated the One as having the role of formal cause in the generation of Forms. (See, for example, *Metaphysics* A 987^{b}18-25.)

Brunschwig suggests that what we have may in fact be, in summary form, a criticism that was developed more fully in Aristotle's own lost work *On the Good*, itself a version of Plato's lectures, no doubt also containing some criticism of Plato's doctrines.

But it is difficult to believe that Plato, or whoever held the theory, thought of the demonstration in question as a means of *discovery* of the goodness of health, wisdom, etc; it is surely much more probable that the aim was to *explain* the goodness of such generally recognized goods by offering a systematic theory. It is hardly an objection to a theory that it has as consequences truths concerning which we are far more certain than we are of the axioms of the theory.

Similarly, the objection that the proposition that numbers seek the One is metaphorical seems too facile.

1218ª19-20: 'numbers and monads'. The use of the term 'monad' is no doubt to be interpreted in the light of what is said by Alexander of Aphrodisias in his commentary on the *Metaphysics* (55. 20f. = Ross, p. 113, fr. 2 of *On the Good*). It is there said that, both for Plato and Pythagoreans, solids are generated out of planes, planes out of lines, and lines out of points (which are there called monads), which were ultimate and not further analysable. Aristotle says that they regard these elements (or rather, no doubt, sets of them) as numbers, and it was thus, presumably, that numbers (conceived of as aggregates of basic elements) were regarded as the ultimate constituents of the universe. If so, in this passage, 'numbers' and 'monads' refer to the same things.

1218ᵃ33–35

This summarizing passage marks the end of the criticism of the Platonic Theory. It parallels the initial summary of his criticism of Plato at 1217ᵇ19–25. The argument that the Platonic Form is of no use to political science, because each science is devoted to seeking to achieve a good specific to that science, is extremely brief. Presumably, when he says here and at 1217ᵇ25, that it is not useful, he means that a *knowledge* of it is of no use. If so, a Platonist might reply with the objection raised at *E.N.* I, 1096ᵇ35–1097ᵃ3, to which Aristotle replies with remarks similar to those he makes here.

1218ᵃ36–38

These lines were excised as a gloss by Cook Wilson, followed by Susemihl. But there seems no good reason for this. The first sentence begins with a reference to 'what is written in the treatise' (*logos*), followed by a brief allusion to an argument, apparently having the form of a dilemma. There follows a further argument against the Platonic Theory: the Form of the good is not 'realizable by action'. The latter criticism is most conveniently considered with the criticism of the identification of common character goodness with the supreme good.

The form of citation in ᵃ36 is strange, and it is probably impossible to reach any firm conclusion about what work is referred to. A similar form of words occurs at VII, 1244ᵇ30–31, which means that it would probably be a mistake either to emend or excise this sentence. The matter is discussed at length by Dirlmeier, both in his note on this passage, and in his article 'Merkwürdige Zitate', in which he also discusses II, 1220ᵇ11 (see Commentary) and VII, 1244ᵇ30–31. The reference may be to some early work, like *On Philosophy*, *On the Ideas*, or *On the Good*: but the form of words is uncharacteristic. Dirlmeier refers to *Topics* 105ᵇ12, and in the article, perhaps more relevantly, to *Topics* 109ᵇ13 f. 'Another rule is to examine classes of which it has been said that something belongs either to all or to no members.'

The argument would then be as follows: (i) The Form of the good, if it exists, is useful (i.e. knowledge of it is useful) either to all sciences or to none. In order to show that it is not useful to every science, one counter-example is enough. So (ii) it is not useful to every science, and therefore (iii), by (i), it is not useful to any science. Therefore, in particular, it is not useful to political science (cf. ᵃ34).

The argument for (ii) may have been not dissimilar to *E.N.* I 1097ᵃ 8–11, where Aristotle says that it is difficult to see how a weaver or a doctor will be helped in his craft by having seen the Form of the good. It is probable that in this passage the term 'science' is used in a broad sense, covering a range which includes higher order disciplines like mathematics, and also practical skills like medicine, gymnastics and generalship. The problem concerns Aristotle's justification for enunciating the original disjunction, (i). Aristotle's argument seems to involve an unwarrantable insistence that, if every good is so, ultimately, in virtue of its relation to the Form of the good, no particular good can be recognized as such except by someone with knowledge of the Form.

1218ᵃ38–1218ᵇ6

It emerges from the summarizing passage at 1218ᵇ7–9 that Aristotle is here arguing against a *second* view, distinct from the Platonic one, that the 'good-itself' is a common character, goodness, shared by all goods. The argument is brief, perhaps because some of the earlier arguments tell as much against the existence of such a common character as against the Platonic Forms specifically, e.g. 1217ᵇ25–35 and perhaps 1218ᵃ1–15. ᵃ38–ᵇ4 seem to give two arguments against the claims of the common character to be the good-itself which Aristotle is looking for. One is that it is not 'realizable', an objection that was also raised against the Forms at ᵃ37–38. The other argument occurs in the clause in brackets in ᵇ1. There then follows, at ᵇ2–4, a further supporting remark. Is this offered as a *third* argument, or is it intended to support one of the two already given?

It is worth noting, first, that the conclusion is stated in a rather surprising way: as it seems to have been Aristotle's view that there is no single common character, goodness, the question of its identity with the good-itself ought not to arise. The earlier argument for the ambiguity of 'good' would have as a consequence that there is no single common character possessed by all good things. It is as if Aristotle were offering here a brief and popular argument for a conclusion already established, in a more fundamental way, by the earlier, more technical, arguments.

That Aristotle discusses the common character at all as a candidate for being the good-itself is rather surprising. He began the chapter by laying down some conditions that any candidate proposed must ᶜulfil (1217ᵇ3–5); the Platonic Form appeared to fulfil them, hence tᵔe discussion of it. These requirements are not abandoned: in 1218ᵇ 9–11 his own candidate is shown to satisfy them (see Commentary

85

on the next section). No such motivating reason is given for the brief discussion of the common character.

In fact, it seems that the common character is thought to deserve discussion because those who accepted that there is such a common character would claim that it is the reason for anything's being a good. Would they also claim that it was first among the goods (cf. 1217^b4, 1218^b11) and highest of all goods? If they accepted the first of these, their position would involve more than bare acceptance of such a common character: they would be treating it as itself the unique possessor of the character, and thus separate from all the possessors of it. Their position would then be that criticized by Aristotle at 1218^a1-15, which involved incoherently separating the common character, and treating it as one of its own instances. Plato's theory tended to include these incompatible strands. Similarly, if the common character, goodness, is regarded as the best thing that there is, it is again being treated as a good, comparable with other things in respect of goodness. Yet Aristotle appears to be considering the claims of the common character as a candidate on its own account, and independently of the Platonic theory. The difficulty is that, if the existence of the common character is treated on its merits, and independently of the Platonic tendency to treat it also as an ideal exemplar or instance, it hardly looks like a candidate for what Aristotle is seeking to identify.

In this matter, *E.N.* is much clearer and more coherent. Although *E.N.* I, 6 is explicitly devoted to a discussion of the Platonic doctrine of the Form of the good, Aristotle seems much clearer about the relation of Plato's theory to the view that goodness is a common character, and the relevance of his arguments against it. At 1096^a11, the view about goodness that he is about to discuss is introduced by the phrase 'the universal good', and most of the discussion of the chapter is concerned with the doctrine that there is a common character, goodness. Throughout, Aristotle recognizes the equivalence of saying that goodness is a single thing (1096^a28, 1096^b32) and that it is common (1096^a23, 28, 1096^b25, 32) and that it is universal (1096^a28). It is also recognized that this view, that goodness is a single universal character, is *one* consequence of the Platonic ideal theory. He speaks of something 'common in accordance with a single Form' (1096^b25-26) and hence arguments against that are arguments against the Ideal Theory. It is also recognized that the argument from categories for the systematic ambiguity of 'good' is an argument against the common character, and thereby an argument against the existence of the Form of the good. In *E.E.* 1217^b25 f, there is no indication of the relevance of the argument from categories for the Ideal Theory. In *E.N.* I, 6, after devoting the bulk of the chapter to the criticism of common character-consequences of the Ideal Theory, at 1096^{b}31, he turns his attention to a distinct criticism of the Form of the good as something separate, and here the objection is made that the Form will not be realizable.

In *E.N.*, too, Aristotle recognizes that, though the thesis that goodness is a common character of all goods is a feature of the theory in the form in which it was held by Plato, a modified version was possible in which the common character represented by the Form belongs only to the things that are good in themselves, other goods being so described in a different sense, and by reference to the goodness of things good in themselves (1096^{b}8–26). No such argument occurs here.

The argument at 1218^{b}1, for the conclusion that the common character *good* is not identical with the good-itself (cf. 1218^{a}15), is that the good-itself would then belong to any good whatsoever, even a 'small' good. We have also seen that such a common character would qualify as the cause of goodness in other things: the point seems to be that it will not be the highest good. In fact there is no reason why a believer in the common character should hold that it is the highest good. But if the common character is treated not merely as that, but also as itself a good, it is unclear why the fact that it belongs to things good only to a small degree should constitute any special difficulty.

The argument that the common character is not realizable is paralleled by the same objection to the Platonic Forms a few lines earlier, and by the argument of *E.N.* I, 1096^{b}34–35; there, however, it is allowed that the objection is not decisive, and Aristotle goes on to consider the reply that knowledge of it would be of value as a guide and a standard.

How much force does this objection have, either against the Platonic Form or the common character? The requirement of realizability seems a reasonable one if what is in question is the final goal of human action: a form of human life which is proposed as the best available, as the 'good for man', must be realizable. But would anyone wish to propose either the Form of the good or the common character as answers to the question 'What is the highest human good?' Plato would certainly have held that the Form of the good is the most supremely good thing, but hardly that it was to be identified with the good-for-man, in Aristotle's sense. Plato would have agreed that the final good for human beings was happiness, a certain sort of life, or possibly a particular state of the soul, attainable by human action. The Form of the good was hardly offered as something *identical with* happiness, though he would no doubt have held that, ultimately, a knowledge of the Form of the good was required for certain identification of one particular life, or state of the soul, as the best attainable by human beings. Aristotle is, of course, correct in saying that the Form of the good is not something realizable; it exists eternally and is not something that human actions can bring into existence. Thus, Aristotle can be presented with a dilemma: either the Form is being identified with the good-for-man in his argument, in which case the requirement of realizability is relevant, but the position is not one that Plato or anyone else would seriously adopt; or it is not being so identified, in which case it is not clear that the complaint that it is not realizable has any force.

In *E.N.*, at least, there is no suggestion that the Platonic Form is among the rival candidates for identification with happiness: the forward-looking reference at 1095ª26–28 represents it as a rather different sort of view from the competing accounts of what the good life consists in mentioned just before. In *E.E.* part of the source of the trouble seems to be the ambiguity of 'best': it may mean 'best among human goods' or it may mean 'highest good *simpliciter*' (which could not be a human good, according to Aristotle, see 1217ª34). The notion of the good-itself, and with it the Platonic Form, only gets introduced into the discussion if 'best' is taken in the second way; but the best in the first sense is what is relevant to Aristotle's concerns in *E.E.*

What of the argument that the common character is not realizable? It is doubtful if it is *true* that the common character is not realizable. For if it is construed as the character shared by human goods, and is held to depend for its existence on their being possessors of that character, its existence *will* be dependent on human action. That point seems to be recognized by Aristotle at ᵇ4–6, where he distinguishes the good in the sphere of action and that in the sphere of the unchanging. But he there undercuts the discussion by implicitly denying that there is a single common character shared by *all* goods.

At ᵇ2–4, he says that no practitioner of a science or skill aims to secure the possession of 'what belongs to anything', but always some specific good (e.g. health). This may be taken as adding further support to the claim that the common character is not realizable; if so, it seems fallacious, since the fact that it is impossible to seek to produce some good except by aiming at producing some specific form of good does not show that that good cannot be produced. If there were a common character, goodness, that would not prevent it from having species. Alternatively, it may be a further argument against the view that the good-itself is a character common to all goods, from the fact that such a character could not serve as an end of human action, which requires always to be directed in a more specific way.

The relevance of ^{b}4–6 is not made clear. The thesis that 'good' is used in distinct senses, which was argued for on a different basis in 1217^{b}25–35, would establish that there is no common character goodness, but that conclusion is not drawn.

Aristotle says that 'good' is used in a plurality of senses, and one part of the good is the fine. He then says (^{b}5) that one sort of good is realizable, the other not. It is natural to relate this to the twofold division of the meanings of 'good' just introduced, and suppose that those goods that are also describable as fine are those that are not realizable by action. The 'good among unchanging things' will then be the same as the fine. However, the interpretation of ^{b}4–6 is controversial (see Notes), and the doctrine implicit in the interpretation just suggested is at least verbally inconsistent with what is said elsewhere about the relation of the good and the fine (see Allan (1971), pp. 64–8). The relation between the good and the fine in *E.E.* is further treated in VIII, c. 3, 1248^{b}16–37 (see Commentary). Here it is perhaps necessary to note only that *Metaphysics* M 1078^{a}31–^{b}6 seems to interchange the uses of 'good' and 'fine', the latter being regarded as the more comprehensive concept. Allan (op. cit., p. 68) regards the usage as being 'an alternative expression of the same view which is developed in *Metaphysics* M and not . . . a substantial deviation from it'.

1218^{b}7–16

Having disposed of the claims of the Platonic Form, and of the common character, to be the good-itself, Aristotle offers his own answer. The reasons for the rejection of the other two candidates are summarized at ^{b}8–9: the reference is clearly to the immediately preceding argument, which thus seems to be treated as the crucial one by Aristotle. The relation between the two concepts introduced is that being incapable of change entails being unrealizable, whereas being capable of change does not entail realizability. The common character is said to be subject to change not, presumably, because it can itself change, but because objects can come to possess or cease to possess it; it is in that sense a changing feature of the world. The reason that it is said, none the less, not to be realizable must be that given at 1218^{b}2–4, which I have argued is fallacious.

The final end of human actions is said (^{b}10–11) to fulfil the conditions laid down at 1217^{b}3–5, and never abandoned. It is (*a*) the best thing there is; (*b*) the reason, in relation to other things, for their being goods; (*c*) first among goods. (*b*) is argued for in the next section (1218^{b}16–22); (*c*), arguably, at 1218^{b}22–24.

I have already said that Aristotle's retention of the phrase 'the good itself' as a description of what he is looking for is a little unhappy. How far can he claim that his good-itself fulfils the requirements which were not met by the other, rejected, candidates? There is, firstly, the ambiguity of 'best' already mentioned in the Commentary on 1218^{a}38–^{b}6, which may mean 'best *simpliciter*' or 'best of human goods': the Platonic Form of the good secured consideration because it was held to be the best thing *simpliciter*; by that criterion, Aristotle's candidate does not qualify at all. Aristotle certainly holds that there are higher goods than human ones (see 1217^{a}31–32). Further, it is hardly accurate to say that, for Aristotle, the final end is the first of all goods; not all goods belong to the human sphere (cf. 1218^{b}4–6). For similar reasons it is not fair to say that that is the reason, in the case of *all* other goods, for their being goods – only for human goods.

It is natural to ask also how far Aristotle has yet given an answer to the question what the good-itself is (1217^{b}1); that followed on the recognition that happiness is the best (1217^{a}40). But happiness itself has figured in the discussion because of its role as a final end: it is crucial to determine what happiness consists in because we need to adopt a final goal with reference to which to orient the conduct of our lives (see Chapter 2). Thus, although, in the *E.E.*, a positive conclusion seems to emerge from the discussion of Plato's theory, nothing at all definite has been established about the character of the final end of human action, which, since early in this book, it has been assumed must be investigated. If the argument for the outline account of happiness which occupies the first part of Book II, Chapter 1, had followed immediately upon the end of c. 7, would Aristotle's argument have contained any lacuna that it does not contain already?

1218^{b}13: 'Supreme'. Compare *E.N.* I, 1094^{a}26, 'most authoritative and most architectonic'. The authoritative and architectonic character is there explained as consisting in the fact that it lays down which sciences are to be pursued in a city, and to what extent. Aristotle employs the notion of a hierarchy of sciences, the higher being more architectonic than the lower, and, as here, some sciences are spoken of as being under others. Political science has its place at the top of the pyramid because it is the science of the good for man. The admission of such a science is not, of course, incompatible with Aristotle's denial of a general science of the good at 1217^{b}34–35: there is no single science of good in general (see Commentary on 1217^{b}35– 1218^{a}1). On Aristotle's conception of political science, see Commentary on 1215^{b}1–14. On this passage, see also Kenny, p. 54.

1218^{b}13–16: the rather awkward wording of ^{b}13–14 reflects the fact that Aristotle wishes to leave open the question whether one science or three is in question. The topic is further discussed in *E.N.* VI, c. 8. There it is said that political science and practical wisdom (to which is added the science of the household) are the same state (i.e. the same *virtue*) but are distinguishable because they have different scope: practical wisdom, in the narrow sense, is concerned with the achievement of the good life for the individual, political science with the securing of the good life by the members of a city as a whole, and hence by political arrangements. The third member of this trio, mentioned in *E.N.* VI, is clearly concerned with the good of members of a family. It is in accordance with his conception of an objective, discoverable good for man, the same for everybody, that he should regard the three virtues mentioned as essentially the same state: each applies the same knowledge of what the good life for human beings is. The forward reference must be either to the passage mentioned in *E.N.* VI, or to something very like it. *Phronēsis* here means 'practical wisdom' (see Commentary on 1218^{a}32).

1218^{b}15: 'in being of that sort': i.e. in being authoritative (architectonic) *vis-à-vis* other virtues.

1218^{b}16–27

^{b}16–22 offer an argument for what has been asserted at ^{b}10, that the final end has a causal role in relation to objects subordinate to it. I have retained the traditional translation 'cause' although 'reason' or 'explanation' might seem more natural, because the point of ^{b}20–22, in which two sorts of cause are distinguished is otherwise lost. The argument is fairly straightforward: some things are good for their own sake, other things are good only as means. The goodness of an end X is the cause of, a reason for, the goodness of things that are means to X. Aristotle argues for this by appealing to the fact that we show that a derivative good is a good by showing that it is a means to something that is underivatively good. There follows the example of health. On this, compare II, 1227^{b}30–36, *Metaphysics* Z 1032^{b}6–9. Among his four causes, Aristotle distinguishes the final cause, involved in teleological explanation, where something is explained by reference to its purpose, and the efficient cause, which corresponds more closely to our conception of cause. Thus the healthy is an efficient cause of (the existence) of health (^{b}20–22), and Aristotle can describe the final goal (^{b}18–19) as a (final) cause. Here, however, he is possibly not envisaging the explanation of the taking of certain health-promoting steps by reference to the aim of health, but the giving of a reason for something healthy's being a good by reference to health, already accepted as one. But it is not entirely clear that he distinguished the two sorts of final explanation.

The relevance of the further argument of ^{b}22–24 is not clear. Perhaps it is intended to support the proposition that the final goal is first among all goods (^{b}11). Health is part of the final good, happiness; so the final good is ultimate and primary among goods. (This assumes that health is already accepted as forming part of happiness, the good for man.) On the reference to the sophist, compare 1216^{b}40–1217^{a}10. But to say that the final goal is the first among *human* goods seems tautological, and to say that it comes first among *all* goods would presumably be regarded as false by Aristotle. So perhaps it is a further argument for the view that the final good is a cause of the goodness of other things: the good for man (or one of its constituents, like health), is what reasoning about what is good or bad starts from, as shown by the fact that there is no proving that health is a good. Compare *E.N.* III, 1112^{b}15–24, and VII, 1151^{a}15–19, where the final goal is described as a starting-point, compared to axioms in mathematics, and said not to be discovered by rational means.

Although no doubt few people would need to be persuaded that health is a good, it is a question how much is being ruled out here. Aristotle ought to allow that it is possible to show that health is a human good, by showing how it forms a part of the good life. It may be that 'show' in ^{b}22 should be taken in a strict sense: that health is a good is not something that could be the conclusion of a formal piece of reasoning, in the way that the proposition that exercise is beneficial could be.

The final sentence (^{b}25–27) is rather ponderous and may well be spurious.

BOOK TWO

CHAPTER 1

This chapter falls into three main parts: (i) 1218^b31–1219^b25. (ii) 1219^b26–1220^a12. (iii) 1220^a13–37. In the first section of (i) an elaborate argument is presented for the outline account of happiness with which the section ends (1218^b31–1219^a39), and in the second part (1219^a40–$^b25$), Aristotle attempts to show that this account harmonizes with commonly held beliefs, and helps to solve some puzzles. (ii) is devoted to a brief discussion of the general structure of the soul, leading to a distinction between two kinds of virtue. (iii) is the start of Aristotle's treatment of virtue of character, and is continuous with what follows.

1218^b31–1219^a39

This passage contains what is clearly presented as a formal argument for the outline account of happiness offered at 1219^a38–39. The argument is considerably more elaborate than the corresponding argument in *E.N.*, as well as differing from it on a number of points of philosophical doctrine. As the solution to some of the problems of individual sections depends on the view taken of the over-all structure of the argument, it will be convenient to begin with that. Aristotle enunciates a number of premisses, for the most part making it clear, by the form of words he uses, that the proposition is being introduced as a premiss. A satisfying interpretation of the passage ought to give all the premisses (thirteen on the analysis adopted here) a role in the argument.

In broad outline, the structure of the argument is fairly clear: goods in the soul are superior to other goods, hence the final good ('the best') must be a state or activity of the soul; activities are superior to the states that give rise to them, hence the best (and therefore happiness) is an activity of the soul, in accordance with the best state of the soul, i.e. virtue or excellence.

The whole argument may be set out as follows:

Tautology (1) All goods are either in the soul or external to it ($^b32$).

Premiss (2) Goods in the soul are better than those external to it ($^b32$–33, supported by 33–35).

Therefore, (3) The best things (highest goods) are in the soul ($^a30$; from (1), (2)).

Premiss (4) The things in the soul are states, capacities, activities, and processes ($^b35$–36; cf. $^a30$–31).

Premiss,
supported
^a1–5
(5) An excellence is the best disposition, state, or capacity of anything that has an exployment or function (^b37–^a1; ^a32–33).

Premiss
(6) The soul has a function (^a5).

Therefore
(7) The excellence of the soul is the best disposition, state, or capacity of the soul (^a5; from (5), (6)).

Premiss
(8) If x and y are states, and x is better than y, the function of x is better than the function of y (^a6).

Premiss
(9) The function of a thing is it purpose (^a8).

Premiss
(10) The purpose of each thing is the best for that thing (^a10–11).

Therefore
(11) The function of a thing is better than the state (disposition) that corresponds to that function. (^a9, 11–13; from (9), (10)).

Premiss
(12) 'Function' is used in two senses: sometimes the function of x is the employment of x, sometimes something over and above the employment (^a13–17).

Therefore
(13) When the function of x is the employment of x, the employment is better than the state that corresponds to the employment (^a17–18, cf. ^a31; from (11), (12)).

Premiss
(14) The function of x is the function of x's excellence (^a18–23).

Premiss
(15) The function of a soul is to make something alive (^a24–25).

Premiss
(16) Living is an employment (^a24–25).

Therefore
(17) The function of the soul is the function of the excellence of the soul (^a25–27; from (14)).

Therefore
(18) The function of the excellence of a soul is a good life (^a27; from (15), (17)).

Therefore
(19) A good life is the final (*teleon*) good (i.e. happiness) (^a27–28; from (18)? (10)).

Premiss
(20) Happiness is the best thing (the highest good) (^a29, 34).

Therefore
(21) An activity is better that the corresponding disposition (^a31; from (13)).

Therefore
(22) The best activity is the activity of the best state (^a32; from (8)).

Therefore
(23) The best thing of the soul is the activity of its excellence (^a33–34; from (4), (7), (13), (22)).

Therefore
(24) Happiness is an activity of a good soul (^a34–35; from (3), (20), (23)).

Premiss
(25) Happiness is something complete (^a35–36).

Therefore (26) Happiness is an activity of a complete life in accordance with complete excellence (^{a}38–39; from (24), (25)).

(3) is not stated before ^{a}30, but follows from (1) and (2). (1), (2), (4), and (5) are explicitly presented as premisses. (21) is an immediate inference from (13), if 'state' (*hexis*) is taken as equivalent in meaning to 'disposition' (*diathesis*). (23) involves emendation.

It will be seen that the conclusion reached at ^{a}34–35 makes use of all the premisses enunciated by Aristotle outside (14)–(19), which for convenience I shall call the Subsidiary Argument. Is the Subsidiary Argument quite separate or are its conclusions used elsewhere? Can the deficiencies of the main argument be remedied by making use of premisses or conclusions of the Subsidiary Argument?

Aristotle first asserts that the function of a thing and of its excellence are the same. (14) is supported by induction from the case of shoe-making. Next (15) the function of the soul is said to be to make a thing alive; the next few words present difficulty, and discussion of them may be postponed. Then (15) is applied to the case of a soul, and then Aristotle concludes (18), that the function of a soul is a good life. So far, the only premisses used have been the two introduced with the Subsidiary Argument, except possibly for the premiss that the soul has a function. The conclusion that the final good, and therefore happiness, is a good life is a fairly unstartling one, and hardly seems to require such argumentation; but if Aristotle is attempting a formal proof of it, some of the required premisses are missing. The remark at ^{a}24–25 that living is an employment is perhaps best taken as an explication of the sense of 'life' in which it is the function of the soul to cause life: by 'life' in this context is meant not merely the state of being alive, but living a life and therefore employing one's capacities and disposition. We may compare I, 1216^{a}2–5.

Before concluding that the Subsidiary Argument is indeed distinct and isolated from the rest, we must consider the validity of the main argument. The main doubts concern (21), (23), and (24). The derivation of (23), on any view, involves a neglect of the capacities and processes that are mentioned, along with states and activities, as 'things in the soul' in (4). This difficulty, would, of course, be removed if 'state' (*hexis*) were being used in a broad sense in which capacities were included under it, and similarly if activities included processes. The derivation of (21) from (13) requires that the employment of a capacity or disposition that has no purpose beyond the employment is properly described as an activity. We are reminded of the distinction between process (*kinēsis*) and activity (*energeia*) as it occurs in *E.N.* X and *Metaphysics* Θ. This, in turn, suggests that

95

Aristotle may be tacitly ruling out the possibility that the final end is a process on the ground that if it were, there would be some purpose to which the process was directed, for whose sake the activity occurred, which would then have a stronger claim to be regarded as the good. It is, however, doubtful if Aristotle was using '*kinēsis*' at $^b36$ in a way parallel to the distinction he later draws between those cases where there is some function beyond the employment and those where there is not. At *E.N.* II, 1105^{b}20, the enumeration of the 'things in the soul' lists affections (*pathē*), capacities, and states, so by 'process' here, he may have in mind affections, a suggestion borne out by some of the uses of the word later in this book, e.g. at 1220^{a}30, 1220^{b}27. If so, Aristotle may have regarded it as too obvious to need argument that final good is not an affection (*pathos*).

The suggestion that Aristotle was using 'disposition' (*diathesis*) interchangeably with 'state' (*hexis*) perhaps needs little argument, despite the sharp differentiation made between them in *Categories*, *c.* 8. We find Aristotle using 'disposition' instead of 'state' at *E.N.* II, 1107^{b}16, 30, 1108^{a}24, ^{b}11, and in this chapter the argument makes no sense unless one is treated as simply a variant of the other (see, for example, ^{a}30 and 31, where Aristotle switches from one to the other in the space of a single line).

Finally, there is the inference to (24), where Aristotle needs to assume only that an activity of the best state of the soul must be the activity of a soul that is in the best state.

It will be seen that at no point are the deficiencies in the main argument to be made up by drawing on the Subsidiary Argument which therefore seems to be independent. What we have is two distinct arguments for the character of happiness, one much more complete and fully elaborated than the other.

Comparison with E.N.

In general, the Subsidiary Argument is closer in content to the argument of *E.N.* I, c. 7. In the main argument, happiness is said to be activity (or an activity), but its character is not further specified, and there is no mention of reasoning, or the rational part of the soul, as there is in the *E.N.* What this argument and the corresponding argument in *E.N.* I have in common is that the turn that the discussion later takes is determined: it must take the form of an examination of excellence (virtue).

We may now consider this part of the chapter section by section.

1218^{b}31-36

Elsewhere, Aristotle tends to make a threefold division between goods in the soul, those in the body, and those external to either.

Cf. *Politics* VII, 1323^{a}21–24^{a}4, *E.N.* I, 1098^{b}12–15, *M.M.* 1184^{b}1–6. Compare ^{b}35 with I, 1214^{a}30–^{b}5. An alternative, less plausible, translation would be ' . . . some or all seem to everyone to be an end'. That one or more of these things mentioned figure on everyone's list of ends will not, of course, show that goods in the soul are all superior to external goods. Further, there is some difficulty in seeing how the criterion is to be applied, as some ultimate goods that might be proposed would seem to involve both the soul and the body, as indeed seems to be the case with the example of pleasure.

1218^{b}34: External discussions'. See Commentary on I, 1217^{b}22.

1218^{b}37–1219^{a}5
In this passage, the premiss that an excellence is the best state of anything that has a function or employment is said to be supported by induction. On the other hand, there is no argument for the proposition that the soul has a function. Later, at 1219^{a}23–24, Aristotle tells us what the function of the soul is, but, again, there is no argument for this comparable with the argument we find at *E.N.* I, c. 7 for the function of man.

The unifying characteristic of the things said, here and in *E.N.* to have a function, is that it makes sense to speak of *using* them.

1219^{a}6–13
Doubts may be felt about (9) and (10), which serve to effect a connection between the notion of function and that of what is good or bad for something. The most nearly parallel passage in *E.N.* I, 1097, ^{b}26–27 simply asserts that the good of something lies in its function.

1219^{a}13–18
Premiss (12) is reminiscent of the opening sentence of *E.N.*, where Aristotle says that ends are distinguished in that some of them are activities, in other cases they are products (*erga*; i.e. things produced) over and above those activities. As already indicated, what is here called an employment (*chrēsis*) is an activity, as opposed to a state or disposition to engage in that activity. The alleged difference of sense is not exploited in the argument. The idea seems to be that a disposition is always a disposition to ϕ, where ϕing is an activity and an employment of the disposition. Some values of ϕ are such that ϕing is essentially the production of something, whether a physical object like a house, or a state like health. Compare *Metaphysics* Θ 1050^{a}23–^{b}2, *M.M.* 1184^{b}9–17.

1219^{a}18–23
The doctrine that a thing and its excellence share a single function is

not found in precisely this form in *E.N.* The closest parallel is I, 7, 1098ᵃ7–12; if the function of *A* is *X*, the function of a good *A* is a good *X*. Presumably here when Aristotle refers to the function in ᵃ22, he means the function *of the excellence*. The function of the art of shoe-making is said to be a shoe, the function of excellence at shoe-making, i.e. of a good shoe-maker ('and' in ᵃ22 = 'i.e.'), is a good shoe.

A further problem is the point of the qualification 'though in different ways' at ᵃ20, which is not further explained. Two suggestions might be made: (i) The qualification is intended to allow for the fact, which the shoe-making example brings out, that where the function of an *X* is a such-and-such, the function of the excellence of an *X* is a *good* such-and-such. (ii) The point is to distinguish the senses in which *X* and its excellence may each be said to have a function.

1219ᵃ23–34

ᵃ23–25 raise textual difficulties. With the reading adopted in the translation, Aristotle here supplies the needed premiss (16); but that involves emendation, and if the manuscript reading is kept, the translation will be: 'and . . . the function of that is an employment and a waking state'. This has the awkward result that Aristotle will be ascribing to the soul a function that itself has a further function, and the text is suspect on independent, linguistic, grounds. Compare *E.N.* I, 1095ᵇ30–33, 1098ᵃ5–7, 1102ᵇ7–11.

1219ᵃ34–39

Aristotle argues from the fact that happiness is something complete (*teleion*) that the same qualification must be applied to 'life' and 'excellence' in the definition of happiness. The sense in which happiness is something complete is not made clear. In *E.N.* I, 1097ᵃ30–ᵇ1 happiness is said to be the most final (*teleios*) end of all because it is not chosen for the sake of anything else. It is also asserted (1098ᵃ18) that happiness consists in rational activity in accordance with virtue in a complete life, where the word used for 'complete' is the same as the word used earlier for 'final', but there is no suggestion that this requirement is derived from the requirement that the account of happiness must make it something 'final'; rather, Aristotle seems to think it sufficient to appeal to our intuition that one would not call someone happy for a short time.

The senses in which a life and virtue may be said to be complete or incomplete do not seem to be the same. The parenthesis in ᵃ37 suggests that in the case of virtue, the contrast Aristotle has in mind is that between having *a* virtue (or some virtues) and having every virtue. But in fact there is no argument offered for the view that happiness is an activity in accordance with complete or total virtue; all that the preceding argument has established is that happiness is *an* activity of a good soul, and there is no reason given for supposing that the activity is one which requires complete excellence. The phrase 'total virtue' occurs later, at 1219^{b}21, where he says that the excellence of the nutritive part is not to be regarded as a part of it; presumably what Aristotle has in mind is that a soul (or a man) is not to be called good *simpliciter* in respect of the excellence possessed by the nutritive part. Compare VIII, 1249^{a}16, where complete excellence is identified with nobility (*kalokagathia*).

In *E.N.*, the closest parallels are I, 7 1098^{a}17–18, 1100^{a}4–5, 1102^{a}6, where the good for man is described as activity according to the best and most complete (*teleios*) virtue; on these passages and the interpretation of *teleios* see Ackrill (1974), pp. 8–12, Kenny, pp. 204 f.

1219^{a}40–^{b}8

In the section that begins here down to 1219^{b}25, Aristotle tries to show that the outline account of happiness that has been given fits what has been commonly thought about it. ^{a}40–^{b}4 claim that the account that has been given conforms to, and reconciles, the two apparently conflicting common views that happiness consists in living well and that it consists in acting well. Aristotle's outline account of happiness reconciles them because happiness has been said to be an activity of a complete life (1219^{a}38–39) and earlier (1219^{a}27–28) a good life. The purpose of ^{b}2–4 seems to be to show that action is a form of employment (and therefore, in accordance with the doctrine of the earlier part of this chapter, an activity); that the good life, with which happiness has been identified, is an activity rather than a state, was already implicit in the earlier argument that an activity is better than its corresponding state. However, the use of the example of the horseman, who uses the products of the blacksmith's skill is puzzling: the only relevant sense in which the life of virtuous action may be reasonably treated as involving employment is that it involves the use of the various good states of the soul which the virtues are, a point to which the example of the horseman's use of the equipment forged by the smith is hardly relevant. In any case, the view that both are living well and acting well are activities seems to be one that emerges from Aristotle's outline account of happiness without appeal to the notion of employment. On ^{a}40–^{b}4, compare *E.N.* I, 1098^{b}20–1099^{a}3.

In ^{b}5–8, Aristotle discusses certain views concerning the temporal restrictions on happiness. These seem to be represented as according

72059

with the account of happiness already given because that contains
the requirement that happiness be an activity of a *complete* life
(1218ᵃ38). There is, however, some doubt about the text (see below).
In view of the parenthetical remark at ᵇ6-8, it is natural to suppose
that Aristotle is saying that a man may not be truly described as
happy at any point *within* his life. This will certainly rule out calling
a child happy. But it is clear not whether Aristotle's point is that
since happiness is (primarily) a characteristic of a whole life, it
makes no sense to speak of a person as happy for a limited period
(just as it makes no sense to speak of someone as exhibiting longevity
in his childhood), or whether it is rather that, since the assessment
is of a whole life, we ought not to ascribe happiness at any period
before the end of a man's lifetime (since we lack the knowledge to
make the assessment before then). The view that one should not call
a child happy suggests the second point, the idea that it is impossible
to be happy for only a single day, the first. Strictly, of course, the
second thesis would not show that it was always false to call a man
happy before the end of his life, only that it might be rash.

   In *E.N.*, the doctrine that it is impossible to be happy just for a
single day is kept separate from the discussion of Solon's dictum.

   Even if, as understood by Aristotle, happiness is primarily a
characteristic of a whole life, as indeed his outline definition suggests,
that would be no obstacle to saying of a man that he was happy for
a period shorter than a whole life-span, if that period had a character
which, if possessed by a whole life, would justify calling that life a
happy one.

1219ᵃ40:   '. . . genus and definition'. What has the genus of happiness been said to be? The most plausible answer is *activity*, in which
case, 8-16 is devoted to confirmation of Aristotle's view of what the
genus of happiness is. But if so, what does Aristotle mean here by
'definition'? It is doubtful if what has been offered qualifies as such.
Perhaps the reference is to Aristotle's claim that happiness consists
in a good life, in which case corroboration is offered at ᵇ1-4.

1219ᵇ6:   '. . . for a stage of one's life'. The translation offered is
the only possible one that makes sense of the sentence, keeping the
reading of the manuscripts. The wording of the Greek is, however,
rather awkward, and textual corruption has been suspected.

1219ᵇ8-11

Three considerations are offered in favour of the view that happiness
is an activity rather than a capacity or state. On the first, compare
E.N. I, 1101ᵇ31-34; on the second, I, 1099ᵃ3-5. The support given

by the third sentence to the view that happiness is an activity is less clear, because, even if happiness were a state, it would still be necessary to judge whether someone was virtuous from his actions. Compare II, 1228^{a}2-18 and *E.N.* III, 1111^{b}6.

1219^{b}11-16

Is this a further corroboration of the outline account of happiness? If so, the argument has to be taken as drawing, from the fact that happiness is not a subject of praise, the conclusion that happiness is the standard to which other goods are referred. But this hardly supports the outline definition of happiness; at any rate, it supports the view that happiness is the highest good, which was a premiss of the argument of the earlier part of this chapter, not its conclusion. In the parallel passage in *E.N.* (I, c. 12) these observations do not form part of Aristotle's confirmation of the outline account of happiness by appeal to commonly held opinions. On the distinction, compare *Rhetoric* 1367^{b}28-36.

1219^{b}16-25

The thought of this section is extremely compressed. ^{b}16-20 seem to be offered as a further confirmation of the doctrine that happiness is an activity rather than a state. The passage most nearly parallel to ^{b}16-19 in *E.N.*, I, 1102^{b}6-7, occurs in the course of the discussion of the divisions in the soul.

^{b}20-25 raise some problems. It is not immediately clear how to understand the reference to *another* part of the soul, when parts of the sould have not been mentioned. Aristotle must have in mind a part of the soul other than those concerning which the generalization just asserted holds, viz. that they are inactive during sleep. According to Aristotle, corresponding to each part of the soul are specific capacities and excellences, and so there will be an excellence corresponding to the nutritive part of the soul. Aristotle argues (^{b}21) that the excellence of this part (i.e. the excellence possessed by someone with a good digestion) must be excluded from 'total virtue'. The latter phrase seems to require interpretation in the light of 1219^{a}37, where he speaks of total, as opposed to partial, excellence and says that happiness requires complete excellence (virtue). If so, the section is indeed relevant to Aristotle's outline account of happiness, as making more precise what is to be understood by complete virtue. The exclusion of the nutritive part in fact belongs more properly to the discussion of the parts of the soul and their corresponding virtues which begins at 1219^{b}26.

1219^{b}22-25: Compare *E.N.* 1102^{b}9-11: for Aristotle's account of the physiology of dreams, see *Parva Naturalia* (*De Somniis*), c. 3, 460^b28-462^a31. In ^b24, the pronoun 'they' is most naturally taken to refer to the perceiving and desiring parts of the soul.

1219^b26-36

This section begins the second part of this chapter, which continues to 1220^a12. Aristotle makes some general observations about the soul, as a preliminary to the discussion of the virtues, which occupies most of the rest of the *E.E.* This part of Chapter 1 thus corresponds to *E.N.* I, c. 13. With ^b27-28, compare *E.N.* I, 1102^a13-14, with 32-36, compare 1102^a28-33.

Broadly, the doctrine of parts of the soul introduced here is similar to that of *E.N.* I, 1102^b13-1103^a3; in both places the distinguishing of a rational and a partly rational part of the soul is followed by the division of the virtues into two classes, for which it forms a basis. In both passages, Aristotle distinguishes a part which commands, and one which obeys. The two books are alike also in dismissing the metaphysical character of the division of the soul as irrelevant to present concerns (^b32-36, *E.N.* 1102^a28-33), and in holding that the obeying part may, with appropriate qualifications, be described either as rational or as non-rational. However, whereas *E.N.* first intoduces that part as non-rational but having a share in reason (1102^b13-14), and then later allows that it may be described as rational (1103^a1-3), here Aristotle introduces his division as one between two rational parts of the soul; but the dismissal at ^b31, of any part that is non-rational 'in any *other* way' implies, rather obliquely, that one of the two rational parts of the soul here distinguished is also properly described as non-rational. The reference is presumably to the nutritive part of the soul already dismissed as irrelevant at ^b20-21, and, on one interpretation, to be dismissed again at ^b37f.

1219^b32-35: Aristotle here dismisses the question whether the soul has parts in a strong sense of 'part', as irrelevant to his present concerns. This is in line with the methodological doctrine that ethics should concern itself with metaphysical questions only in so far as they are relevant. (Compare 1214^a12-14.) This passage is only partly parallel to the comparable passage in *E.N.* The two examples given here seem to be different from each other, and the second seems more apt for Aristotle's purposes. What Aristotle seems to be contrasting with the case of two physically separate parts is the case when there are two things distinguishable only in thought. If so, Aristotle, in speaking of the rational or desiring part of the soul, ought to regard himself as committed only to the existence of

102

certain capacities. In fact, however, when Aristotle speaks of parts of the soul, here and in the psychological works, the structure is represented as *explaining* the various capacities that are to be found, and thus as not simply reducible to them. Here when he postulates that the soul has two parts he seems to mean more than that the soul may be considered as a source of both rational and non-rational behaviour.

1219ᵇ35-36:   The translation, which attempts to reproduce the Greek as closely as possible, may be made more intelligible by the following paraphrase: 'yet the straightness is not identical with the white, (except incidentally) and it is not in essence the same as it'. In Greek, the neuter of an adjective like 'straight' or 'white' can be used to designate either the property ascribed by the adjective or the bearer of the property.

1219ᵇ36-1220ᵃ4

There are some fairly close similarities with *E.N.* I, 1102ᵃ32-33, ᵇ11-12, even closer if certain widely accepted emendations are made in ᵇ37 and 39. The conclusion is that, just as physical well-being is composed of particular excellences (i.e. presumably those of particular bodily parts and functions), the virtue of the soul, mentioned in the outline account of happiness, is composed of particular virtues. Aristotle is once more operating with the notion of total virtue, as at 1219ᵇ21. Earlier, certain virtues had been excluded as forming no part of it: it is now argued that this comprehensive excellence is made up of a plurality of particular excellences. It would seem to follow that, not only the total virtue that figured in the outline account of happiness is good in itself, but also the particular virtues that compose it are desirable in themselves, to be pursued for their own sake. Compare *E.N.* VI, 1144ᵃ1-6, 1145ᵃ2-4, where intellectual virtues are argued to be goods on the ground solely that they are virtues of certain parts of the soul.

At ᵇ39-ᵃ2 he argues broadly in the following way: reason belongs essentially to a human being, in particular the sort of reason that is able to initiate and govern action; but this direction is not of reason itself, but desires and appetites, hence a human being must possess both a reasoning and an appetitive part. If so, 'those parts' at ᵃ2 means 'those parts *of the soul*' (i.e. ᵃ2 is not saying that *virtue* must have these parts). Further, the two parts that Aristotle here says are necessary are in fact the same as those introduced at 1219ᵇ28 f., although the quasi-rational part is not there called the appetitive element.

The conclusion of the final section is (ᵃ2-4) supported by the argument that since certain elements are ascribed to the human soul, the inclusive virtue that is desirable for itself must comprehend a plurality of virtues, corresponding to the distinct elements of the soul. The purpose of the section is to show that the virtues of each of the two parts of the soul distinguished earlier are part of total human excellence. That both rational and quasi-rational parts of the human soul have specific virtues would follow immediately from what is said in the previous section, by Aristotelian principles; what the present section does is to show that the virtues of each of these parts is a component in the inclusive excellence mentioned in the outline account of happiness.

Different textual readings at ^{b}37–38 begin the sentence either with 'but' or with 'for'; since 'the parts of the soul we have mentioned' must refer to rational and quasi-rational parts distinguished at 1219^{b}28 (because the sentence immediately before refers to only one part of the soul, not regarded as peculiar to human beings), 'but' is preferable and has been adopted in the translation. At ^{b}38–39 there are four alternative readings: (i) 'the nutritive and the appetitive part', (ii) 'the nutritive and growing part' (a commonly accepted emendation), (iii) 'the nutritive part', (iv) 'the appetitive part'. (i) involves a designation of two parts of the soul, the others only one part. (ii) and (iii) are equivalent. With none of these alternatives does the following sentence (^{b}39–^{a}2) support what is said here, and it must therefore be treated as parenthetical; but ^{b}37–38 must provide an explanation for what is said in ^{b}38–39, and this rules out (i) and (iv), since the appetitive is one of the parts mentioned as peculiar to human beings at ^{b}38. I have therefore adopted (ii). The point of ^{b}38–39 is that not only that part of the soul, but also its virtues, are not peculiarly human.

Alternative readings to that adopted in the translation of ^{b}39–^{a}2 yield the following translations: 'For it is necessary that reason and direction and action should belong to a man *qua* man' or 'For it is necessary, if there is a man, that reason and direction and action should belong.' Neither of these yields an argument for the exclusion of the nutritive ((ii) and (iii)), and independent reasons for rejecting (i) and (iv) remain.

With the reading adopted, ^{b}39 f support smoothly ^{b}37–38, which says that the parts are peculiar to the human soul; the intervening sentence may, as I said before, be taken as parenthetical.

1220^{a}5–12

In this passage, which is parallel to *E.N.* I, 1103^{a}3–10, *M.M.* 1185^{b}5–12, Aristotle distinguishes two kinds of virtues corresponding to the two parts of soul just distinguished. (Compare the recapitulation at 1221^{b}27 f.) The purpose of the argument is to show that not only characteristics like justice, but also those ascribed when men are called intelligent or wise, must be reckoned as virtues. The characteristics ascribed when people are called just or intelligent are dispositions rather than actual activities. So intelligence and wisdom must be accounted as virtues. Virtues like justice, courage, etc. are virtues of character, wisdom and intelligence, intellectual virtues. Virtues of character are the main topic of the remainder of this book, and of Book III; intellectual virtues are treated in the 'common' book, *E.N.* VI. It seems clear from the course of the argument of this section that ·those things' in ª7 must refer to the characteristics presupposed in the reference to the just, the intelligent, and the wise in ª6. We note that the part of the soul that has been described as rational at 1219ᵇ30, on the strength of its capacity to obey reason, is called non-rational here (ª10). A similar variation is noticeable in *E.N.* I, c. 13. See Commentary on 1219ᵇ26-36.

1220ª13-22

The third section of this chapter begins here, and is continuous with what follows. If the translation 'amounts to' is correct, only two questions are distinguished: (*a*) What is virtue of character? (*b*) How is it produced? The 'parts of virtue' are not the individual virtues, but the elements in the definition of virtue of character, so the question what its parts are is not to be distinguished from (*a*). The answer to (*b*), in so far as an answer is given at all, occurs in the course of giving an answer to (*a*).

ª15-22 contain a methodological observation followed by an illustration. Aristotle says, here as elsewhere, that philosophical inquiry must start from opinions that are true but imprecise and not well grounded, and aim to arrive at conclusions that are at once true and precise; thus we already possess something in the way of knowledge or opinion when inquiry begins. On the doctrine, compare I, 1216ᵇ31. ª18-22, in which the doctrine is illustrated, raise more problems. It is not clear whether Aristotle is here offering *two* illustrations or only one. On the first alternative, presumably the point is that we may have enough knowledge of health to compare it with other states and enough knowledge of swarthiness to pick Coriscus out, but lack full knowledge of these properties. On the view that only one illustration is given here, the superlatives are not specially significant; the point is that we know empirical truths about individuals, and a very general truth about health, but lack the knowledge of the intermediate terms to connect the two.

Which interpretation is adopted makes a difference to what the reference of 'either of these things' is in ª20. On the view that two illustrations are given, the reference must be to health and swarthiness; on the other view, reference would have to be to health and virtue.

1220ᵃ22-29

In this section, Aristotle enunciates three principles: (i) The best state (disposition) results from the best things (22-23). (ii) The best things are done, in each case, from a thing's excellence (ᵃ23-24). (iii) Every state (disposition) is both produced and destroyed by the application, in a certain way, of the same things (ᵃ26-27).

Despite the fact that Aristotle (ᵃ28-29) says that these propositions are supported by induction, (i) and (ii) appear to be necessary truths: the only standard for evaluating what produces a state is the state produced (or, at any rate, other standards are irrelevant) though, of course, food (one of Aristotle's examples) can be evaluated not solely on the basis of its tendency to produce health. Equally, the only ground for deciding whether a disposition is a virtue is the actions which it leads to. (iii), however, seems to be an empirical thesis. The point of Aristotle's examples for (iii) is presumably that, just as the right sort of food promotes, so the wrong sort ruins, health, and similarly with exercise. If so, the example of time of life (*hōra*) is rather strange: it is not something that can be applied either in a beneficial or a deleterious way.

That (iii) is the substantial thesis is borne out by the fact that in *E.N.*, it is that which is asserted, and illustrated with a wealth of examples, at II, 1103ᵇ6-25, 1104ᵃ11-27. There is nothing corresponding precisely to (i) and (ii).

1220ᵃ29-37

ᵃ29-30 apply thesis (i), ᵃ30-31 thesis (ii), and ᵃ31-32 thesis (iii) of the previous section to the case of virtue. ᵃ32-34 could be taken in two ways: (*a*) (The interpretation adopted) 'Virtue's employment has to do with the very things just mentioned (which produce or destroy it), and in relation to these it is the best disposition'. (*b*) 'Virtue's employment has to do with the same things (by which it is produced and destroyed) as those in relation to which it is the best disposition.' (*a*) seems better, in view of what follows: the main point seems to be the identity of a virtue's 'field' and what promotes and destroys it.

The final sentences of the chapter have been interpreted in the following ways:

(i) (the one adopted) 'That (sc. what is said in the previous sentence) is a sign that both virtue and vice have to do with pleasant and unpleasant things; for . . .'

(ii) 'There is evidence that *both* virtue *and* vice have to do with pleasant and unpleasant things; for . . .'

(iii) 'It is a sign of that that both virtue and vice have to do with pleasant and unpleasant things; for . . .'

With both (i) and (ii), the 'that'-clause specifies what evidence is being given for, but with (i), the evidence is given in what precedes (with the 'for' sentence explaining the connection), whereas with (ii) the evidence occurs in the following 'for' clause. With (iii) the 'that'-clause itself adduces evidence for something said in the previous sentence.

The main difficulty with (ii), accepted by Solomon, is that it is not apparent what the relevance of the observation here is, and Allan (1961) suggests the passage is in the wrong place. Against (iii), the interpretation of Rowe and Dirlmeier, is the fact that the connection of virtue and vice with pleasure and pain will then be appealed to as established doctrine, though it is introduced here for the first time. In favour of (i) is the fact that this connection is taken up immediately at the beginning of Chapter Two, and at 1221ᵇ37-39 Aristotle implies that evidence in favour of the connection has already been given; and it is difficult to see where, if not in this passage.

On (i), the argument is that the character of punishment shows that the application of painful or pleasant treatment has the effect of instilling virtue (or vice, if differently applied); hence, by the thesis of ª32-34, it is with pleasures and pains that virtue is concerned. Pleasure and pain are treated as instruments of moral therapy.

Aristotle's own example of physical health shows that the principle that a disposition has to do with (manifests itself essentially in) what produces or destroys it, is not in general true. One's diet can affect one's health favourably or adversely, but is hardly (except in the case of morbid cravings) a manifestation of one's state of health. Again, choosing to live in a healthy climate may improve a person's health, but it will not be a manifestation of this, but of the desires and beliefs of the relevant kind. In the case of physical exertion it is, of course, true that the health may be sustained by the same physical performances that it gives one the capacity to perform, as Aristotle himself recognizes at *E.N.* II, 1104ª31-33.

For a parallel to the doctrine of ª31-34, see *E.N.* II, 1104ª27-ᵇ3.

CHAPTER 2

This chapter is not well integrated into its context, as Rowe has observed (p. 39). The first section, to 1220ᵇ6, ends with the conclusion that character is a quality of the non-rational part of the soul, a conclusion that scarcely advances beyond what was agreed at 1220ª10; the second section raises the question in respect of what features of the soul these qualities are ascribed. It is more closely connected with Chapter Four than Chapter Three, and only in the former are the conclusions of this chapter taken up.

1220ᵃ38–ᵇ6

The exact manner in which the observation that character results from habituation supports the conclusion of ᵇ5–6 is not clear, and the problem is aggravated by doubts about the text (see Notes). The argument seems to be that since character results from habituation (and not teaching) it belongs to the non-rational part of the soul; since the character that results is something permanent, it is a quality and not a mere affection. Moreover, the fact that the human soul is susceptible of this sort of training indicates that the non-rational element that is subjected to it is capable of being influenced by rational means, unlike wholly non-rational things, such as inanimate objects, which are not susceptible of habituation. But the argument suffers from a failure to mention the form of acquisition of qualities with which habituation is being contrasted. In the parallel passage in *E.N.*, II, 1103ᵃ14–23, Aristotle is explicitly concerned with the acquisition of virtues rather than character, and contrasts virtues of character, which are acquired by habituation, with intellectual virtues which result from teaching. The purpose of the discussion is to show that virtue is not innate. Our passage, too, may be thought of as implicitly answering the question raised at I, 1214ᵃ19–21, and again in the previous chapter at 1220ᵃ14–15, though the conclusion is not explicitly drawn.

The word translated 'character' is used in the singular in much the same way as the English word, and also, unlike 'character', in the plural meaning, roughly, 'traits of character'. I have therefore adopted the latter translation of occurrences of the word in the plural.

1220ᵇ7–20

On Aristotle's notion of a quality, see *Categories*, c. 8, with Ackrill's notes. There Aristotle distinguishes within the class of qualities, between states, conditions, and capacities, and affective qualities, and, on the whole, distinguishes all of these from affections. The first three of these would naturally be ascribed in answering the question what someone is like, hence they are required by Aristotle to be relatively long-lasting, unlike affections, which belong rather to what *we* might assign to the category of events.

One of the most striking features of this chapter is that Aristotle appears to assign some traits of character to the class of capacities, others to that of states.

Two questions naturally arise: (i) What is the distinction between capacities and states? (ii) How do what Aristotle calls 'traits of character' relate to virtues and vices? Aristotle elsewhere in this book, as in *E.N.*, classifies virtues and vices as states rather than capacities. (Cf. 1222ᵃ6 f.) We might therefore think that virtues and vices are a sub-class of those traits of character classifiable as states, and this is borne out by the examples in ᵇ19–20. On the other hand, three of the five capacity-ascribing adjectives correspond to abstract nouns occurring in the list of vices in the next chapter. Aristotle here treats some vices (and presumably also virtues) as capacities and some as states. Certainly, the term 'capacity' is not used in quite the same way as it is in *E.N.* II, Chapters 1 and 5, where virtues are firmly put in the class of states: there capacities are said to be distinguished by the fact that they are present before the activities that they are capacities for occur, whereas states are engendered by habituation, involving these activities before the state has been produced. Capacities are thus treated as innate, whereas here, being treated as a class of traits of character, they are acquired. (Compare *E.N.* II, 1103ᵃ26-ᵇ2; 1106ᵃ6-9.) Perhaps Aristotle recognized that some character traits crucially involve the capacity for certain emotions, or for being moved in certain ways. A callous man is incapable of certain kinds of sympathetic response; those who are excitable or irascible are more readily roused to certain emotions than others are. But if we suppose that those traits that are ascribed because of a person's susceptibility to affections of a certain kind are capacities, we find that this seems to fit Aristotle's specification of the class of states at ᵇ9-10. On the other hand, the mere capacity to feel anger at all, as opposed to being capable of being aroused to it a specific degree will presumably be an innate human characteristic, and therefore not a trait of character, and certainly not a vice or a virtue.

If we look at the two sets of examples, the main difference appears to be that those traits classified as capacities are such that the propensity to exhibit certain sorts of emotions is much more central in their ascription than in the ascription of what are classified as states. Aristotle's view in *E.N.* is that the virtues and vices are concerned with actions and affections, but clearly the relative importance of each of these two will vary from case to case. In any case, if the basis for the distinction is the importance of the emotional aspect, it is not very appropriate to mark it by use of the categorial terms 'capacity' and 'state'.

1220ᵇ14:   The remark about the accompanying of affections by pleasure and pain raises two problems: (i) What does Aristotle mean when he says that they as such give rise to pleasure and pain? (ii) What is the force of the qualification 'perceptual'? (i) It may be suggested that there is a conceptual connection between these occurrences and a state of pleasure and distress, or at least unease, a connection that would be revealed by appropriate analysis. Thus shame might be thought of as a state of unease arising from the thought that one has behaved wrongly. The feelings of desire and anger are quite generally held by Aristotle to be unpleasant (1225^{b}31). A difficulty will then be that it is not clear how the consequent pain could occur only 'usually'. In *E.N.* a longer list is given (II, 1105^{b}21–23) and, as here, specified as being accompanied by pleasure and pain, without the qualification 'perceptual'. Both in the *E.N.* and here, it looks as if the class of affections is defined by reference to the concomitance of pleasure and pain. If so, Aristotle must mean that it is true of each of these affections that it is mostly accompanied by pleasure and pain, not that affections are occurrences which, most of them, are followed by pleasure and pain. We find definitions in the *Rhetoric* that would imply a conceptual connection between anger and fear, and pain. Anger is defined (1378^{a}31–32) as 'a painful desire for vengeance, resulting from an apparent indignity'; fear is defined as 'a pain or disturbance resulting from the imagination of a harmful or painful evil in the future' (1382^{a}21–22). Further, an affection fairly similar to that denoted by the word here translated 'shame' (*aischunē*) is defined (1383^{b}12–14) as 'pain or disturbance at present, past, or future evils that bring disgrace'. Again, *E.N.* defines shame as 'a kind of fear of disgrace' (IV, 1128^{b}11–12). In *E.N.* IV, c. 9, it is said to be not really a virtue, but rather an affection. Here, his position seems to be that the word 'shame' refers sometimes to an affection, sometimes to a virtue, as it is without qualification listed as a virtue at 1221^{a}1, III, 1233^{b}26 f. It seems odd to speak of shame as a virtue, but the oddity is probably absent with the Greek word.

The connection between desire and pleasure is not the same as its connection with pain. Aristotle does, indeed, offer a definition of desire that mentions pleasure as its proper object. But this can hardly be in point here, as pleasure is the normal sequel, not of the desire itself, but its satisfaction. What Aristotle must have in mind here is the unease or discomfort associated with (presumably physical) desire and the pleasure accompanying certain *other* affections. Compare 1225^{b}30, where desire and anger are both said to be accompanied by pain.

(ii) The phrase '*perceptual* pleasure and pain' does not occur elsewhere, and is absent from *E.N.* Following Kapp, we may elucidate it by reference to *Physics* VII, 246^{b}20–247^{a}19, where Aristotle seems to be taking much the same view of the relation of the virtues of character to pleasure and pain as is taken in the *E.E.* Virtue is said to consist in the right dispositions towards bodily pleasures and pains. Pleasures and pains are said, unlike good or bad states of character themselves, to be changes resulting from something's acting on the perceiving part of the soul. Bodily pleasures and pains are said all to arise either from action, memory, or expectation, and the last of these ties in well with the way in which, following the *Rhetoric*, pain has been said to be essentially involved in fear, anger, and shame. This is clearly a much wider notion than our notion of *physical* pleasure and pain, as clearly none of the examples normally involve pain in the ordinary sense. One feature of the examples given here is that they involve characteristic physical symptoms, and are naturally described as physical reactions, like blushing, trembling, etc. This is not true of envy, which occurs on the *E.N.*'s longer list, which may account for the absence of the qualification under discussion from that work.

CHAPTER 3
1220^{b}21–27

Compare *E.N.* II, 1106^{a}26–^{b}16. In this passage, Aristotle offers an argument for the possibility of discerning a mean in the sphere of actions. The word translated 'mean' is the normal Greek word for 'middle', but, like the French *moyen* has a wider range of application, meaning 'intermediate', 'medium', and so 'mean'. As in the corresponding passage in *E.N.*, Aristotle claims that in every divisible continuum, it is possible to identify a mean point, and claims that this will show that virtues of character are mean states, since actions are changes, and all change is continuous. The argument is complicated by the fact that Aristotle wishes to distinguish between the mean between extremes 'in relation to one another' and the mean 'relative to us'. Aristotle writes as if both sorts of mean are to be discovered in any continuum, but it is difficult to see what argument could be offered for that, if the notion of a continuum is construed in a purely general way. In any case, it is not true that every continuum will have a mean point: the end points of the continuum would first need to be determined. If, on the other hand, Aristotle is *not* claiming that both sorts of mean are to be found in every continuum, the existence of a mean relative to us in the cases relevant to virtues of character would require a separate argument, which would in turn render the appeal to theoretical considerations about continua superfluous. The examples mentioned at ^{b}23–25 of practical arts might be thought to constitute such an argument.

The contrast between the mean 'relative to one another' and the mean 'relative to us' would appear to be the same as the contrast drawn in *E.N.* II, 1106^{a}26–28 between the mean 'in respect of the thing itself' and that 'relative to us', and we must therefore turn to *E.N.* for further explanation of the contrast, as it is not further explained here. The contrast seems to be that between the midpoint on some scale, which is a matter of calculation and can therefore be

111

ascertained in abstraction from particular circumstances, considering solely the scale itself, and the rather vague notion of what is intermediate between excess and defect, which clearly may depend on a host of variable factors, and is not open to mathematical calculation. (The possibility of such a contrast depends on the ambiguity of the Greek word already mentioned, which may refer either to a midpoint, or what lies between two other things.) The second mean involves an evaluative element, since it refers to what is intermediate between excess and defect, i.e. what avoids what is too much or too little, and therefore cannot be determined without reference to human needs or purposes, — hence the phrase 'relative to us'.

The other term of the contrast is marked here by a somewhat unfortunate phrase, since the excess, defect, and mean are *always* so described relative to one another, and therefore also in the case where they are 'relative to us'; hence it is not an apt term for marking one of the two kinds of mean.

The argument for the doctrine is that action is a kind of change, and every change is continuous (26–27); hence in every action, there is a mean. This argument raises two problems: (i) The only clear sense in which all change, and therefore all actions, are continuous, is that discussed in Aristotle's physical writings (e.g. at *Physics* IV 219^a10 f., where it is argued that changes are continuous because magnitudes, and therefore the magnitude bounded by the terminal points of the change, are; and *Physics* V 228^a20 f., where the same conclusion is drawn from the fact that every change can be divided up into smaller changes). But what is relevant here is not the possibility of finding a midpoint or mean in a particular change (e.g. by determining the half-way point in the stretch of time that it occupies), but whether each action can be regarded as falling within a range of alternative actions which are capable of being ranged in a quantitative scale. In the example given, of medicine, it is plausible to suppose that a large part of the physician's task consists in administering just the right amount of a particular form of treatment; similarly, acts of generosity involve giving precisely the right amount (cf. Plato, *Politicus, Republic*). But the rather abstract considerations about the continuity of change do nothing to support the conclusion that there is such a scale associated with *every* action. 'Action' in ^b25 must be taken as meaning 'type of action', but the following argument purports to establish a conclusion about every particular action.

(ii) The argument speaks of actions, as if hitting the mean were always a matter of choosing the right action from a spectrum of alternatives of the sort indicated in (i). But the predominant thought in *E.E.* is that virtue consists in hitting the right point on a scale of feeling: virtue is concerned with the affections, notably pleasure and pain (cf. 1220^{a}34-37). Even in *E.N.* actions and affections are mentioned as providing distinct scales in which there is a correct point to be aimed at, but this argument refers only to 'actions'. It may be, as Kapp suggests (p.45), that 'action' is here being used in a broad sense in which affections can also be so described; but this suggestion fits ill with 1222^{b}28-29, where the proposition that actions are changes is repeated, in a context in which 'action' is clearly being used in a narrower and more normal sense.

The contrast between two sorts of mean may be related to a contrast drawn in Plato, *Politicus* 283 E.

1220^{b}27-36

On the thought, compare *E.N.* II, 1108^{b}11-23, where, however, the observations about the 'opposition' of the extremes to one another, and to the mean, are not, as here, exploited as part of the argument for the mean doctrine.

This passage appears to contain two arguments:

Argument I

(i) The mean relative to us is as science and a rational principle prescribe (^{b}28).

(ii) In all cases, the states that are in accordance with these principles (sc. the prescriptions of science and a rational principle) are the best ones (^{b}29).

(iii) Therefore, the mean relative to us is best (^{b}27-28).

But, (iv) virtue is the best state.

Therefore (v) Virtue has as its object certain means, and is itself a mean state (^{b}34-35).

The argument suffers from uncertainty about the referent of 'that' in ^{b}28 and 29. On the interpretation adopted above, the referent of 'that' in ^{b}28 is the mean relative to us (not the best, as Dirlmeier holds), and in ^{b}29 it seems to refer neither to the mean nor to 'knowledge and a rational principle' but rather loosely to the guidance of the rational part of the soul. This enables the argument to be construed as an argument for the thesis that virtue is a mean through the notion of what reason prescribes. (i) may be regarded as having been supported by the examples given in ^{b}23-26. There is, however, a pervasive uncertainty about whether what is in question is the thesis that the best choice is choice of some mean, or the thesis that virtue is itself a mean state. (i) and (iii) could be taken as referring either to the mean that is the object of the virtuous man's choice, or to the mean state that Aristotle thinks that virtue is, but (i) is perhaps most naturally taken in the former way. Only so can it be readily thought to derive support from ^{b}23-26.

On the other hand, (ii) seems to be saying something about what the best settled state of character is, and hence to be aimed at the conclusion that virtue is itself a mean. It may, therefore, be better (bearing in mind the presence of 'also' in ^{b}29) to suppose that the argument that the best choice is *of* a mean is complete at ^{b}28, and that ^{b}29 asserts further, as something needing no further argument, that the best state is always *constituted* by a mean. This involves taking the referent of 'that' in ^{b}29 as the mean. The argument is then as follows:

(i) The mean relative to us is always as science and rational principle prescribe (^{b}28).

(ii) What is prescribed by science, etc. is best (supplied).

Therefore (iii) the mean relative to us is best (^{b}27–28).

Also (iv) The mean state always constitutes the best one (29).

(v) Virtue is the best state.

Therefore (vi) Virtue is concerned with certain means (from (iii) and (v)) and is itself a mean (from (iv) and (v)) (^{b}34–35).

The alternative of taking 'that' in ^{b}28 as referring to what is best fails to yield any satisfactory argument, as it will then make no mention of the mean but be offered in support of a conclusion that concerns it.

Argument II

In ^{b}30–35, there appears to be another argument for the same conclusion (cf. 'for'), which at ^{b}30 is said to be evident both from induction and argument. The reference to induction may be a reference to the manner in which premiss (i) of the preceding argument is supported; see previous paragraph. The argument appears to be of the following form:

(i) Each of two opposites rules out the other.

(ii) Extremes are opposed both to each other and the mean (supported by the argument of ^{b}32–33).

Therefore (iii) Each extreme rules out the mean state.

This, as it stands, does not support any conclusion about the character of virtue as a mean. It may be supplemented as follows:

(iv) Every virtue is such that there are two vicious states associated with it that rule it out.

Hence (v) Virtues fulfil the condition stated in (iii).

What may be extracted from the argument is that each virtue has two vices associated with it, which lies between in the sense that it is closer to each of them than either is to the other. Even a minimal version of Aristotle's theory of the mean would seem to require at least this.

1220^b28: 'Rational principle': Compare 1219^b30, 1222^a8, 1222^b7, III, 1229^a1–11, 1233^a22.

1220^{b}36–1221^{a}15

In *E.E.* we have a table of virtues and vices, followed by a brief description of the virtues and vices in III. In *E.N.*, the table is missing from our text (though a reference to such a table is made at II, 1107^{a}33), but the brief description of the vices at 1221^{a}15–^{b}3 corresponds to *E.N.* II, c. 7, just as *E.E.* III corresponds to *E.N.* III, c. 6–IV; the discussion of justice occurs in *E.N.* V.

The list of virtues here is much the same as the virtues of character to be found in *E.N.* and *M.M.* I, c. 7; a rather shorter list is given in *Rhetoric* I, 1366^{b}1–22. The main discrepancies with *E.N.* are the following: *E.N.* has in addition a virtue which is the mean between excessive ambition (*philotimia*) and lack of ambition (II, 1107^{b}24–1108^{a}2; IV, c. 4); in *E.N.*, the virtues of friendliness and dignity are not treated as two, though servility and flattery are distinguished; most important, endurance is not treated along with other virtues of character, but appears in VII, c. 7, and there is no suggestion in *E.N.* that practical wisdom (*phronēsis*), treated at length in *E.N.* VI, is a virtue to which the doctrine of the mean applies. These two virtues are also absent from *E.E.* III, which does, however, include a discussion of 'ready wit' (*eutrapelia*), a virtue also found in *E.N.* (cf. *E.E.* III, 1234^{a}4–23). For these reasons, some have held that these trios did not figure in Aristotle's table; and certainly, whatever view be taken about endurance, it is hard to believe that, at any stage of his thought, Aristotle held that the doctrine of the mean was applicable to intellectual virtues as well as virtues of character. Although the unworldly (*euēthēs*) man may lack the intelligence with which the practically wise man is properly endowed, that is surely not something with which it is possible to be over-endowed; hence there is no symmetry in the characteristics of the unscrupulous and unworldly man *vis-à-vis* the man of practical wisdom. I have therefore enclosed these two trios in square brackets in the translation.

The one- or two-word translations given are inevitably misleading in some cases. In general, a translation has been given that conforms to Aristotle's own descriptions of the virtue or vice in question, rather than one that fits the normal usage of the terms in other Greek authors. Difficulty has been found in the fact that at 1221^{a}13, Aristotle speaks of 'these affections', as if that were what had been listed; whereas, the items on the list are, of course, virtues and vices, and therefore settled states (though some of the words used (e.g. 'shame', 'envy') can also be used for the affection that manifests the disposition). But each trio may be regarded as defining an affection or feeling which may be had either to the right or the wrong degree. An exception to that is practical wisdom, which I have argued should be excised, and also the justice-trio, where, strikingly, instead of finding two vicious states of character, we find simply 'gain' and 'disadvantage'. This strongly suggests that Aristotle, at the time of composing this passage, already accepted that justice was a different sort of mean from the other virtues: at *E.N.* V, 1133^{b}33 he says that justice is distinctive in being 'of the mean', and at 1132^{b}18-19, the just decision is said to be a mean between gain and disadvantage. However, the description of the two extremes opposed to justice at 1221^{a}23-25 suggests a wider notion of justice than simply rectificatory justice, to which the notion of mean is applied in *E.N.* V.

On what basis was the list of virtues and vices constructed? Clearly, what we have could not pretend to be an exhaustive list of the virtues and vices recognized in Greek vocabulary. Nor can they be regarded as a representative sample, intended to confirm the doctrine of the mean, since Aristotle concedes in one case that one of the extremes lacks a name, and in a number of cases he has had either to invent a word or use an existing term in something other than its normal meaning. A full discussion of the individual virtues and vices, and the words used to distinguish them is beyond the scope of this book.

1221^{a}15-^{b}3

1221^{a}15-17:   cf. III, c. 3.

1221^{a}17-19:   cf. III, c. 1.

1221^{a}19-23:   cf. III, c. 2. See Notes on the question of possible lacunae in the text.

1221^{a}23-24:   The words translated 'acquisitive' and 'self-harming' are cognate with the words translated 'gain' and 'disadvantage' in the table of virtues and vices.

1221^{a}24-25:   cf. III, 1233^{b}38-1234^{a}3.

1221^{a}25-27:   cf. III, 1233^{b}29-34.

1221^{a}27-28:   cf. III, 1233^{b}34-38.

1221^{a}28-31:   This section has been thought to be spurious. See Commentary on 1220^{b}36-1221^{a}15.

1221^{a}31-33:   cf. III, c. 5.

1221^{a}33-34:   cf. III, c. 4.

1221^{a}34-36:   cf. III, c. 6.

1221ᵃ36–38: See Commentary on 1220ᵇ36–1221ᵃ15 for reasons
for thinking this section to be spurious.

1221ᵃ38–1221ᵇ3: cf. III, 1233ᵇ18–26. A literal translation of
ᵃ38–39 would be 'the man is spiteful through being upset in more
cases of good fortune than he should', a description which makes the
case of spite appear to fit the mean theory more closely than it does,
since the point is not really that the spiteful man is upset by *more*
cases of good fortune than the man in the mean state, but that he
is displeased in the *wrong* cases—those when the good fortune is
well-deserved.

1221ᵇ4–9

Aristotle says that it would be superfluous to add into each definition
that the conditions are fulfilled 'not incidentally'. He then adds that
it is not necessary for any science, properly so-called, to insert such
qualifying clauses into definitions; such a procedure is needed only
when dealing with those who deliberately produce paradoxes by
ignoring the natural sense of what is said. For similar phrases, compare *De Interpretatione* 17ᵃ36, *Rhetoric* 1402ᵃ15, 27, *Metaphysics*
Δ 1005ᵇ21. A verbal form of the word translated 'chicaneries' occurs
at *Topics* VI 139ᵇ26, 35, VIII 157ᵃ32.

Although the general point made in the second sentence in this
section is clear, it is difficult to see what the significance of requiring
that the conditions specified should hold essentially is. Other somewhat puzzling uses of the qualification 'not incidentally' occur at
1225ᵇ6 and 1219ᵇ27. Is Aristotle saying that it is superfluous to
specify that the character-states in question are essentially, not
merely incidentally manifested in behaviour of the sort described
(because that is how the virtues and vices are defined)? Or is he
saying that it is superfluous to add that it is no accident that persons
who are truly described by the adjective concerned act in the specific
fashion (sc. because their actions result from a settled character
disposition)?

1221ᵇ4: An alternative translation would be: 'It would be superfluous to add that they stand in such a relation to each thing (sc. to the
affections with which virtue and vice are concerned) not incidentally.'

1221ᵇ5: 'Productive': see Commentary on I 1216ᵇ17–19.

1221ᵇ7: Literally '. . . the verbal chicaneries of the practical skills',
where Aristotle presumably means by 'practical skills' what he means
at *Rhetoric* 1402ᵃ27, namely the skills of rhetoric and eristic, or
skill in debate.

1221^{b}9:   By 'the opposing states', Aristotle presumably means the virtuous means, which have yet to be discussed. They were said to be opposed to the extremes at 1220^{b}31–32.

1221^{b}10–17

There is some correspondence between ^{b}10–15 and *E.N.* IV 1126^{a}8–31, and between 15–17 and III, 1118^{b}16–21. Excess in respect of time would naturally suggest, in the case of anger, a person who is angry for too long, as at *E.N.* IV, 1125^{b}32, 1126^{a}10–11, but here it consists in getting angry too quickly (i.e. sooner than the circumstances warrant). The first group of vicious states are clear sub-forms of irascibility, the second (though this is not said explicitly) are apparently sub-forms of intemperance or dissoluteness. Excess in time and in intensity are illustrated in the case of anger by the sharp-tempered and the bad-tempered and the choleric man; differentiation by the object of the affection is illustrated by the vices associated with eating and drinking. The cases of the bitter and violent man do not readily fit any of the initial specifications, though they both involve, in a sense, excess. (This may support Ross's view that the text is corrupt at 1221^{b}11–12.)

As I have translated ^{b}11–12, Aristotle is saying that, among vicious traits of character that err through excess, sub-forms are distinguished *either* by the degree of excess (in one of two dimensions) of the associated affections, *or* by their objects (which are here assumed also to be causes of the affections). Alternative translations would be '. . . by differences in excess either of time or intensity or relation among the things that produce the affection' or '. . . according as the excess is in time or intensity or in the object producing the affections'. (So Solomon and Rackham.)

The first of these is open to the objection that the notion of intensity in respect of relation has no clear sense, and it makes Aristotle attribute the excess to the object of the affection rather than the affection itself; the second is open to the objection that it is doubtful if the Greek can be thus translated, and it does not accurately represent how, according to Aristotle, these sub-forms are differentiated.

1221^{b}10:   'Affections': the word translated thus here (*pathēmata*) is cognate with, but not the same as, the word regularly so translated, but is normally used synonymously with it (cf. 1220^{b}8–9, 11, 1221 ^{b}36, 1222^{b}11, III, 1234^{a}26), and probably is so here. In fact, however, what Aristotle is concerned to do here is not to differentiate affections, but certain settled unvirtuous dispositions on the basis of differences in the associated affections. To say that a person is quick-tempered is not to report the occurrence of a feeling, but ascribe a disposition.

1221^{b}18–26

With this passage should be compared *E.N.* III, 1107^{a}8–27, which is a considerably fuller treatment of the same topic. More examples are given there, including the case of adultery, which occurs in this passage, but not the case of assault. In *E.N.* affection-descriptions which 'incorporate badness' (*Schadenfreude*, shamelessness, envy) are distinguished from action-descriptions with the same feature (theft, adultery, murder). Here, on the other hand, no such distinction is made: the first example is of a character-description, applicable to a person ('adulterer') and the second ('assault') is an action-description; but the general account of the phenomenon in question suggests that the primary concern is with affections (cf. ^{b}19).

The passage is perhaps most readily intelligible if taken closely with what precedes. (The phrase 'things said' is best understood as relating to character-descriptions of the sort exemplified in the previous section.) There, sub-forms of a given unvirtuous characteristic, marked by distinct character-ascribing adjectives, were distinguished by a difference of object or degree in the affection associated with the character-state in question; Aristotle now appears to be saying that the relevant differences in the affection have in some cases led to the introduction of distinct affection-descriptions, which incorporate the implication that the affection occurs in a reprehensible degree or manner. With such an affection, it is not possible to experience it more than one should (or less, or the right amount): the reason, not explicitly stated by Aristotle, is that such a description incorporates a reference to the *right* degree, which would be inconsistent with the implication of reprehensibility contained in the description.

That account fits reasonably well with what he says at ^{b}18–19, and also 22–23. Although such affections will be examples of more generic ones that can be experienced either in an acceptable or an unacceptable degree, etc., the *specific* affection in question cannot ever be of an acceptable degree. This also seems to be the point of the examples of envy, *Schadenfreude*, and shamelessness at *E.N.* III, 1107^{a}10–11, and the remark that certain things are '*immediately* given a name incorporating badness' (1107^{a}9–10): the point of that seems to be that there is no non-evaluative name of the specific affection. This comes about because the introduction of a name which incorporates badness is treated as involving the recognition of a sub-form of the affection in question.

Clearly, once it is accepted that the features which distinguish certain manifestations of an affection as reprehensible define sub-forms of the affection, there will be some sub-forms that will not be identifiable independently of their reprehensibility; but whether there are such sub-forms will not depend on whether their existence has been marked by the introduction of names. Moreover, there will be such distinguishable sub-forms in the case of all the affections relevant to defining the virtues of character. However, Aristotle seems mainly interested in those cases where a single name has been introduced, and thus although the doctrine is presented as if it were a doctrine about a certain class of affections, his interest seems to be in the fact that certain *names* for affections 'incorporate badness'.

Unfortunately, construed as a doctrine about affections and the names for them, what he says is not illustrated by his examples. 'Adulterer' is clearly presented as a description which incorporates badness, but it ascribes a character-state to a person. (This is hardly true of the English word, but it is a feature of the Greek word as is apparent from *E.N.* V, 1·134ª22.) That will not show that the corresponding affection is called by a name that incorporates badness. Someone is not an adulterer solely, or perhaps at all, on account of his affections, but his actions. This lack of harmony between Aristotle's general remarks and his examples is similar to the case of the violent and truculent man of 1221^b14–15, who does not fit any of the categories distinguished at the beginning of the section, because these descriptions are applied on the strength not of the intensity, duration, etc., of feelings of anger, but of the actions that result.

1221^b23–25:   The case described is more plausible than appears, because, according to Aristotle, for adultery to occur a man must act voluntarily and know enough about the identity of the partner to be aware that he is committing adultery. Cf. *E.N.* V, 1134ª20.

CHAPTER 4

In this chapter, Aristotle takes a further step towards the preliminary account of virtue of character presented at 1222^b9–14 by establishing the connection between virtue and vice and pleasure and pain. This is argued for at 1221^b35–1222ª2, and based on material introduced from 1220ª22 onwards.

1221^b27-34

The division of the soul into two parts was made at 1219^b26–1220ª4, and the distinction of two sorts of virtue, corresponding to these two parts of the soul, introduced at 1220ª5–12. New to this chapter is the doctrine that the intellectual virtues are all concerned with arriving at truth (see ^b30, and its distinction between the truth about how things are and how something is to come about). This is similar to the distinction drawn in *E.N.* VI between the highest part of the soul employed in theoretical inquiries, whose characteristic virtue is

sophia (theoretical wisdom), and that part of the rational soul concerned with action, whose virtue is *phronēsis* (practical wisdom).
Compare *E.N.* VI, cc. 1 and 2. The idea that all intellectual virtues
have as their function the reaching of truth recalls the reference to
'practical truth' at *E.N.* VI, 1139ᵃ26-31. (Cf. also 1139ᵇ12.)

1221ᵇ31-32:   For inclination as characteristic of the part of the
non-rational soul that is capable of obeying reason, cf. 1220ᵃ1-2.
The parts of the soul which lack inclination include both the rational
part, and those parts dismissed as irrelevant to virtue at 1219ᵇ31–
32, 36-37.

1221ᵇ34-1222ᵃ5

This section down to ᵃ2 contains the arguments for the propositions
that traits of character are good or bad through the pursuit or avoidance of pleasures and pains (ᵇ32-34), or, equivalently, that virtues
of character have to do with pleasures and pains (ᵇ37-39). Aristotle
then says that this may be established by appeal to 'division tables'
of affections, states, and capacities. The reference seems to be to the
same tables of definitions as are mentioned at 1220ᵇ10 and III,
1234ᵃ26. Although the exact form of these tables cannot be reconstructed, presumably they gave definitions by division of individual
capacities, states, and affections and were regarded by Aristotle as
embodying established doctrine, on which he could draw for the
premises of an argument. The *first* argument, to which 'these considerations' at ᵇ37 refers, would seem to be as follows:

(i)   Capacities and states are differentiated by the affections
      that result from them.
(ii) Affections are defined by pleasure and pain.
(iii) Therefore, states, and in particular virtues, have to do with
      pleasure and pain.

Although the vagueness of the conclusion makes the argument
difficult to assess, it is not a valid argument for what Aristotle is
trying to establish, viz. that virtuous dispositions are dispositions to
pursue pleasures and avoid pains (i.e. to pursue certain pleasures
only, and in certain circumstances, etc., cf. ᵃ2). If that conclusion is
to be supported, (ii) must be construed as saying that affections are
defined by reference to the different sorts of pleasure and pain which
the subjects of the various affections pursue. But that, in its turn,
involves treating all affections as consisting in, or crucially involving,
desire for pleasure or the avoidance of pain. But it is not at all plausible to reduce all affections to desires, nor to suppose that all the
affections are differentiated by the pleasures and pains towards which

or against which they are directed. The definitions which we find in the *Rhetoric* (see Commentary on 1220^{b}14) do not so define them, though pleasure and pain enter into the definitions in so far as the affections are themselves pleasant or disagreeable states. It would seem that Aristotle, in order to reach his conclusion, would have done better, instead of considering affections, to concentrate on desires: desires are distinguished by their objects, and if desires are essentially for the pursuit of pleasure and avoidance of pain (cf. 1223^{a}34, III, 1235^{b}22), they will indeed be distinguished by the pleasures and pains that are their objects. The point will be clearer if we take the example of anger. One of Aristotle's virtues consists in a habit of feeling anger to the right degree, at the right time, etc. Anger does seem to include, conceptually, certain desires, e.g. the desire for retaliation, or compensation for an injury, but it would be absurd to suggest that the virtue of good temper was crucially a matter of coming to pursue in the right way the pleasure of revenge. The only passage in *E.N.* corresponding at all to this first argument is II 1104^{b}13-16, where, in order to show that virtue has to do with pleasure and pain, Aristotle argues that every affection (and action) is followed by pleasure and pain: here too we might object that the fact that they accompany each action and affection will not show that virtue consists in the right pursuit of them. See Commentary on 1220^{b}14.

At ^{b}37, Aristotle says that the conclusion about virtue follows not only from the considerations just mentioned but also from the things that have been asserted before. We then have a *second* argument corresponding closely to *E.N.* II, 1104^{b}18-26, with, apparently, the following structure:

   (i)   The nature of a soul's state relates to and concerns those things that make its state better or worse (^{b}39-^{a}1).

  (ii)   Men (and therefore the states of their souls) are worse on account of pleasures and pains by pursuing or avoiding the wrong ones, or doing so in the wrong manner (^{a}1-2).

 (iii)   Therefore good states of a soul (i.e. virtues) concern pursuit and avoidance of pleasures and pains.

My translation of ^{b}39-^{a}1 involves emendation (on which see the Notes) and it is therefore not certain that (i) occurs in the text as represented. According to the text that I have translated, (i) corresponds reasonably closely to 1220^{a}32-34. (ii), on the other hand, does not seem to represent anything asserted earlier. As stated, (ii) might be regarded as a kind of conceptual truth: by the wrong sort of indulgence in pleasure and shunning of pain, a state is produced which essentially involves a disposition to the same behaviour with respect to them. But the difficulty is that he will not then be saying that it is the *only* way in which men become worse, which is what is required if it is to support (iii); he will merely be saying that pleasures and pains *can* make people worse, by leading to the wrong pursuit and avoidance patterns.

The passage in Chapter 1 (1220^{a}22-37) which contains the assertion which (i) recapitulates is itself an earlier argument (based on the character of punishment) for the conclusion of this chapter. Thus there seem to be *three* arguments for the connection of virtue and vice with pleasure and pain.

1222^{a}2-5: Aristotle here mentions an erroneously sweeping conclusion drawn by some philosophers from the facts mentioned in the preceding lines. If the reading 'everyone' is correct, he must mean only that it is a generally held view. The word translated 'lack-of-disturbance' occurs in a definition of courage in the pseudo-Platonic *Definitions* 412^{a}8; that translated 'unsusceptibility' occurs in a definition of the same virtue at *Topics* 125^{b}23.

CHAPTER 5

This chapter begins with a preliminary account of virtue, incorporating the conclusions about it arrived at so far (1222^{a}6-17) and ends with a fuller summarizing paragraph (1222^{b}5-14), which surveys the course of the discussion from the beginning of Chapter 2, and marks the end of a section in the treatment of virtue. In between stands a discussion of some particular points connected with the doctrine of the mean.

1222^{a}6-17

1222^{a}6-8: Compare 1218^{b}37-38, 1219^{a}6. It was laid down in Chapter 1 that virtue is the best state, and that the better a state, the better is what it produces.

1222^{a}8-10: This is the first occurrence of the phrase 'the right principle', but the word translated 'principle' (*logos*) has also occurred at 1220^{b}28, in the passage where the notion of the 'mean relative to us' is first introduced, but is there translated 'rational principle'. The word *logos* can refer either to the rational faculty of the soul, or to the principle or rule which the faculty prescribes. For a discussion of the use of the expression here translated 'right principle' in *E.N.* VI see Smith and Stocks.

Other passages in which the phrase is used are 1222^{b}7, 1227^{b}17, III, 1231^{b}33. Compare also 1222^{a}34, III, 1233^{b}6, 1234^{a}11, where *logos* alone seems to be used in the same sense.

1222^a10-11:   On the 'mean relative to us', see 1220^b27-29, with Commentary. The translation '... each virtue is essentially a mean state' involves emendation of the text, on which see Notes.

1222^a12:   '... certain means in pleasures and pains, and things pleasant and unpleasant'. Aristotle here appears to distinguish two ways in which virtues, as well as being intermediate states themselves are concerned with means. They involve a settled disposition to avoid excess and defect in the having of pleasures and pains, and also to avoid excess and defect in the pleasant and unpleasant things chosen. He thus takes account of the fact that a virtue like liberality has to do more with giving and receiving the right amount of money and in the right circumstances, than with having feelings of generosity to the right degree and in the right circumstances. The *E.N.* lays much greater stress on the fact that virtues and vices have to do with means in actions as well as affections. Compare *E.N.* II, 1106^b16, III, 1109^b30.

1222^a16-17:   By 'going to excess without qualification', he means 'exceeding the right amount', i.e. going beyond the mean, just as in English, calling something excessive, without specifying in relation to what normally means 'exceeding what ought to be the case'.

1222^a17-22

The argument is that, since excess and defect in the objects towards which the virtuous man has the right disposition are opposed both to one another and to the mean, the virtuous state itself is opposed to each of the two unvirtuous states and they are opposed to one another. (Compare 1220^b31-32.) 'Thing' in ^a19 presumably has to be taken in a neutral sense to cover both such things as fear, of which the brave man has just the right amount, and things like money, which the liberal man gives and receives the right amount of. Compare III, 1228^a29-31, *E.N.* II, 1108^b11-15, *M.M.* 1186^b13-14. The text translated contains an emendation — the insertion of 'not'; without it, Aristotle will be referring to *a* (single) state that leads sometimes to deficiency, sometimes to excess, thus uncharacteristically treating the unvirtuous states of character as exemplifying a single generic state, defined as one that deviates from the mean.

1222^a22-36

Compare *E.N.* II 1108^b30-1109^a19. Aristotle says that, in some cases, one extreme is closer to the mean than the other, and in such cases, the other extreme is regarded as more opposed to the mean. In ^a24-28, the reason given is that in some cases it is the transition from excess to the mean, in other cases, the transition from deficiency; that is more quickly made. Aristotle's examples in ª28–36, suggest that which extreme is nearer the mean is determined by which of the extremes is less reprehensible and therefore nearer the best state.

1222ª36-1222ᵇ4

Aristotle offers as a reason for the asymmetries mentioned in the previous section that human beings commonly deviate from certain virtues in one direction only. In fact, this has no tendency to show that in these cases one extreme is nearer the mean than another.

The facts alluded to here reflect two more general issues concerning the doctrine of the mean. The theory requires, at least, that for each virtue of character there are two associated vices; but (i) in some cases it is not easy to name two such vices since one of the two is not found in the field of human behaviour; (ii) in some cases, there seems to be only one vice that is naturally regarded as opposed to a virtue: it is the cowardly man, not the foolhardy, who lacks bravery, and the extravagant man is not naturally described as ungenerous. It looks as if the mean theory can be made to apply as widely as Aristotle claims it does apply only by having as the virtue what is in fact an amalgam of *two* virtues, one opposed to one extreme, the other opposed to the other. On these issues see Hardie, Urmson, and Pears.

1222ᵇ5-14

In this section, Aristotle summarizes the conclusions of the discussion from 1220ª13. The translation adopted involves emendation: Aristotle recognizes that from the fact that virtues are all mean states it does not follow that *all* of these mean states are virtues. With the reading of the MSS he will be recognizing the possibility either that not all virtues are means *between pleasures and pains* (so Kapp and Dirlmeier) or that not all virtues are means at all (sc. because intellectual virtues are not).

CHAPTER 6

This chapter raises a number of internal difficulties, but it is at least clear that it forms a prelude to the investigation of the voluntary and involuntary (cc. 7, 8, and 9), and of choice, (c. 10). The chapter attempts, in a way more characteristic of *E.E.* than *E.N.*, to apply systematic considerations concerning objects of change to the subject of human origination of action (1222ᵇ15-20). Since origins of *changes* are controlling origins, and actions are all changes, human beings are controlling origins. There follows (ᵇ25-41) an attempt to give a quite general characterization of the notion of an originative principle, one that does not appeal to the special features of the origination of change. The conclusions are then applied to human action.

1222ᵇ15-20

Aristotle begins with the doctrine that substances are 'starting-points'. The word thus translated (*archē*) is the normal word for a beginning or starting-point—often the starting-point of a temporal sequence. From that it comes to mean 'origin', in the sense of the ultimate terminus in a chain of explanation. But the associated verb, in the active rather than the middle voice, commonly meant 'rule' or 'command', and the noun, in non-philosophical contexts, commonly means 'command', 'authority', or even 'form of government'. On this see Kirwan on *Metaphysics* Δ 1013ᵃ10. Both uses clearly influence Aristotle's philosophical usage: something is called a starting-point if it controls or determines what follows, as well as occupying a terminal position in a chain of explanation. Here, human beings, among animals, are said to be starting-points not only because they can reproduce their kind, but also because they are the source, by their decisions, of changes in the world.

The proposition that human beings are starting-points of action is plainly regarded as evident without argument: equally, acceptance of it does not prejudge the question whether human action is voluntary, for which argument is offered later in the chapter. Although there is nothing closely corresponding to this chapter in *E.N.*, at III, 1113ᵇ17-19, Aristotle describes a human being as an origin or begetter of his actions 'like a parent'. Compare also III, 1112ᵇ31-32.

1222ᵇ18-20:   Compare *E.N.* VI, 1139ᵃ20.

1222ᵇ20-29

Aristotle now singles out a class of starting-points that are called controlling (*kuriai*)—those that are origins of change. Since actions are changes, human beings, as origins of action, are *controlling* origins. Accordingly, later in the chapter, he feels justified in referring to human beings as *controlling* (1223ᵃ5-7). In this section, human beings are contrasted with, on the one hand, Aristotle's god, who is the source of changes that occur necessarily, and, on the other hand, the basic principles of mathematics, which are also called starting-points. For a defence of this translation of *kurios* ('controlling'), see Notes.

Aristotle's god is most naturally taken as the unmoved mover (compare *Metaphysics* Λ, *Physics* VIII), the source of changes that occur in accordance with necessary laws, but himself unchanging.

This creates a difficulty in $^b23$, as Dirlmeier notes, where the basic principles of mathematics are referred to as unchanging origins, as if God were not unchanging. This led Dirlmeier to suggest that the deity is here conceived of in a semi-popular way. It seems better to suppose that Aristotle is writing loosely, and by 'unchanging starting-point' he means 'principle governing the unchanging': the principles of mathematics are principles governing a class of objects not subject to change.

1222^b25-28:   On the interpretation here adopted, the purpose of this section is simply to explain how, in a stretched sense, mathematical starting-points may be described as 'controlling'. This is preliminary to the use of the geometrical example to illustrate the notion of a starting-point at $^b29-41$. It is, admittedly, difficult to separate the grounds for calling the first principles *controlling* starting-points from those for calling them starting-points at all. The point seems to be that if a starting-point A has consequences B and C, then, if A had not been the case, B and C would have been different also. To this, it is natural to object that it assumes that B and C each entail A rather than conversely. $^b26-28$ seem to be making the point that, if B and C are consequences of A, in general neither B nor C, will entail the other (hence B will have no claim to be counted the starting-point of C, instead of A, nor C of B). He then takes account of the case where B *does* entail C, and points out that the falsity of B would require the falsity of C, but only on condition of the falsity of A. The difficulty is that he seems to envisage a case where A, B, and C are each mutually entailing; but that alone provides no ground for singling out any one of the three propositions as a starting-point of the other two.

1222^b29-41

This section appears to be intended to explain the notion of a starting-point in a quite general way by reference to the case of a geometrical proof. The proposition that the sum of the interior angles of a triangle is equal to two right angles is said to be the starting-point of the propositions that the sum of the interior angles of a quadrilateral is equal to four, of a five-sided figure six, and so on. Aristotle is appealing to the fact that any n-sided rectilinear plane figure may be divided into an $n-1$ sided figure and a triangle; so, given that the sum of the interior angles of a triangle is two right angles, the sum may be calculated for a plane figure of arbitrarily many sides: the sum of the interior angles of an n-sided figure is $2(n-2)$ right angles. There is no *similar* calculation of the sum of the angles of a triangle: no figure with fewer than three sides can enclose a plane. It is in this sense that the proposition about the triangle may be called a starting-point.

There is, indeed, a problem in making sense of the contrary-to-fact supposition of the sum of the interior angles of a triangle totalling three right angles, since the proposition in question holds necessarily; it is perhaps best to construe the conditional epistemically. 'If we had found that the interior angles of a triangle totalled three right angles, we should have been able to infer that the angles of a quadrilateral totalled six . . .' This is in line with Aristotle's calling something a starting-point of something's being the case if it contributes to the most fundamental *explanation* of its being the case. Compare *Metaphysics* Δ 1013^{a}14-17. In this case, one acquires knowledge of the sum of the interior angles of, say, a quadrilateral, by way of knowledge of the corresponding truth about the triangle. One difficulty is that, although there is no other knowledge *of the same* sort on which our knowledge of the sum of the angles of a triangle depends, that proposition is certainly a theorem rather than an axiom, and depends on other truths of geometry. Why then does he suggest at ^{b}39-40 that the proposition about triangles depends on nothing else?

1222^{b}38:   For references to the *Analytics*, compare I, 1217^{a}17, and 1227^{a}10. The reference here may be to such passages as *Posterior Analytics* I, c. 4.

1222^{b}41-1223^{a}9

The course of reasoning in this section is not at all easy to follow. Aristotle clearly wishes to apply the general doctrine about origins to the case of human action. He first says that if there are things that can come about in opposite ways, their starting-points must be of such a kind (^{b}41-42). The reason is then given (^{a}1) that, from necessary starting-points, the results must also be necessary. What exactly is the property, implied by the phrase 'of that kind', which he says that a starting-point must possess if it is to be the source of results which may take either of opposite forms? To say that the origins must be such that either of two opposite outcomes can flow from them would be trivial, and ^{a}1 suggests that the starting-points must at least be non-necessary. When, therefore, he says (^{a}2) that what results 'from these' can come about in opposite ways, he must be referring to outcomes flowing from starting-points of the appropriate non-necessary sort.

So far Aristotle has simply said that *if* there are outcomes that can be of either of two sorts (which we may conveniently call *contingent outcomes*), their starting-points must be contingent also.

This conditional principle seems to rest on the doctrine that a starting-point completely determines its outcome, which Aristotle has sought to establish, perhaps rather unhappily, by the mathematical illustration of ^{b}29-41, from which it follows that variability in outcomes requires a variability in their source. He now (^{a}2-4) says that the antecedent of the conditional is fulfilled: many such things (i.e. contingent occurrences) are in human power, and things of which human beings are themselves the origin.

At 4-7, Aristotle says that two things follow: (a) all the actions of which a human being is the controlling origin are capable of either coming about or not (^{a}4-6), and (b) all those things concerning which a man controls whether they are the case or not are such that it is within his power whether they come about or not (^{a}6-7). It would seem that on no interpretation does (a) follow from what precedes; for all that had been said before was that many contingent occurrences are things of which human beings are the source, and it does not follow from that that *everything* that has its source in human agency is contingent. Similarly (b) which seems to be saying that everything determined by human agency is contingent, does not follow from ^{a}2-3, where nothing was implied about *all* occurrences of which human beings are the source. (I have made a small excision at ^{a}2, but the present point is unaffected by that.)

It seems to me that the lacuna in the argument can be explained, if not excused, if we supposed that Aristotle was assuming that if an origin is sometimes the source of contingent outcomes, it must always be so; hence it is enough to appeal to what Aristotle takes to be a fact, that some results of human agency are contingent, to establish that all human actions are. We can now explain how, in ^{a}7-9 Aristotle feels entitled to say that something is within a person's power to do or not to do if and only if it is one of which he is the cause. This rests on the connection, just asserted, between being the result of human agency and being contingent, and the connections between being a starting-point and being a cause (cf. ^{b}39-40).

That some occurrences, notably human actions, are contingent, appears to be regarded by Aristotle as simply a matter of observation. Plainly it requires more argument than is given here.

1223^{a}9-20

In this section, Aristotle argues from the fact that virtue and vice, and the deeds resulting from them, are praised and blamed, and the fact that praise and blame are bestowed on those things of which the recipient of the praise or the blame is the cause, that virtue and vice have to do with those things of which the agent is the cause; these must therefore be defined (^{a}9-16). This leads on to the investigation of the voluntary and involuntary, and choice, which occupies the next few chapters.

This section does not appear to depend at all on the conclusions of the earlier part of the chapter. It is taken as evident without argument that praise and blame are bestowed only on actions that we cause, and that only the latter are voluntary. The conclusion of the earlier part of this chapter was that actions that human beings cause are actions which it is within their power to perform or not, and this is taken up later in Chapter 10, at 1226ª21 f.

CHAPTER 7
1223ª21-28

In this section, three possible explanations of the voluntary and involuntary are suggested. Aristotle says that the voluntary (i.e. voluntary actions) would seem to be what is in accordance with one of three things, viz. inclination, choice, or thought (24-25); the voluntary, on the other hand, is what is *contrary* to one of those things (presumably, though Aristotle does not say this, contrary precisely to that which the voluntary is defined as being in accordance with). The first option (inclination) is said to divide into three species, and the remainder of this chapter is devoted to disposing of the three corresponding accounts of the voluntary and involuntary one by one. 1223ª29-ᵇ17 discuss *desire*, ª29-ᵇ3 offering arguments *in favour* of defining the voluntary and involuntary in terms of it, and ᵇ4-17 presenting arguments *against* the suggestion, which are clearly intended to be decisive. 1223ᵇ18-28 deal more briefly with the *second* species of inclination, spirit, and ᵇ29-36 attempt to dispose of the third form, wish.

1223ª24-26:   The first two suggestions for defining the voluntary are intuitively plausible and have often been proposed: it seems natural to regard a voluntary action as one which the agent wanted to do, or again as one which he chose to do. The third alternative *thought* (*dianoia*) is less clear; on this see Commentary on 1224ª7-9.

1223ª26-27:   The term that has been translated 'inclination', *orexis* has already occurred at 1220ª1 (on which see Commentary) and 1221ᵇ31-32. It is sometimes translated 'desire', but that translation has been reserved for *epithumia*, which is one of the forms of *orexis*. Inclination forms part of the systematic doctrine of the *De Anima* and *De Motu Animalium*. Inclination serves to distinguish a part of the soul possessed by all living organisms that have perception. At *De Anima* II, 413ᵇ21 f, it is argued that everything that has perception is capable of pleasure and pain, and that this involves desire and hence inclination. There, as here, desire is treated as a species of inclination, which all animals possess, unlike plants (414^{a}32–^{b}2). In this last passage we find the same threefold division of inclination into desire, spirit, and wish. (Compare also *De Motu Animalium* 700^{b}22-23.) Elsewhere in the *De Anima*, at III, 432^{a}23 f., desire and anger are regarded as non-rational, whereas wish is rational. See also *Rhetoric* 1369^{a}1-7, where again wish is classified as a rational inclination, and said to have the good as its object, while spirit and desire are non-rational.

There are two problems with Aristotle's way of disposing of the suggestion that the voluntary may be defined as that which is in accordance with inclination. (i) If 'voluntary' means simply 'in accordance with inclination', it will follow that every voluntary action is in accordance with one of the trio mentioned in this section, but not necessarily the same on each occasion. Yet Aristotle argues as if the proposal under consideration can be broken down into three alternative suggestions, requiring separate refutation; and these are much less plausible suggestions than the simple suggestion that the voluntary is what is in accordance with *some* inclination, which may be any of the three kinds. It is as if Aristotle were unaware of an ambiguity of scope in the statement that, for an action, to be voluntary is to be in accordance with some species of inclination. (ii) Is Aristotle here assuming that the voluntary and involuntary are both exclusive of one another and exhaust the class of actions? That he held that they were exclusive is indicated by 1223^{b}35-36; but since inclinations may conflict, the suggestion that voluntary actions are those in accordance with inclination will have the consequence that an action may be both voluntary (being in accordance with some inclination) and involuntary, through being contrary to another inclination in conflict with the first. Further, given the different species of inclination, an action may fail to be in accordance with a desire without therefore being contrary to some desire; so the voluntary and involuntary will not exhaust the class of actions. These difficulties would have been avoided if Aristotle had simply attempted a definition of one of the pair *voluntary-involuntary* and then defined the other class by exclusion from the first. This, on the whole, is the line he takes in *E.N.*, III, c. 1 where involuntary actions are defined as those done under compulsion or through ignorance, and voluntary actions are explained as those which are not involuntary in either of the two ways that Aristotle mentions.

1223^{a}29-36

In the text as it stands, the argument may be set out as follows:

(1) Everything involuntary is compelled (29-30).

	(2)	Everything forced or compelled is unpleasant (30–32).
So	(3)	Something is compelled if and only if it is unpleasant (33) (? from (2)).
But	(4)	Desire is of the pleasant (34).
So	(5)	What is contrary to desire is always unpleasant (33–34) (from (4)).
So	(6)	What is contrary to desire is compelled (34–35) (from (3) and (5)).
and	(7)	What is contrary to desire is involuntary (34–35) (? from (1) and (6)).
But	(8)	The voluntary and involuntary are opposites (35–36).
So	(9)	What is in accordance with desire is voluntary (35) from (7) and (8)).

To consider first the argument down to (7), the step from (2) to (3) seems to involve a blatant fallacy; moreover, not (2) but its converse, which (3) incorporates, is used in the argument. Further, (7) cannot be validly derived from (1) but only from its converse. These difficulties beset the attempt to find a valid argument for the conclusion that being contrary to desire implies being involuntary. But is (7), thus interpreted, sufficient to lead to the conclusion, in conjunction with (8)? Aristotle is considering an argument for the view that identifies the voluntary with the in-accord-with-desire, which is, of course, a stronger conclusion than (9). But he may have been attempting to argue for nothing stronger than (9), which he may have regarded as providing intuitive support for the definition of the voluntary in terms of desire. But does (9) follow from (7) and (8)?

If (8) is taken, for the purposes of the argument, as implying no more than the incompatibility of 'involuntary' with 'voluntary', (9) cannot be derived. But it is possible that (7) is meant to support the definition of the involuntary as what is contrary to desire, in which case (9) does follow, on any interpretation of (8), provided that it is accepted that every action is either in accordance with, or contrary to, what the agent desires.

The difficulties with the derivation of (7) are mitigated if an emendation proposed by Mr J. O. Urmson is accepted at 29–30, which would yield the translation '. . . Everything involuntary seems to be compelled, and what is compelled is involuntary, and everything which men do or undergo under necessity is unpleasant . .' On this reading, the argument would contain, instead of (1), (1)′, 'Everything involuntary is compelled, and everything compelled involuntary', from which, together with (3) and (5), (7) can be validly derived. In support of this is the fact that (1)′ is explicitly stated at 1224ª10-11. But the glaring fallacy in the derivation of (3) from (2) would remain.

If (5) rests on (4), the argument presumably is that, if X is contrary to desire, not-X is desired; hence, by (4), not-X is (thought of as) pleasant, and hence X is unpleasant. It is assumed that if not-X is pleasant, X is unpleasant. For the doctrine that desire is of the pleasant, see VII, 1235ᵇ22, *Rhetoric* 1370ᵃ17, *E.N.* III, 1111ᵇ16-17, *De Anima* 414ᵇ5-6. For the idea that actions in accordance with desire are pleasant, involuntary actions unpleasant, see also *E.N.* III, 1111ᵃ32-33.

1223ᵃ36-1223ᵇ3

Up to ᵇ2, the structure of the argument is reasonably clear, and may be summarized as follows:

(1) Vice always makes a man less just (ᵃ36).

(2) Incontinence is a (form of) vice (ᵃ36-37).

(3) A man acts incontinently (if and) only if he acts in accordance with desire contrary to reasoning (ᵃ37-39).

(4) Unjust action is voluntary (ᵃ39).

Therefore (5) The incontinent man acts unjustly, through acting in accordance with desire (39-ᵇ1) (from (1, (2), and (3)).

Therefore (6) The incontinent man acts voluntarily (ᵇ1-2) (from (4) and (5)).

and (7) What is in accordance with desire is voluntary (ᵇ2) (from (3) and (6)).

Clearly, the argument does not purport to establish anything stronger than (7); but to support the proposed definition of the voluntary it would evidently be necessary to establish the converse proposition that every voluntary action is in accordance with desire. However, the argument is not valid as an argument for (7), as (3) does not imply that all action in accordance with desire is incontinence; that is so even if (3) is construed as a biconditional, because of the crucial qualification 'contrary to reasoning', without which (3) would have little plausibility, and it is obviously so if it is not thus construed. As it is, the argument supports only the conclusion that *some* actions in accordance with desire are voluntary.

Various transpositions have been proposed of the sentences in ᵃ36-ᵇ2, but all seem quite unnecessary, and none has any effect on the validity of the argument. The final sentence ('It would be strange ...') is puzzling, and it has been thought that it really belongs elsewhere, e.g. after 1223ᵇ12 (on which see Notes), or that there is a lacuna before it. With the present text, we have to suppose Aristotle is pointing to the absurdity that would result from denying that incontinent action is unjust (thus denying (5), and therefore (1) or (2)). But someone who denied that incontinence is voluntary would deny that it is a vice (thus rejecting (2)), and would not be committed to the absurdity that men become more just (or less unjust) when they become incontinent. In view of these difficulties, there seems much to be said for transferring ᵇ2–3 after ᵇ12. (1) may be surprising, but can perhaps be found intelligible if we suppose that Aristotle has in mind the broad sense of 'justice' and 'injustice' in which they are identical with the whole of virtue and vice respectively. See *E.N.* V, 1129ᵇ25–1130ª13. However, it is doubtful if the word translated here 'vice' (*mochtheria*) is interpretable so as to make (1) and (2) each true. If Aristotle is using it as a synonym for *kakia*, it will refer to the man of established bad character, whose dispositions have a settled direction towards the wrong kind of life; (1) will then be true, but incontinence will not be an example of it, and (2) will be false. 'Incontinence' is the conventional translation of Aristotle's *akrasia*, and it has been adopted because it is less question-begging than 'weakness of will'. *Akrasia* is the state of a person who is led by desire to act in a way contrary to what he knows (or believes) to be the best; he thus 'acts in accordance with desire 'contrary to reason'. The *locus classicus* in Aristotle is *E.N.* VII, cc. 1–10, where Aristotle starts from the difficulties that the phenomenon of *akrasia* presents for the Socratic equation of virtue and knowledge. On *akrasia* see also Commentary on c. 11 and VIII, c. 1.

1223ᵇ3–10

This section and the next each contain an argument *against* the identification of voluntary acts with those in accordance with desire. The argument of this section is as follows:

(1) A person acts voluntarily if and only if he does what he wishes to do (ᵇ5–6).

(2) No one wishes for what he thinks bad (ᵇ6–7).

(3) A man acts incontinently if and only if he acts contrary to what he thinks best as a result of desire (ᵇ8–9).

Hence (4) A man who acts incontinently does not do what he wishes to do (ᵇ7–8) (from (2) and (3)).

Therefore (5) The same person will simultaneously act voluntarily and involuntarily. (From (1) and (2) and the doctrine of the previous section that voluntary action is in accordance with desire).

This argument is valid: (3) is put forward as a definition of incontinence, which is verbally different from, but substantially the same as, the account used in the previous section. (1) in effect introduces the alternative version of the view that voluntary action is action in accordance with inclination (see Commentary on 1223a21-28), which is argued against at 1223b29-36. For Aristotle's concept of *wishing*, see Commentary on that section.

1223b10-17

The argument of this section is as follows:

(1) Continence is a virtue (b11-12).
(2) Virtuous conduct is just (b12).
Therefore (3) The continent act justly (b10-11) (from (1) and (2)).
(4) A man acts continently if and only if he acts in accordance with reason against desire (b12-14).
(5) Just action is voluntary (b14).
Therefore (6) Continent action is voluntary (from (3) and (5)).
(7) Acting against desire is involuntary (b16-17).
Therefore (8) The same man will simultaneously act voluntarily and involuntarily (b17) (from (4), (6), and (7)).

The argument is similar in structure to that of the previous section; (4) represents a definition of continence similar to that of incontinence at b8-9. The same contradiction is derived from the combination of the thesis of the first two sections of the chapter, that acting against desire is involuntary ((7)), with certain views on continence. (2) presupposes, as before, a broad conception of justice (see Commentary on previous section). (6) is not stated in the text. (1), like the statement of the previous section that incontinence is a vice, may provoke qualms: for Aristotle's ideally virtuous man, who has a settled virtuous disposition and whose desires are all rightly directed, will not have desires opposed to reason. Continence is a lesser virtue than temperance (*sophrosunè*). On this contrast, see 1227b16 f., with Commentary, *E.N.* IV, 1128b34, VII, 1145a17-18, 1145b15 f, 1151b23 f.

Although presented inside a hypothetical clause, (5) is evidently something that Aristotle accepts. The argument that just and unjust actions are such that if one of them is voluntary, so is the other, is reminiscent of *E.N.* III, 1114b12-25.

1223b11: The remark at 1223b2-5 that it is strange if incontinence should make men more just is more naturally inserted here if the manuscript reading is retained (see Notes).

1223b18-28

The first part of this section, down to b21, similar in form to 1223a29-b3, argues for the identification of the voluntary with action in accordance with spirit. It has the following form:

            (1) What is opposed to spirit is unpleasant (^{b}19–20).
            (2) What is unpleasant is compelled (cf. 1223^{a}33).
Therefore   (3) What is opposed to spirit is compelled (^{b}2) (from
                (1)).
            (4) What is compelled is involuntary (^{b}20–21).
            (5) The voluntary and involuntary are opposites (cf.
                1223^{a}35–36).
Therefore   (6) What is in accordance with spirit is voluntary (^{b}21)
                (from (3), (4), and (5)).

In (4) we have the right premiss for the argument, whereas at 1223^{a}29–30 we had its converse, which made the argument invalid. See Commentary on 1223^{a}29–36.

The word *thumos*, here translated 'spirit', is elsewhere translated 'anger'. It is here evidently treated as a source of action co-ordinate with desire, in a way reminiscent of the spirited element of the soul, *to thumoeides*, in Plato's *Republic*.

For continence and incontinence, in respect of anger, compare *E.N.* VII, 1145^{b}20, c. 4. In the later passage, as here, it is made clear that continence and incontinence *tout court* are to be regarded as continence or incontinence *in respect of desire*; thus the reference to incontinence in respect of desire at ^{b}19 refers back to the preceding arguments, which exploit a definition of continence as action opposed to desire. However, the argument that follows parallels 1223^{a}29–36, which does not mention incontinence, unlike the preceding arguments.

1223^{b}22:   The citation of Heraclitus is made in support of (1). The meaning of the passage of Heraclitus emerges from *Politics* V, 1315 ^{a}30, where it is also cited: the impulses generated by anger are so strong that men are willing to act at risk to their lives. This is here taken to be a measure of the unpleasantness of its repression.

1223^{b}24–28:   The suggestion is that the same sort of argument can be developed against the identification of the voluntary with acting in accordance with spirit as was developed against the parallel thesis with desire at 1223^{b}3–18. The first part of that section suggested the positive thesis that acting voluntarily consists in doing what one wishes to do (see premiss (1) in the Commentary on 1223^{b}3–10). That is in turn supported by the observation of ^{b}27–28.

What qualification is intended by 'in respect of the same aspect of the situation? (The word 'aspect' is added in translation: the Greek has simply the neuter article.) If the point is that in some way the same action may be both voluntary and involuntary, it would be natural to suppose that Aristotle is alluding to the possibility that an action may be voluntary under one description and involuntary under another, a possibility allowed by the non-philosophical use of the Greek word thus translated. If so, the proposition that the same action cannot be both voluntary and involuntary would need qualification, but the argument of this chapter would be undermined; for the apparent contradiction arises from the fact that an action would be in accordance with one moving impulse but contrary to another; but then it will be generally possible to associate different descriptions or aspects of an action with each of the impulses. This is particularly plausible in the case of conflicts between desire and wish, given that a desire's object is said to be pleasure, and a wish's object is the good. Thus a man may be said to visit the dentist voluntarily (the action being in accord with his long-term and settled wants) but also involuntarily (= reluctantly).

1223^{b}29-36

Aristotle now investigates the *third* version of the view that the voluntary is in accordance with inclination. The intuition that the voluntary is in accordance with wish had figured in the arguments against the other two suggestions. First we have (^{b}29-32) a recapitulation of the argument that incontinence involves injustice (cf. 1223^{a}36-^{b}3) with the conclusion left unstated. Then we seem to have the following argument:

(1) No one wishes for things that he thinks are bad (^{b}32-33).

(2) The incontinent man does things that he thinks are bad (^{b}33; cf. 1223^{b}8-9).

Therefore (3) The incontinent man does things that he does not wish to do (from (1) and (2)).

(4) Unjust action is voluntary (^{b}33-34).

(5) Action is voluntary if and only if it is in accordance with wish (^{b}34).

Therefore (6) Incontinent action is not voluntary (from (3) and (5)).

Therefore (7) The incontinent does not act unjustly (^{b}34-36) (from (4) and (6)).

The inference to (3) requires the assumption that if no one has a wish for things believed bad, no one wishes *do do* something he believes bad.

Although it seems clear that the argument is of this form, and intended to yield a conclusion in conflict with the doctrine that the incontinent man acts unjustly, the conclusion actually stated is that the incontinent man will cease acting unjustly when he becomes incontinent (and so be juster than before).

CHAPTER 8
1223^{b}37-1224^{a}4

On Aristotle's claim to have shown that the voluntary is not definable as that which is in accordance with inclination, and the involuntary as contrary to it, see Commentary on 1223^{a}26-27.

The general form of the argument is reasonably clear: many actions are performed in accordance with wish, but in a flash (i.e. straight off, without reflection or deliberation); nothing in accordance with choice is performed in a flash. So not all actions in accordance with wish are in accordance with choice. But all actions done from wish are voluntary; so some voluntary actions are not in accordance with choice. So the present definition must be rejected. For the doctrine about actions done on impulse, cf. *EN* III, 1111^{b}9-10. The word translated 'in a flash' is a word normally meaning 'sudden'.

At ^{b}39-^{a}3, the reference is to 1223^{a}29-36: the case of the incontinent man has provided an example of a man acting voluntarily but contrary to wish, not an example of a wished action that is not voluntary; hence the thesis that if an action is in accordance with wish it is voluntary is allowed to stand. The translation of ^{b}39 to ^{a}1 involves an emendation: the MSS have 'that which is in accordance with wish has been shown to be not involuntary (? i.e. voluntary)'. But that has not been *shown*. For further discussion, see Notes.

1224^{a}5-13

This section introduces a discussion which continues to the end of the chapter. The doctrine that an action is done under compulsion if and only if it is involuntary is in marked contrast to *E.N.* III, where actions done under compulsion (*bia*) constitute only *one* of the two classes of involuntary action there distinguished.

1224^{a}7:   For the argument, see 1223^{a}25. Why does Aristotle assume that the voluntary must be defined in terms of one of these three things? Presumably the reason is that action results from a combination of thought and inclination (*orexis*) whose interaction results in choice, hence the voluntary and involuntary must be explicable in terms either of one of these or of what results from their co-operation.

1224^{a}13-30

The main theme of this section is the close connection between the notions of compulsion and necessity. The word translated 'compelled' is the adjective formed from the Greek word for force (cf. ^{a}14).

The argument is that we can best understand what it is for human beings to be compelled, or to act under compulsion, if we examine the application of the notion of force to inanimate things; to speak of *them* as being forced to behave in a certain way is to say that they are behaving in a way contrary to their natural tendency. This can be applied also to living things (^{a}20-24), but the situation is complicated by the duality of natural impulses in human beings (^{a}26 f.). The final sentences of this section seem to be of a parenthetical character.

1224^{a}14:   'Persuasion'. Compare 1224^{a}38-1224^{b}1.

1224^{a}16-18:   According to Aristotle's physics, objects have natural places and hence move in certain directions unless prevented from doing so. Thus fire goes upwards, and solid objects like stones go downwards. For this see, for example, *Physics* VIII, 253^{b}33 f, *De Caelo* IV, c. 3.

1224^{a}22-23:   On this compare *E.N.* III, 1110^{a}1-^{b}17, where Aristotle simply says that an action is done under compulsion if the starting-point (*archē*) of the action is outside the agent and he contributes nothing. Here, as we have seen, the definition of an action done under compulsion is reached on the basis of a general consideration of changing phenomena. He has said that compulsion and necessity imply that what occurs is contrary to a thing's natural and essential impulse (^{a}18), i.e. those essential to the kind of thing in question; in the case of human beings, this is said to involve change contrary to the agent's internal impulse, under the impact of something external to him. We might still question whether change contrary to a thing's natural impulse is necessarily change resulting from external pressure. It is commonly objected to Aristotle's treatment in *E.N.* III, c. 1 that he leaves no room for exculpation for actions done under *internal* compulsion, for example a neurosis. There we seem to have behaviour that is in some sense contrary to natural human tendencies, resulting from a morbid condition, but not from anything external.

1224^{a}25-27:   For the division of the soul, see 1219^{b}26 f., with Commentary. The two parts of the soul concerned with action give rise to a duality of natural impulses to action.

1224^{a}28-30:   Aristotle is, of course, here using the verb 'act' (*prattein*) in a strong, philosophically loaded sense (cf. 1222^{b}20). The present restriction corresponds to the denial of action (*praxis*) to children and animals, cf. *E.N.* VI, 1139^{a}20.

1224^a30-^b2

The fact that there are two impulses to action in human beings, having their source in the rational and the non-rational parts of soul, which can come into conflict in the case of the continent and the incontinent man, means that there are two grounds on which an action may be naturally described as performed under compulsion, and a plausible case can be made for saying that the continent and incontinent man each act under compulsion. Aristotle now argues that the view that the incontinent man acts under compulsion conflicts with the view that actions done under compulsion are unpleasant (compare 1223^a29 f), while the view that the continent man acts under compulsion conflicts with the view that compulsion is opposed to persuasion (compare 1224^a13–15). For the conception of continence and incontinence presupposed here, see Commentary on 1223^a36-^b3.

1224^a31:　The remark that that is why so much dispute has arisen over the continent seems to refer back to the argument of 1224^a23–27, rather than to the immediately preceding remark.

1224^a37:　cf. 1223^a34.

1224^b2-15

The general drift of the argument is reasonably clear even though the exact translation raises problems. The conception of compulsion that is applied also in the sphere of inanimate objects, namely that an object acts under compulsion if its behaviour goes against a natural tendency, makes it appear that the continent and incontinent men's actions are involuntary (^b2–5; the reference is to the argument of 1224^a31–36, not the ensuing passage casting doubt on the doctrine). Aristotle now points out that if we are careful to include in our conditions for an action's being involuntary the requirement of 1224^a23 that actions against impulse result from something *external*, the problem vanishes: neither the continent nor the incontinent man act under external pressure. He then gives an example of an action that *does* qualify as involuntary by his criterion, when something external opposes *both* the impulses which are in conflict in the continent and the incontinent man.

1224^b2-3:　The translation involves an emendation. The text of the MSS would run: 'That these seem to be the only men to act under compulsion and involuntarily . . .' See Notes.

1224^b5-7:　The translation involves an emendation, and a different punctuation from Susemihl's text. A translation of that would be: 'If we add the further element in the definition, then there too the problem is solved.' See Notes.

1224^{b}13-14:   For the example, compare *E.N.* V, 1135^{a}27.

1224^{b}15-21

In this passage Aristotle argues, in a straightforward fashion, that both pleasure and pain are present in both the incontinent and continent man.

1224^{b}21-29

Aristotle seems here to be producing a *new* reason for the plausibility of the thesis that both the continent and the incontinent man act involuntarily: each experiences pain, as argued in the preceding section. (The fact that each experiences pleasure as well is strictly irrelevant to his immediate purpose.) He now adds (^{b}24-29) that to say that these people act involuntarily involves applying to the whole soul what can, quite correctly, be said of each of the conflicting elements. Thus Aristotle is here ready to allow that reason and desire *do* act under compulsion in cases of continence and incontinence, presumably because (e.g.) in the case of the continent man, the natural tendency of the desire is thwarted by something external to it, hence what is true of desire and reason separately fulfils the already accepted definition of the involuntary. Similarly, *mutatis mutandis* in the case of the incontinent man. What we seem to have in this section is thus a diagnosis of the error of those who hold that continence and incontinence are involuntary, using the account of the involuntary that has already disposed of the paradox at ^{b}6-7.

However, a problem remains about exactly *what* desire and reason can legitimately be said to do under compulsion. In the case of the continent man, desire, and in the case of the incontinent, reason, are frustrated, and it is far from clear that either can be said to have *done* anything.

On the relevance of the final clause of the last sentence of this section see Commentary on next section.

1224^{b}29-1225^{a}1

This section is devoted to showing that both desire and reason are natural: desire is present from birth, and human beings acquire reason if their development is not interfered with, these being the marks by which the natural is distinguished. On this doctrine, see 1220^{a}11, *De Generatione Animalium* V 778^{a}16-28. On the basis of this, he argues that it is possible to say without qualification that

141

the continent and the incontinent man each act in accordance with
nature, but in a qualified way, that each acts contrary to nature.
(This last statement requires emendation of the text, but a reasonably certain one, in view of the need for a contrast with 'without
qualification' in ᵇ35.) It seems that he is saying that the people in
question in a qualified way act against nature: they act against a
natural tendency.

How is the discussion of whether these elements are natural
relevant to the context? The conclusion that both the persons in
question act in accordance with nature seems to be intended as a
further reinforcement of the view that they act voluntarily, based
on the explanation of behaviour under compulsion given at 1224ᵃ18.
But it is not clear, in view of the conclusion of 1224ᵇ5–11, that the
denial that either reason or desire are natural would cast doubt on
the conclusion that they act voluntarily; nor has the view that they
are natural been questioned in the previous discussion.

1224ᵇ36–1225ᵃ1:   Aristotle here summarizes the whole discussion
from 1224ᵃ30.

1225ᵃ2–8

Having completed the treatment of the problems raised by continence
and incontinence, Aristotle now considers the sort of case considered
at *E.N.* III, 1110ᵃ4; such actions are there called *mixed* actions – a
phrase not used here. It is plausible to say that someone who performs an action only under threats is acting under compulsion; but
he does not fit the account of acting under compulsion that Aristotle
has given.

1225ᵃ4:   '*Either* unpleasant *or* bad' would be what we should have
expected Aristotle to say.

1225ᵃ8–19

This passage presents considerable difficulties. The first sentence ᵃ8–
9 may be translated (*a*) 'Perhaps one would say some of these things
are true others not', or (*b*) 'Perhaps one would say some of these
actions are voluntary others not.' The second interpretation is adopted
both by Solomon and by Dirlmeier, presumably in view of the next
two sentences, but the first seems linguistically easier.

The main problems of interpretation are:
    (i)   What is meant by 'within the agent's power' in this passage?
    (ii) What is the bearing of the distinction between the agent's
choosing what he does and choosing his end? (ᵃ13)
    (iii) How is the magnitude of the evil to be avoided or good to
be secured thought to be relevant?

Aristotle, as is made clear in the previous section, is discussing cases in which an agent claims to have been compelled to do something bad or unpleasant under threats, to which the reply made at ª6-8 is that the action is voluntary because the agent might have chosen to undergo the evil threatened. The central difficulty of interpretation lies in the fact that there are two sorts of case that fit this general description, in which the language of necessity and compulsion is naturally used, and it is not clear how far he is considering one, or the other, or both of them. Two main lines of interpretation may be proposed, corresponding to (a) and (b) above:

(a) A person may claim to have been compelled to do something, for example under threat to his life, when the agent would offer his plea of necessity as a *justification*; his choice was the right one as the choice of the lesser of two evils. There is no suggestion that it was not within the agent's power to act differently; the choice was necessary with the options then open to the agent, if one alternative is so bad that the action chosen was plainly preferable. Thus, in such a case, when an agent claims that he acted in the way he did by necessity, or that he had no choice, the judgement of necessity is relative to the alternatives available, and an evaluation of them; so the magnitude of the evil to be avoided or the good to be secured is highly relevant. The example of *E.N.* III, 1110ª8–9 of the cargo thrown overboard in a storm can readily be interpreted as a case of this sort. It is clear, too, that such cases are ones where there is 'no conflict between reason and inclination' (ª3). Aristotle accepts some, but not all, of what has been said: it has been suggested that people in these circumstances act voluntarily because they can choose to accept the threatened evil; Aristotle replies that they do choose the action they perform, but they did not choose to pursue the end (ª13) (sc. circumstances forced them to take steps to avert some threatened evil, rather than act to promote some positive end, as they would have preferred).

(b) With the other reading of ª8-9, Aristotle had two sorts of case in mind. If a man is threatened with death or severe personal injury, the situation may inspire a degree of fear that deprives the man of the power of choice, and he may claim that he was *psychologically* incapable of acting differently. He need not, of course, then be claiming that his action was justified as the choice of the lesser of two evils. This offers a reasonable reading to the phrase 'within the agent's power', and moreover reads it in a way that is in line with what we have in the following section (ª19-33). The mention of love and anger is intelligible if the primary case that he had in mind is the case of someone acting in a state of extreme fear. Above all, the remark at ª25-26 that what is in someone's power is what his

143

nature can bear suggests that what is in question is a psychological state that deprives the agent of the power of choice. Again, the magnitude of the evil to be avoided or the good to be secured will be relevant on this interpretation, since whether the fear (or other psychological state) is intense enough to remove from the agent the power of choice will obviously, in general, depend on its object. The absurdity mentioned at 14-15 will consist in the fact that it would be absurd for someone to claim that fear of some minor inconvenience so overwhelmed him as to deprive him of the power of choice: absurd, because such a claim would be too incredible to be believed. (With (a) the absurdity would be a moral or prudential one.)

On objection to (a) is that it is not clear why the statement (ᵃ6-8) that all actions are voluntary should not have been allowed to stand, since all actions of the kind under discussion are evidently voluntary in the sense that has been used up to now. An objection to (b) is that these cases of action under necessity are said, at the beginning of the whole discussion at 1225ᵃ2-3, to involve no conflict between reason and inclination, whereas an agent's acting wrongly under overwhelming psychological stress *is* a case of such a conflict: in this respect, the examples would be like cases of incontinence. With (b) in ᵃ9-11 he specifies those cases in which the agent acts voluntarily, and at ᵃ11-14 the cases of involuntary action (though even here the agent acts involuntarily only with qualification).

Whether (a) or (b) is accepted will make a crucial difference to the interpretation of ᵃ12-14. He there says 'in a way he acts under compulsion, but not simply because he does not choose the very thing that he does, but that for whose sake he does it'. This is ambiguous, in Greek as in English, between (i) 'he acts under compulsion, but that is not simply because he does not choose . . .' and (ii) 'he acts under compulsion in a way, but not unqualifiedly so, because . . .' In the one case the 'because'-clause serves to explain why the man acts under compulsion (though in a qualified sense), in the other Aristotle is denying that his acting under compulsion has the explanation given. With interpretation (a) of the whole, it is natural to adopt (i), so that Aristotle is saying: 'He acts in a way under compulsion, but not simply because he does not choose the actual act that he performs <he does choose that>, but <because he does not choose> the final end'. With (b), (ii) is easier: he will then be saying that the person acts under compulsion, but only with qualifications, because, although he does not choose the particular action he performs, he does choose the end. The point, admittedly obscurely expressed, might be that the ultimate origin of the action is (e.g.) the agent's desire for his own safety; that distinguishes this case from the central case of compulsion, when the origin is outside the agent. But the agent has no choice, in the circumstances, about the performance of the action.

What precedes this passage seems to favour (*a*), what follows the (*b*). It is probable that Aristotle did not clearly distinguish the two alternative grounds for saying that a man acts under compulsion when he acts under threats, no doubt because the typical cases are similar in each involving substantial danger of harm.

1225ᵃ14-15: The reference seems to be a game like blind man's bluff.

1225ᵃ19-36

On the wider bearings of this passage, see Commentary on the last section. With this section, the excursus, which began at 1224ᵃ8, on the relation of the voluntary to compulsion, ends.

The previous section had introduced (on one interpretation) the idea of a state of fear that takes away the agent's power of choice. Aristotle now generalizes the conclusion to other similar psychological states like love and anger, and certain cognitive states where human beings are in a state akin to divine possession.

1225ᵃ21: Aristotle here seems to be expressing himself in a deliberately paradoxical fashion. These psychological states are natural, in that it is part of the human constitution that they should occur, but 'beyond nature' in the sense that it is beyond the power of the human constitution to control them.

1225ᵃ30: 'Nor is it done as a result of desire'. The sentence as it stands is extremely elliptical. Dirlmeier supposes that Aristotle is saying 'Nor is everything done from desire voluntary', but this is rather difficult in view of ᵃ27, where it is implied that inclination, of which desire is a species, is such that everything that is within a person's inclination is voluntary. It seems better to take him as saying that poets and other divinely inspired do not act from desire.

CHAPTER 9
1225ᵃ36-1225ᵇ8

Aristotle now resumes the discussion of the conclusion, arrived at at 1224ᵃ7, that what differentiates voluntary acts is some feature of the agent's thought at the time of action. The term translated 'thought' applies to cognitive states generally; but it now turns out that the cognitive state regarded as relevant is knowledge, and we now have a brief discussion of the relevance of knowledge and ignorance to the voluntariness of an action. We seem to have an argument of the following form:

(i) The voluntary is opposed to the involuntary (^{b}1-2).

(ii) Acting with knowledge (of a specified kind) is opposed to acting in, and through, ignorance of the appropriate sort (^{b}2-6).

(iii) Acting through ignorance is involuntary (^{b}6-7).

So (iv) Acting with knowledge is voluntary (^{b}7-8).

The argument raises a number of problems:

(*a*) Its validity depends on a principle that each thing has only one opposite. (iii) says only that actions done in ignorance are among those that are involuntary, but, for the argument to be valid, they would need to be assorted to be coextensive, which is both implausible in itself and contrary to Aristotle's view. If 'voluntary' is here regarded as the contradictory of 'involuntary', his position here contrasts with his position at *E.N.* III, 1110^b18 f. Premiss (i) has already appeared at 1223^a36.

(*b*) Although it does not affect the formal validity of the argument, it is rather surprising that he here contrasts ignorance of *all* of a specified list of things with knowledge of *at least one* of them. We should have expected him to speak instead of being ignorant of one thing in contrast to having knowledge of all. This looks like a slip.

(*c*) Aristotle here lists three possible items of knowledge or ignorance—*whom, with what*, and *for what result*. At *E.N.* III, 1111^a3 the list given is rather longer, and includes *how* the action is being (? or ought to be) performed, and *what* is being done. At *E.N.* V, 1135^a23 the list is, interestingly, the same as that given here. *Whom* refers to the identity of the patient, *with which* to the instrument, *for what result* to the consequences of the action. Plainly, which among the things true of the person acted on (if any) or the instrument (if any) is relevant will vary from case to case, as also will the other factors that may be relevant. He does not show any awareness of such facts as that the identity of the person affected by an action may be known under one description but not under another. However, the qualification 'because of ignorance' may indicate some recognition that it is *relevant* knowledge that is in question (see next paragraph).

(*d*) What is added by the requirement that the agent acts not merely in, but also through, ignorance? It is natural to suppose that a man's action is not due to his ignorance of X if, had he known X, he would still have acted in the same way. Thus Aristotle would be making the reasonable point that only ignorance that affects what someone does is relevant to whether an action is voluntary. However, the matter is rather more complicated than this, since we may regard a man as having acted unintentionally, and therefore absolve him from responsibility even if, had he had the knowledge lack of which

146

made his action unintentional, he would still have acted in the same way, though with a different intention. What is relevant is ignorance that affects the execution of the intention he has, even if it does not make a difference to what is done.

However, although this is a plausible reading of the phrase 'through ignorance' it hardly fits the way in which the terminology is used at *E.N.* III, 1110ᵇ24 f., where the contrast between acting through ignorance and acting in ignorance seems to be a contrast between knowledge of particular facts and knowledge of general principles.

The phrase translated 'for what result' is that elsewhere translated 'for the sake of what'. The same phrase occurs in the parallel passage in *E.N.* The expression in Greek might suggest that Aristotle is requiring, oddly, that a person should not be ignorant of the *end* of his actions, whereas, as the examples make clear, the ignorance is of the result of the action.

(*e*) There is a serious problem in understanding the point of the qualification 'incidentally' at ᵇ6. The nearest parallel is at *E.N.* V, 1135ᵃ26, a parallel all the more relevant if it refers back to the *Eudemian* account of the voluntary. There are at least three lines of interpretation according to what 'not incidentally' is taken with:

(i) It could be taken with 'opposite', so that the point will be that what is done in ignorance is essentially and not merely incidentally opposite to what is done with knowledge. It is not very clear what the point is, but Aristotle may mean that it is possible to infer the definition of the voluntary from the specification of the opposite class of cases. But the qualification would seem largely redundant.

(ii) It could be taken with 'in ignorance of what . . .' in which case he is requiring that the agent's ignorance of these specific facts should not be merely incidental. Although this interpretation makes this passage most closely parallel to the *E.N.* V one, it is far from clear what could be meant by being ignorant of something incidentally.

(iii) It could be taken with 'because of ignorance', a phrase which immediately precedes it. The point will then be that the ignorance in question should have affected how the person acted, and not be merely incidental to what he did (see (*d*)). This would give a reasonable sense to 'incidental', at the cost of making it have a very different point from that of the *E.N.* V passage.

1225ᵇ8-16

We have in this section Aristotle's fullest account of the voluntary, given in ᵇ8-10. The general structure of the argument, from the beginning of Chapter 7, is somewhat puzzling. Aristotle began by considering three plausible suggestions for defining voluntary action (1223ᵃ23-25), and then rejected two of them, leaving in the field

the alternative that voluntary action is that involving thought (1224
^{a}7–8). There follows an excursus on the topic of compulsion (1224^{a}8
to the beginning of this chapter). The suggestion that the voluntary
may be defined as action with thought (i.e. in terms of a cognitive
state) has just been explicated in terms of the requirement of knowledge, and an argument, admittedly fallacious, has been offered,
apparently for the conclusion that action with the relevant knowledge
is voluntary. He now draws together the results of the arguments
concerning compulsion and knowledge and ignorance into a comprehensive definition embodying both elements. It now appears that,
despite ^{b}7–8, knowledge is necessary but not sufficient for voluntary action: the action must be one that is in the agent's power not
to do. (Likewise, ignorance is sufficient but not necessary for an
involuntary action, but Aristotle does not point this out.) It will be
noted that the definitions here have the consequence that not every
action is either voluntary or involuntary, despite the argument of
the previous section; also that, despite the argument of Chapter 7,
the voluntary is not defined in terms of the agent's cognitive state
but involves another element which seems to be something very
like the requirement that it be in accord with the agent's inclination;
none of the three things mentioned at the beginning of the whole
discussion proves adequate by itself for defining the voluntary.

1225^{b}9:   What is meant by 'through his own agency' (*di' hauton*)?
If this introduces a *further* condition beyond the requirement that
it be in the agent's power not to perform the action, it is not clear
what it is. The phrase may, however, be amplificatory of that
condition.

1225^{b}11–14:   He here deals with a complication which is not mentioned in the parallel passage in *E.N.* 'Know' has two senses, corresponding to the distinction between potentiality and act: in one
sense a man may be said to know something if he possesses the
required knowledge even if he is not using it. Hence ignorance has
a similar duality. At ^{b}14, he mentions the case of someone's failing
to use knowledge that he has through negligence, but of course
whether such a person may be described as ignorant in one sense
only is independent of *why* he was ignorant.

1225^{b}13–16:   Aristotle here discusses someone who is open to
censure despite his ignorance, because his ignorance is culpable.
Compare *E.N.* 1113^{b}30–1114^{a}10. When Aristotle speaks at ^{b}15
of what it was necessary to know, he presumably has in mind the
sort of information that people are expected to acquire; and certainly

whether a person is held to have acted negligently when he acts in ignorance depends crucially on what degree of knowledge we expect people to have. It is hardly correct to say that someone may be blamed for acting in ignorance of something that he could easily have ascertained if the information is not of the sort that people are expected to acquire. Again, often the question is not whether it was *easy* for the person in question to acquire the information but whether it was *possible* for him to do so (given his circumstances, his capacities, etc.). On this see Hart.

CHAPTER 10
1225^{b}17–24

Both opinion and inclination are said to accompany choice. Presumably, the opinion that is the invariable concomitant of choice is the belief that the action in question is the best one to perform; the inclination, will of course, be an inclination for the performance of the action in question. 1225^{b}24–36 argues against the view that choice is an inclination, 1226^{a}1–17 against the view that it is an opinion. The answer to the question in what genus it falls comes at 1226^{b}30, where it is said to fall within the class of the voluntary.

1225^{b}24–37

In this discussion of the suggestion that choice is identical with inclination, we encounter once again the trio into which inclination is divided at 1223^{a}26–27, on which see Commentary. Five arguments may be distinguished:

(i) Animals have spirit and desire, but not choice (^{b}26–27).
(ii) Choice occurs without spirit or desire (^{b}27–29).
(iii) Even when desire and spirit are present, choice may not occur (^{b}29–30).
(iv) Spirit and desire are always accompanied by pleasure and pain, choice occurs without either of them (^{b}30–31).
(v) We wish for things we know to be impossible, but do not choose them (^{b}32–36).

(i) shows no more than that choice is not identical with either spirit or desire in general; it might, for example, be identical with a particular sort of desire, not to be found in animals. (ii) and (iii) appear to be intended as complementary to one another, (ii) showing that neither desire nor spirit are necessary for choice, (iii) that they are not sufficient. However, the case of the man who fails to act on his desires is not really an example of desire not followed by choice, as in such a case the man presumably chooses not to act on them. Thus the case would in fact be similar to those under (ii). The sort of case mentioned under (ii) is that of the continent man.

The remark that spirit and desire are always accompanied by pleasure and pain is a little puzzling. We should expect him to say that both are accompanied by pain; pleasure results from *satisfied* desire. (v), likewise, will show that choice is not to be identified with wish in general, not that it may not be identified with a specific sort of wish. With (i), compare *E.N.* III, 1111ᵇ12-13; with (ii), ibid., ᵇ14-15; with (iii), ibid., 13-14; with (v), ibid., ᵇ19-26.

In *E.N.* III, 1111ᵇ16-18 he says only that desire is *of* the pleasant and painful, but choice is essentially neither of the pleasant nor the painful.

1225ᵇ35-37:   Strictly, what Aristotle should have said is that the object of choice is what is *thought* to be within the agent's power.

1226ᵃ1-6

Aristotle here presents two arguments against the identification of choice with opinion. (i) An opinion may be about things not in our power. (ii) An opinion, but not a desire, may be true or false.

(i) is, of course, effective against the view that any and every opinion is a choice, but not against the view that choice is identifiable with an opinion that a certain action ought to be done, or that a certain course of action is the best in the circumstances. That suggestion is refuted only at ᵃ4-6. A similar argument occurs at *E.N.* III, 1111ᵇ31-33.

(ii), likewise, is hardly effective against the thesis that choice consists in an opinion about what should be done: why should we not say that correctness of choice consists in the truth of some judgement of the form *X ought to be done*? On this compare *E.N.* III, 1111ᵇ33-1112ᵃ1. It appears that he *does* regard (ii) as refuting the weaker, and plausible, thesis that equated choice with particular sorts of opinion. For a modern view not dissimilar to the view that Aristotle here attacks compare Grice.

1226ᵃ6-17

What we appear to have here is a further argument for the distinctness of choice from both wish (as already argued at 1225ᵇ32-36) and opinion (as already argued at ᵃ1-6), as becomes clear at ᵃ16-17: wish, like opinion, is 'of the end', which choice is not, i.e. the end is something wished for, and something concerning which one may believe that it ought to be pursued (cf. ᵃ14-15) whereas choice is only of means. This interpretation involves taking 'this' in ᵃ6-7 as referring to what follows rather than what precedes, and its referent only becomes clear several sentences later; he has not mentioned the means-end distinction in the previous section. If we make 'this' in a6 refer to what precedes, the only thing that can plausibly be referred to is the fact that both opinion and wish may have to do with what is not within our power. But those features of belief and wish have already been mentioned, and, more important, this interpretation gives no obvious point to a7-8, which are offered as an argument in favour of whatever is asserted at a6-7.

This doctrine, and the similar view about deliberation (cf. 1226 b10 f.) that ends are not chosen, has been much discussed. In *E.N.* III, 1111b26-29 the same doctrine is stated as here, rather more briefly, with the same example, in the context of an argument for the non-identity of choice with wish. It will be convenient to consider this along with the corresponding view about deliberation, without prejudging the extent of the parallelism.

It has been objected to Aristotle's account that we can and do deliberate about and choose which ends to pursue, and not merely the means to an end already given. Thus, when at *E.N.* III, 1112b11 it is denied that we deliberate about ends, the reason offered in support is that the doctor does not deliberate about whether to cure people, nor does the political man about whether to promote political stability. To this, it is objected that the most that can be said is that a doctor *qua doctor* does not deliberate about that question; it is plainly possible to deliberate about whether to make the practice of curing people one of one's pursuits. In general, a person's central projects may be a matter of choice and of deliberation.

Two things that might be meant by 'choosing an end' or 'deliberating about an end' are (i) deciding whether to adopt something as an end at all, in the way that someone deciding what profession to go into is considering whether to adopt certain projects at all, and (ii) deciding, in a particular situation, which of several ends that I already have to promote in a given case, when different alternative courses of action open to me will promote different ends. Aristotle has been accused of neglecting (i) particularly.

In reply to this it may be said: (*a*) The phrase used at a7-8, *ta pros to telos* (here translated 'the things that contribute to the end, cf. 1226b11, *E.N.* III, 1111b27, 1112b12) is wider than the notion of means in English: the preposition (*pros*) signifies the relation believed to hold between *A* and *B* when *A* is chosen for the sake of *B* (e.g. when *A* is a *component* of *B*). So Aristotle is not regarding all deliberation as of the prudential or means-end sort.

(*b*) He may mean only that ends are not as *such* objects of choice or deliberation, so there need be nothing that is *never* the object of choice or deliberation, apart from *eudaimonia* itself, which at *E.N.* I, 1097b1 is said never to be chosen for the sake of anything else. If I am deliberating about something I am not *then* treating it as an end.

Against (*b*): (i) This interpretation does not provide a *justification* for the observation (itself sensible enough), that we do not choose health (^{a}8; cf. *E.N.* 1111^{b}27 f.): health could still be chosen as an element in happiness.

(ii) If the idea of one thing's contributing to another is made wide enough to include 'component means', Aristotle's model of deliberation, — starting from a goal, and working out how it is to be achieved — seems inappropriate: it suggests that the deliberator has a determinate conception of the end before evaluating alternative choices, but if the question is precisely whether something is to be a component of the end, the end itself is, to that extent indeterminate.

(iii) How well armed is Aristotle against the objection that he makes no allowance for deliberation and choice concerning *which* of a number of alternative ends, already accepted as such, a person is to seek to promote in a particular situation? (On this topic in general, see Ackrill, Wiggins, and Cooper.)

1226ᵃ18-28

This marks the end of the section which began at 1225^{b}18, in which problems were raised about the concept of choice. Aristotle now continues with his positive account of choice, taking up points that were made in Chapter 6, and in the discussion of the voluntary that followed it. On the restriction of deliberation to a part of what occurs not by necessity, compare *E.N.* III, 1112^{a}18-31.

1226^{a}25: 'Other causes'. Aristotle has in mind luck. On the notion of luck as a cause, see VIII, c. 2. At *E.N.* III, 1112^{a}27, luck, as exemplified by the case of the finding of treasure, is explicitly mentioned as being outside the scope of deliberation.

1226ᵃ28-1226ᵇ2

The text translated involves the transposition of the sentence beginning at ^{a}32 to an earlier position than it occurs in the MSS, as indicated by the marginal lineation in the translation. For the arguments for the change, see Notes.

Aristotle has already restricted the sphere of deliberation to what it is in our power to affect (though what may be outside the range of influence of one human being may be within another's, as the example of the Indians shows). He now says that not even all of that is a matter for deliberation. This leads on to a puzzle about why the doctor deliberates but not the scribe. The point presumably is that it is a matter of philosophical debate what distinguishes those actions done in exercise of a skill which involve deliberation and those which are not.

The final section (^{a}33–^{b}2), discussing the doctor and the scribe, raises a number of difficulties of detail, though the general point is clear. Wherever conscious deliberation is involved, there is room for one kind of mistake (perhaps through a mistake in reasoning, perhaps through a false belief), but there is room for a second kind of mistake ('in perception') in applying the results of deliberation. Thus someone may misexecute what he has decided to do after deliberation through failure to attend sufficiently closely to his actions, as when a surgeon fails to notice what sort of incision he is making. In the case of the scribe's art, there is no deliberation, hence only one possibility of mistake. However, that two sorts of mistake may be made by the doctor and only one by the scribe, is a symptom, not an explanation, of the fact that deliberation occurs in the one case and not in the other.

In *E.N.* 1112^{a}34–^{b}11, he does confront the question what distinguishes those crafts or sciences in which there is deliberation and those where there is not, and mentions both the examples given here, along with gymnastics and money-making. There is less deliberation in those sciences that are precise and independent, more when there is imprecision, uncertainty, and variability in the way things occur. There is no mention of the two sorts of mistake.

Despite the use of the same examples, the contrast drawn in *E.N.* does not seem to be quite the same as that drawn here. There, the contrast is between skills in which the working out of what to do involves the application of routine procedures yielding a definite answer and those where there is room for uncertainty, the exercise of judgement, and weighing of alternatives. Deliberation is opposed to calculation. Here, the contrast is between cases where we need to work out what to do, and cases in which the person can 'just see' what needs to be done.

At ^{b}1-2, he adds, rather obscurely, that if 'perception and action' are made subjects of deliberation, there will be an infinite regress. The point seems to be the following: At some point deliberation must terminate in a judgement about what is to be done; action needs to take place in accordance with the judgement, and this requires the ability to see what falls under the description contained in the judgement, and the relevant practical skill required to act in the specified way. If, at every stage, a further piece of deliberation may be interposed concerning how the practical judgement is to be executed, deliberation will never come to an end: at some point action must ensue, unmediated by further deliberation. This passage should be connected with those, notably in *E.N.* VI, where excellence at perception is stressed as something needed by the practically wise man. Cf. *E.N.* VI, 1142^{a}27–29, 1143^{a}35–^{b}14; see also III,

1112ᵇ34-1113ᵃ2, when the regress argument is mentioned briefly in connection with the point that *particulars* are not subject of deliberation.

The reason for the difference between the two crafts mentioned by Aristotle seems to be that the scribe's craft is an executive skill, to be distinguished from the many skills involved in deciding what to write; whereas the art of medicine is thought to include not only the ability to reason out what is required but the executive ability to do it.

1226ᵇ2-5

Aristotle's elaboration of a positive account of choice, which continues to 1227ᵃ5, involves a series of preliminary assertions about it. In this section he argues that, although choice is not *identifiable* with opinion or wish, or a combination of the two, it is *constituted* of those two things. What he means by this can perhaps best be understood from what he finally says at 1227ᵃ4-5, where choice is finally said to consist in opinion and inclination *arrived at in a certain way*. So it seems that the point rather obscurely expressed at ᵇ2-4 is that the combination of opinion and wish (i.e. the combination of a belief that a certain action is the best to perform with wish to perform it) is a necessary but not a sufficient condition of choice. That it is not sufficient is briefly argued in ᵇ3-4 from the case where the appropriate combination of opinion and wish arises without reflection. That no one chooses 'in a flash' has already been said at 1224ᵃ4, as part of the argument for the non-identity of choice with wish by itself.

1226ᵇ5-9

Having arrived at the conclusion that choice involves an opinion, Aristotle in this section asks what sort of opinion. The Greek word here translated 'choice' (*prohairesis*) and the corresponding verb, have the form of a compound of a word meaning 'taking' with a preposition meaning 'before'; the latter may have a purely temporal sense or it may have the force of 'in preference to' (cf. English 'I'd sooner do *A* than *B*'). Hence, he argues, the opinion that is a component of choice is a deliberative one. By this he means, as becomes clear later, one arrived at in a certain way—having a certain history. The same etymological observations occurs also at *E.N.* 1112ᵃ16-17, where Gauthier and Jolif, following Aspasius and Joachim, hold that the preposition has a temporal sense: i.e. the object of choice is that which comes *first* in the sequence leading to the end. But it seems clear that the prefix has the other sense in this passage, and the same is indisputably true at *M.M.* 1189ᵃ12-16 (which may be held to be decisive against Gauthier and Jolif's reading of the *E.N.* passage: in *M.M.* there is a reference to choosing the better *instead* of the worse). The argument here is that since choice involves putting one thing before another, it requires investigation and debate; hence it is a deliberative belief/judgement that is involved. 'By deliberative belief' he seems to mean a judgement arrived at by a process of reflection and conscious weighing of competing considerations, and that reading of 'deliberative' (*bouleutikos*) is confirmed by ^{b}19-20.

But it is doubtful if Aristotle in fact wished to restrict *prohairesis* cases in which there was a conscious weighing of alternatives. On this, see Cooper, pp. 6-8.

1226^{b}10-20

For a discussion of the view that only means are objects of deliberation, see Commentary on 1226^{a}6-17.

Having introduced deliberation into the discussion, Aristotle examines it and arrives at a further preliminary definition of choice as 'deliberative inclination for what is in one's power' (^{b}17). In thus mentioning inclination, he is taking up something accepted at ^{b}4-5 (except that there he speaks of 'wish'). A deliberative inclination is here explained as one whose occurrence has a certain explanation. Compare *E.N.* III, 1113^{a}10-12.

1226^{b}10-13:   Compare *E.N.* III, 1112^{b}15-24, 1113^{a}5-7. The contrast in ^{b}11-12 seems to be between a case where someone is deciding which among the candidates that suggest themselves really do contribute to the attainment of the end, and a case in which someone is trying to find something that does so. In the *E.N.* passage, he mentions, at 1112^{b}16-17, a situation in which there may be alternative ways of promoting the end, and the agent has to evaluate them. This will clearly bring other ends into play (e.g. the saving of time and energy) though Aristotle does not explicitly recognize that. But the present passage does not mention such a possibility. At ^{b}13, he means that deliberation ends when we have found something that we can do which will initiate the process leading to the end.

1226^{b}15-16:   *E.N.* 1112^{a}18-31 contains a more elaborate narrowing down of the sphere of deliberation to what is in our power.

1226^{b}21-30

In this section, Aristotle argues for the restriction of choice to mature and sane human beings, and connects the theory of deliberation with the four causes (which cannot be discussed fully here). The notion of cause (or reason) is connected by Aristotle with what would count as an appropriate answer to a 'why-question'. (Compare $^b27$ and, e.g. *Physics* II 194^{b}19 f., 198^{a}14 f.) One sort of answer to a why-question explains by reference to the purpose sought, and so the end to whose realization deliberation is directed is treated as a cause (the *final* cause). On Aristotle's four causes, see *Physics* II. At *Physics* II, 194^{b}33-35 the same example of a final cause occurs as is used at 1226^{a}8. (Health may be a final cause of a man's walking.)

Aristotle tends to treat of final and efficient causes as distinct types of cause, each of which may be found to operate in producing a given change. In the case of human actions, the final cause will be the goal of the action, the efficient cause the inclination for the achievement of the goal that led to the action. But plainly a full specification of the inclinations that were operative will need to mention the ultimate goal, which will be precisely what an explanation in terms of final causes would need to mention. Thus a full explanation in terms of efficient causes would seem to leave no room for further explanation in terms of final causes. Moreover, the state of affairs that was the goal of someone's action need not be actually produced in order for the action to be explained by reference to that goal: the agent's purpose may be frustrated. Thus the final cause may be regarded as the intentional object of the most fundamental desire or inclination that was operative in producing the action.

The connection of thought in this section is not entirely clear. ^{b}26-30 are presented as if they supported the restriction of choice to human beings. But the doctrine of final causation hardly does so, since lower animals were thought by Aristotle to be subject to final causation also; the reason for not attributing choice to animals is their inability to *reason* (^{b}25). At ^{b}29-30, he says that those who lack a goal (*skopos*) are not capable of deliberation; but how is it shown that animals are incapable of acting for a goal? The restriction of choice to human beings is also to be found at *E.N.* III, 1111^{b}8-9.

1226^{b}27:   The distinction between that for whose sake something is and that for whose sake something comes about corresponds roughly to the distinction between formal and material causes on the one hand and final and efficient on the other. Explaining why something is may be interpreted as explaining why it exists, or Aristotle may have in mind explaining why it is *as* it is. On the first alternative, the material and formal causes are explanations of there being something of a certain sort, since (in the case of material substances) the existence of something of a certain kind consists in certain matter's having a certain form (e.g. the existence of a house consists in the disposition of bricks, etc., so as to have a certain structure); on the second alternative he will have in mind a substance's matter and form as the source of the properties that are due to the possession of that matter and form. Similarly, the final and efficient causes may be regarded as explaining either changes in objects or the coming into existence of things: both are covered by the verb here translated 'come about'.

1226^{b}28-29:   The same example occurs at *Physics* II, 196^{b}33 f.

1226^{b}30-1227^{a}2

This section may be regarded as answering the question raised at 1225^{b}20-21 and 1226^{a}19-20, of the relation between choice and the voluntary. The answer is that chosen actions are a subset of voluntary ones. Compare *E.N.* III, 1111^{b}7 f., 1112^{a}14-15, V, 1135 ^{b}8 f., *M.M.* 1189^{a}33-36. At ^{b}30-33, he reiterates the definition of the voluntary already given in Chapter 9, 1225^{b}8-10, from which it follows, in view of what has been said about choice, that all chosen actions are voluntary.

1226^{b}33:   'Not after deliberation nor with premeditation'. The wording at this point suggests that premeditation was regarded as something distinct from deliberation, but it is doubtful if Aristotle wished to make any such distinction, since what is in question is simply the deliberation that has already been shown to be an element in choice.

1226^{b}36-1227^{a}1:   The point seems to be that the threefold legal distinction is correct in that it recognizes that not all voluntary acts are preceded by premeditation, incorrect in that actions preceded by premeditation are treated as a species co-ordinate with the voluntary and the involuntary and not treated as a sub-species of the voluntary.

1227^{a}2-5

In this section Aristotle summarizes the conclusions reached on the subject of choice in the course of Chapter 10. The denial that it is either wish or opinion corresponds to 1225^{b}19-1226^{a}19; the positive assertion incorporates conclusions reached at 1226^{b}4, ^{b}9, ^{b}17, on which see Commentary. The reference to a conclusion at ^{a}5, however, brings a new element into the discussion: the word used is a technical term of Aristotle's logic and suggests that he regarded the process whereby wish and belief yield a choice as their upshot as a piece of reasoning. The passage is reminiscent of the discussion of practical reasoning as it occurs at *E.N.* VI and VII, but nothing further is made of the point here.

1227^{a}2–3:   A reference forward to a discussion such as is found in *E.N.* V, c. 8. Nothing can be inferred from this brief reference about the 'Eudemian' or 'Nicomachean' origin of the *E.N.* V that we have: the allusion is too unspecific.

1227^{a}6–13

Having completed his account of choice, Aristotle returns once more to the subject of virtue. The present passage leads up to the final definition of virtue, presented at 1227^{b}5–11. In this section up to 1227^{b}1–2 he seems to have yet another argument in favour of the thesis that virtue and vice have to do with pleasure and pain. The argument exploits the result already reached that virtue and vice are of things within the sphere of choice; choice has already been seen to involve deliberation, which occurs with a view to an end already given. Aristotle then (^{a}18 f) introduces the notion of the good, as the natural end of action, and the contrast between the genuine and apparent good. This in turn (^{a}38) leads to the topics of the pleasant and unpleasant, as the guise in which the apparent good presents itself to the agent.

In the present section, he recapitulates the doctrine about deliberation already presented at 1226^{b}10 f. On this see Commentary on 1226^{a}6–17. The example that he gives, of deliberation on whether to go to war or not is not naturally construed as a matter of deciding whether war or peace is likely to be the best way of achieving an already determinate end.

1227^{a}9–11:   Just as in theoretical reasoning certain propositions, called here hypotheses, are taken for granted and not subject to examination, in practical reasoning a certain end is taken as given from the start. Compare 1227^{b}28–30, *E.N.* VII, 1151^{a}15.

The reference to an earlier discussion of this topic 'in the beginning of this treatise' is uncertain. Both Dirlmeier and Solomon mention I, 1214^{b}6 f, where Aristotle says that everyone ought to adopt some general aim in life by reference to which all his choices are made. But the similarity is only of the most general sort: there is no statement about what deliberation essentially involves, according to Aristotle, nor is the analogy between theoretical and practical reasoning introduced. A much closer parallel is the recent passage 1226^{b}10–12. Alternatively, we might take the reference to be to Chapter 6, which is, and is marked by Aristotle as being, the beginning of a new section of the work. (Cf. 1222^{b}9 f.)

The reference to *Posterior Analytics* must be to a passage like I, 72^{b}19 f.

1227ª13-18

Aristotle says that the end always comes first in order of reasoning. Reasoning then always seems to relate this end to something in the agent's power. It is not clear whether at ª16-18, he is distinguishing two directions in which practical reasoning may go: in the one case the person deliberating recognizes that X will contribute to the realization of the end, and then asks what will produce X, and so on until he reaches an action that he can perform himself; in the other, he starts with the range of actions open to him in the particular situation, and inquires which will have a bearing on the end.

1227ª18-30

Aristotle claims in this section that the ultimate end and therefore the object of wish is naturally (*phusei*) the good, but if wish is not directed upon the natural object, it is for what *appears* good (ª22) (but is not so in fact, though he does not add this qualification). This section brings in three contrasts that are found elsewhere in *E.E.* and *E.N.* (i) The contrast between the good (sometimes called 'the good by nature' or 'the good in truth') and the apparent good. For this see VII, 1235ᵇ24-29, 1236ª9-10, *E.N.* III, c.4. Since for Aristotle it is an objective matter what is good and bad there is room for mistake, when someone pursues something that only appears to him to be good. (ii) The contrast between what is 'good without qualification' and what is good for a particular person in special circumstances. For this, see VII, 1235ᵇ30-32, 1236ª9-10, 1236ᵇ27-1237ª2, 1237ª26-27, 1238ª3-4, 1238ᵇ5-9, VIII, 1248ᵇ26-30, 1249ª1-7, 17-18, 25; *E.N.* V, 1129ᵇ3-5, VII, 1152ᵇ26; *Politics* VII 1332ª21-25. The evidence that this contrast is in question in this passage is the reference to 'the best without qualification' at ª21. (i) and (ii) are distinguished by Aristotle at VII, 1235ᵇ30. What *appears* good to someone need not *be* good, even for him. What does each individual want—what appears good to him or what is good for him? Aristotle, both in *E.E.* and in *E.N.* thinks that each of these answers is correct, if understood in a certain way, and this involves the third contrast, (iii) which might be described as that between the *formal* and the *material* object of wishing. Each agent has as his object of pursuit always what is good in reality in the sense that that is what he intends that his object of pursuit should be. It is in this sense that Aristotle can say that everyone pursues happiness, however, diverse their conception of it is. The actual object of pursuit and wishing, on the other hand, need not be (really) good, but is simply something that *appears* good. Thus for someone with an erroneous conception of what happiness consists in, the object of pursuit will not be the happy life, but something inferior to it.

His view is that, in the case of the virtuous man, what appears good to him coincides with what *is* good, and similarly what is good for him coincides with what is good without qualification. In *E.N.* III, 1113ª25, 33, the good man is explicitly set up as a standard and canon: what appears good to him is so. The good man's judgements of goodness are correct, and the circumstances of his life are such that the unqualifiedly good things are good for him. Thus what is good without qualification is what would be rationally wanted by someone whose circumstances of life were the best available to human beings. Wealth, for example, is regarded by Aristotle as one of the natural goods, but it is not beneficial for someone who is not intelligent enough to use it well, or whose circumstances are such that it is of no use to him. Thus Aristotle says at VII, 1236ᵇ36 that what is good without qualification and good for an individual ought to be made to coincide. Similarly, at *E.N.* V, 1129ᵇ4–6 he says that men pray that what is good without qualification should be good for them, but pursue what is good for them.

Instead of distinguishing the material and the formal object of wish, he says that what is naturally wanted is that which is really good, but wish, if not in its natural state, may be for something that appears good but is actually bad. At *E.N.* III, 1113ª22 f, he says that in reality and in an unqualified way, it is the good that is wished for, but for each person it is the apparent good. Since in the case of the good man whose dispositions are in the naturally best state, the formal and material object coincide, it is perhaps understandable that he should have regarded the good and apparent good as respectively the objects of natural and corrupt wishing; but the question whether the object of wish is the good or the apparent good can only be properly answered by drawing the distinction between the formal and the material object of wish.

He seeks to explain the fact that wish can be both for the good and the bad by assimilating wish (which is here treated as a psychic faculty, presumably a constituent of the appetitive (*orektikon*) (cf. 1223ª26–27)), to knowledge. It is a standard Aristotelian doctrine that opposites fall under the same knowledge. See *E.N.* V, 1129ª11–16, *Prior Analytics* I, 24ª21, *Physics* VIII, 251ª30, *De Anima* III, 427ᵇ6, and *Metaphysics* Θ 1046ᵇ1–20. The *Metaphysics* passage gives some indication of the reasons for the doctrine. Capacities like knowledge, unlike certain others, involve reason (*logos*), and reason reveals both a thing and its privation (*sterēsis*): a specification or determination of what constitutes being φ determines at the same time what counts as being non-φ; hence knowledge of (what is) φ is at the same time knowledge of (what is) not-φ, and knowledge of how to make something φ will, in general, include knowledge of how to make something non-ϕ. In the *E.N.* V passage, crafts and skills are contrasted with settled dispositions like virtues as being capacities for opposites. Aristotle's reasons for saying that medical knowledge is not in the same way knowledge both of health and disease are presumably that medical knowledge is directly knowledge of health and only indirectly knowledge of disease: disease is known about only *qua* absence of health.

The application of this to the case of wish is not entirely clear. If Aristotle's point is simply that, when the appetitive part of the soul is in the state that is naturally best for it, wishing is directed towards the good, but wish can also be misdirected, that may be correct, but is hardly parallel to the case of knowledge: it is not being suggested that human beings can simply direct their endeavours to the good or the bad at will, nor does Aristotle's thesis follow from the fact that wish involves rationality, and that knowledge of the good involves also knowledge of the bad.

1227^{a}31–^{b}4

In this section, Aristotle discusses how wish is distorted from its natural, good-directed state, appealing to a general theory of corruption and degeneration. If something declines from the optimal state, the decline is always into the opposite state, or into some state on the spectrum between the optimal state and its polar opposite. Thus degeneration from health must be to some state lying between health and disease; similarly, we can say that something, from being black, has come to be white or grey. See *Physics* I, 188^{a}30–^{b}26, *De Caelo* IV 310^{a}24–27.

Aristotle apparently generalizes this into a thesis not solely about the conditions for something's *changing* from an optimal to a degenerate state, but the conditions from something's *being* in a sub-optimal state: a thing can be in a sub-optimal state only through being in a state that lies on the spectrum from ϕ to its polar opposite.

This is now applied to the particular case of error concerning the best thing to do in a particular situation. The doctrine of the mean treats every choice as involving something intermediate between extremes, one being more and the other less, each of which can be said to be opposite to the mean (^{a}37–38; cf. 1222^{a}17 f.). When he speaks of 'the error and the choice' (^{a}36), presumably he has in mind the error about the good that is involved when something appears good that is not, and the erroneous choice resulting from that.

Aristotle now appeals to the connection between something's being pleasant and its appearing good, and its being unpleasant and appearing bad. Given that virtues and vices are dispositions determining choices, and choice always involves the taking of what appears good or avoidance of what appears bad, virtue and vice are once more shown to be concerned with the pleasant and unpleasant (cf. 1220 ª34–35, 1221b37–39, 1222ª11–12). The connection between the pleasant and unpleasant and the apparent good and bad is asserted at VII, 1235b26, 1236ª10. As the second of those passages makes clear, the identity claimed is between what *appears* good to X and what *is* pleasant for him; Aristotle distinguishes between what is pleasant *for someone* and what is pleasant without qualification; the second of these in fact coincides with what is good without qualification. It is difficult to avoid the impression that in this passage, Aristotle introduces unnecessarily elaborate apparatus for the purpose in hand.

Clearly, Aristotle can not be saying that everything judged to be good must be thought of as pleasant to the person judging (and similarly, *mutatis mutandis*, with the bad and the unpleasant) and indeed at VII, 1235b27–28, he explicitly distinguishes a thing's *appearing* good from its being *judged* to be so. Presumably something that appears good will present itself as pleasant when it appears good *as an end*; when something appears good only as a means, the error may be a fault in reasoning, and the thing in question need not appear pleasant. Given that wish is always of the end, and Aristotle is trying to explain how wish comes to be misdirected, it is cases of delusion over what is good as an end that most concern Aristotle here.

1227b5-11

Aristotle now states his final account of virtue, which incorporates the elements of the various preliminary definitions.

1227b9–11:   This qualification, to which nothing corresponds in *E.N.*, is a consequence of the fact that he defines the mean as an intermediate state in the matter of what is pleasant and unpleasant. It then becomes necessary to restrict the things in question to those which are indicative of a person's moral character. A person's concerns and pursuits manifest themselves in what he finds enjoyable or the reverse; but not all such pursuits and concerns reflect his character in the sense in which virtue and vice are states of character. He does not attempt to specify what distinguishes those tastes and predilections that are relevant from those that are not. Although it is reasonably clear that being sweet-toothed is not a character-trait (*ēthos*), what about the enjoyment of convivial gatherings? Would gregariousness be a trait of character?

CHAPTER 11

This chapter is something of an appendix to the discussion of virtue of character and choice. It falls into two parts, $1227^b12-1228^a2$ and 1228^a2-19, the first of which presents the greatest problems of interpretation. The second part corroborates the conclusion of the first part by referring to our actual practice in judging a person's character and awarding praise and blame; this view of the chapter's structure is confirmed by its last sentence.

The argument of the first parts is in places very compressed, to the point of obscurity, and raises problems that go to the heart of Aristotle's moral philosophy. Some ground is gone over that has already been covered in earlier sections of this book, without any retrospective reference, which may suggest that this chapter is fairly loosely attached to what precedes, despite the connection of general theme. The main interest lies in the argument of the first part – the respective roles of reasoning and virtue of character *vis-à-vis* the determination of the final end and what contributes to it. The general topic of the connection of virtue-of-character and choice has figured in the preceding chapters and virtue-of-character has been said to be a state determining choices, and indeed the view taken on the main issue of the chapter might be said to be already implicit in what is said in the earlier chapters of this book.

To this chapter as a whole nothing corresponds in *E.N.*, but the topic of the respective roles of virtue of character and reasoning in determining ends of conduct is discussed in *E.N.* VI, cc. 12 and 13, and it is instructive also to compare 1227^b12-13 with some passages in *E.N.* VII. The discussion of the second part is paralleled by a brief passage in E.N. III, 1111^b5-6. There is also a fairly close parallelism between the chapter as a whole and *M.M.* I, 1190^a9-^b6, which occurs in the same place in that work as this chapter occurs in *E.E.*, viz. between the treatment of choice and the voluntary and the discussions of individual virtues of character.

1227^b12-25

This passage raises difficulties because the problem announced for discussion at the beginning does not seem to be the same as that which is evidently the dominant theme of the chapter, and because the subsidiary discussion in $^b15-19$ of an alternative view held by 'some people' is hard to relate to the main theme. My understanding of this section has been greatly helped by Kapp.

Aristotle begins by raising the question whether virtue makes the choice and the end 'free from error', or whether it makes the reasoning (*logos*) correct (as is thought by some). Two preliminary points should be mentioned: (i) It is clear that here, and throughout the chapter, 'virtue' means 'virtue of character', as often, and notably in *E.N.* VI, cc. 12 and 13. (ii) When he speaks of the correctness of

163

of choice, he has in mind, not making the correct choice of an individual action, but being correct about the end towards which one's choice is directed. That being so, the first of the two alternatives introduced does not mention two independent sorts of correctness, but one, since the correctness of choice that is in question is the correctness of the final goal towards which it is directed, and the 'so that' clause in ᵇ14-15 is explicative of the single condition mentioned as the first alternative. That this is so is apparent from the fact that in 1228ᵃ1-2 the conclusion of this part of the chapter is summed up as that virtue is responsible for the end of one's choice's being correct, and by the fact that Aristotle clearly does *not* think that virtue is sufficient to ensure that the individual choice is the right one in the circumstances, requiring as that would a correct assessment of what contributes to the end. (Compare ᵇ35-36, 39-40.)

In ᵇ22-23, once again we have an alternative question ('Does virtue make the goal right, or what contributes to it?'), which is evidently a somewhat telescoped way of presenting the question 'Does virtue make its possessor correct in the goal he pursues or about what contributes to it?' The *first* alternative of the question at ᵇ12-15 is clearly the same as that of the present one, but the second alternatives in the two questions appear to be different. Between the two passages occurs first a brief rejection of the second alternative raised in the *first* disjunctive question, with an indication of how the view came to be held (ᵇ15-19), followed by a short passage (ᵇ19-22), in which a distinction is drawn between two places at which error can occur in practical reasoning, permitting three possible types of case. This last passage raises no special difficulty of its own, and seems to correspond to what is said more fully at *Politics* VII, 1331ᵇ26-38. It leads on naturally to the question raised at ᵇ22-23.

If the suggestion of ᵇ14-15 is that virtue makes reasoning correct, and it is also assumed that reasoning has to do only with ascertaining what contributes to an already accepted end (compare ᵇ24-30), the two alternative questions will amount to the same. But is this interpretation reconcilable with the passage dealing with those who espouse the second alternative (ᵇ15-19)?

Aristotle says simply: 'That state is continence ... but virtue is different from continence.' (For Aristotle's views on continence and incontinence generally, see Commentary on 1223ᵃ36-ᵇ3.) It seems, then, that those who accept the second alternative — that virtue makes reason correct — are accused of failing to distinguish virtue and (mere) continence. A brief hint is then given on how the view that virtue is simply continence is arrived at: incontinence is 'of that kind' and is praiseworthy. Presumably, the second of these observations alludes to an argument that continence is the same thing as virtue of character because it is a praiseworthy state of character. The other remark, that continence is of such a sort, suggests an argument linking the identification of virtue with continence with the view that virtue renders reason correct; such an argument must appeal to the essential features of continence. Presumably 'of that kind' must refer to the feature mentioned at ^{b}15-16 that it 'does not corrupt reason'. What this means can best be approached by considering what can be meant by virtue's rendering reason correct.

If that is equivalent to 'making reason*ing* correct', then in view of the scope of reasoning in the practical sphere mentioned later, ^{b}12-15 will raise the same question as ^{b}22-23. But Aristotle seems to be objecting that the supposition that virtue makes reason correct would (implicitly) make virtue no more than continence, and it seems clear that correctness of reasoning about what contributes to the end will not be enough even for continence: correct reasoning is compatible with incontinence, when the results of such reasoning are not acted on, and even with intemperance (*akolasia*), where the reasoning is directed towards the wrong end. It is essential to continence that the right choice is made, and the reasoning gone through impeccably; its only demerit is that the correct choice is made in the face of contrary inclinations, such as the fully virtuous man (the *sōphrōn*) would be without; the continent man's desire structure is not fully integrated so as to be directed in a unified way towards the good life. This means that the continent man's choices are directed towards the right end, and it is now difficult to see how the second criticized alternative of ^{b}12-15 is different from the first.

It has often been held that 'some people' refers to Socrates, or anyone who identifies virtue with knowledge. Such a person would hold that a cognitive state is sufficient for virtue, and that knowledge (though perhaps not true belief) will never be overmastered by contrary desires. If it is allowed that knowledge may come under pressure from such contrary inclinations, though never decisively, and virtue is identified with knowledge, it will be a consequence that virtue need be no more than continence.

In *E.N.* VII, c. 3, Aristotle takes Socrates' view that knowledge can never be overmastered very seriously at least, and, on one interpretation, actually accepts it. The present passage does not mention knowledge; but if we suppose that the second alternative of ^{b}12-15 is that virtue ensures that the agent reasons correctly from the right conception of the end, and we assume that Aristotle would agree that under such conditions an agent would never act against the conclusions of such practical reasoning, it would seem that the only objection Aristotle would have raised to the identification of such a state as virtue would be that, as specified, virtue need not

165

amount to more than continence: the correct choice might be made in the face of opposing inclination.

This over-all interpretation will make sense of the passage. We have to suppose that the question raised at ^{b}12-15 concerns a choice between rival accounts of that virtue *consists in*. Although 'makes' suggests that what is in question is simply alternative theses about what virtue is a sufficient condition for, on the view adopted, the point at issue will be rather the converse: Is correctness of reasoning sufficient for virtue? This is most easily taken care of if both 'makes' at ^{b}13 and 'renders' at ^{b}17-18 are glossed in the way suggested. Against the view that virtue consists in correctness of the reasoning element, he insists that the proper development of the inclinations is required also, otherwise the agent may be no more than continent. As he is accepting the view that incontinence occurs only when the reason has been impaired, his only objection to the 'intellectualist' view is that it fails to distinguish virtue of character from mere continence.

If this interpretation is correct, we can now see how the view that continence is the same thing as virtue should lead to the view that virtue consists in correctness of reason. For one who accepts a 'Socratic' view of incontinence, continence will consist specifically in the state in which the agent's reasoning is unimpaired: desires can overmaster only by producing a distortion of the agent's reasoning. Hence ^{b}15-16 have to be understood as saying 'continence is the state in which reason is unimpaired' in a way parallel to ^{b}13. On this view *logos* in ^{b}15, 16, and 17 can be construed as (*pace* Kapp) the faculty of reasoning (= the rational part of the soul) or as reason*ing*, but then correctness of reasoning will have to include more than simply a correct calculation of what contributes to the goal adopted; it will have to include a correct understanding of what goal ought to be adopted.

The general drift of the argument of the chapter will then be as follows: Aristotle first asks whether virtue consists simply in correctness of the reasoning element or in an integrated pursuit of the right end. He decides in favour of the second alternative. This leads on naturally to the question whether virtue is what is responsible for an agent's having the correct goal or whether it is *also* responsible for absence of error about what leads to the goal. This view about what question is being raised in the alternative question at ^{b}22-23 relies on the fact that Aristotle has already pronounced in favour of the role of virtue in making the goal right in the earlier part of the chapter.

1227^b25-33

In this section Aristotle corroborates the view that the role of reasoning is confined to what contributes to the end by appeal to his theory of practical reasoning. Compare I, 1218^{b}17-24, 1226^{a}7-15, 1227^{a}6 f., *Physics* I, 194^{b}32 f. For the comparison of the goal in practical reasoning with the hypotheses of theoretical reasoning, compare *E.N.* VII, 1151^{a}15-17. A mathematical example occurs at *E.N.* III, 1112^{b}20 f., but whereas there the appeal seems to be to reasoning about how to carry out a certain construction (e.g. to draw a figure fulfilling a certain specification), here the illustration must be from *theoretical* reasoning. But it is not clear whether the proposition that the sum of the interior angles of a triangle is equal to two right angles is here being treated as a proposition for which a proof is being sought, or as something regarded as axiomatic (at any rate for the purposes of the particular demonstration) from which consequences are deduced. In favour of the first alternative is the fact that the proposition in question was clearly *not* axiomatic in Aristotle's geometry, and it is plainly the process of proof-discovery that was in question at 1222^{b}31 f. On the other hand, the most natural analogue of the fact that the ultimate goal in the practical sphere is not within the scope of reasoning is the status of the basic axioms in the theoretical sciences. Compare also *E.N.* VI, 1142^{a}25, 1143^{a}32 f., where the mention of *nous* indicates that the axioms are in question. If so, the analogy with practical reasoning from an already accepted goal is only partial; sometimes reasoning takes the form of looking for what is *required* if the goal is to be achieved, but very often it is a question of what would be *sufficient*, perhaps in conjunction with certain other factors.

1227^{b}29: 'Productive sciences': see Commentary on I 1216^{b}17-19.

1227^{b}34-1228^{a}2

In this section, Aristotle reinforces the conclusion that virtue of character is what is responsible for the rightness of someone's ultimate goal, but not for his choice of what contributes to it; that is said to belong to 'another capacity' (^{b}40), a phrase reminiscent of *E.N.* VI, 1144^{a}22, where the capacity is identified as astuteness (*deinotēs*).

The observation that virtue makes the end correct, but some other capacity is responsible for the right choice of what contributes to that is similar to three passages in *E.N.* VI, cc. 12 and 13: 1144 ^{a}7-9, 20-21, 1145^{a}5-6. In this passage, neither practical wisdom nor astuteness (*deinotēs*) are mentioned, as they are in *E.N.*, but there is no reason to doubt that astuteness is the 'other capacity' mentioned at ^{b}40. Whether or not Aristotle, when he wrote this passage would have been willing to allow that practical wisdom has a part to play in determining the end is unclear; if, as appears to be the case, such a role is assigned to practical wisdom (*phronēsis*) in *E.N.*, that is there regarded as consistent with holding that the end is not arrived at by reasoning. (See 1142^{a}25 f; 1143^{a}35 f.)

1227^{b}36-39:   For the distinction in ^{b}36-37, see 1226^{a}11-14. While stressing the connection between virtue and both choice and the pursuit of the right end, Aristotle needs to make it clear that this is not inconsistent with his doctrine, expressed at 1226^{a}7-8, that the end is not chosen.

1228^{a}2-11

The point of the first part of this section (^{a}2-5) seems to be that the main thesis of the chapter, that virtue (or vice) are a matter of the rightness (or wrongness) of the final end towards which a person's actions are directed can be confirmed by our actual practice. ^{a}5-11 appears to argue as follows: (i) Someone who acts badly when it is in his power to act well, evidently has a bad character (^{a}5-7) (sc. because in such circumstances the agent has a bad end.) (ii) In such circumstances, there is no need for him to act badly (^{a}8-9); so (iii) virtue and vice are voluntary (^{a}7-8). This is confirmed by our practice in praising virtue and reprehending vice (^{a}9-11). The reasoning appears to be that voluntary actions reveal an agent's final end, which is in turn an index of good or bad character (cf. ^{a}2-4); and the voluntariness of actions requires the voluntariness of their origin. Compare E.N. III 1113^{b}7-14, and see Ackrill (1978).

1228^{a}11-19

The main thesis of the chapter is now supported by two observations: first that we award praise and blame by looking to the choice (or, as we might say, intention) rather than what is actually done. He then qualifies this by saying that the activity (resulting from a virtue) is more worth having than the virtue itself, although virtue is more praiseworthy. The reason seems to be that virtue is valued because of the actions (activities) that flow from it (compare 1219^{b}9); but unfortunately these do not always occur because even the virtuous sometimes act in the wrong way involuntarily; so possession of virtue is not by itself the best of all possible situations. Secondly, he argues that phenomena apparently conflicting with the view that character is appraised by reference to a person's ultimate choices can be explained by the fact that we are forced to make people's actual deeds the evidence for such appraisal because evidence for choice is necessarily indirect. (This represents a qualification of what had been said, in support of the outline account of happiness, at I, 1219^{b}10-11.) Compare E.N. III, 1111^{b}5-6 and X, 1178^{a}34-^{b}1.

BOOK EIGHT

CHAPTER 1

This chapter raises considerable difficulties, firstly because of the state of the text, and secondly because it is itself a fragment: the first sentence clearly does not follow on from the end of Book VII, nor does it introduce a new topic. The opening words of the book are characteristic of Aristotle when he is raising a difficulty in the course of the discussion of a problem, and exactly what preceded the opening of this chapter must be a matter of speculation. It is, however, possible to discern the main course of the argument of the chapter, as a result of the work of Jackson, Dirlmeier, and Moraux.

The chapter may be divided into three parts: (i) 1246^{a}26-35, in which Aristotle argues that knowledge can be used in two alternative ways—either as knowledge or 'as ignorance'. It is then argued (ii) 1246^{a}35-^{b}4 that, if it is impossible to 'use justice as injustice', it follows that virtue is not to be identified with knowledge. Then (iii) 1246^{b}4-36, Aristotle goes on to detail the absurd consequences that would ensue from the supposition that practical wisdom could be misused. The chapter ends with a statement of Aristotle's own attitude to the Socratic thesis, and to the doctrine of the unity of the virtues. For a rather different view of the structure of the argument of ^{b}4-25, see Kenny, pp. 184 f.

1246^{a}26-31

Despite the difficulties about the text, it is clear that Aristotle is raising the question whether what holds of the eye holds generally, viz., that it is possible to use it either for its natural purpose or in another way; and if in another way, either 'as itself' or 'incidentally'. There are, therefore, three cases: the first sort of use is exemplified by normal seeing, the second by seeing double as a result of deliberate pressure on the eye. The second case counts as a case of using the eye *as an eye* because it is still a case of seeing, unlike the third case.

The example of the eye is not an altogether happy one, if his interest is in possible uses or misuses of capacities, rather than physical objects. Perhaps his purpose in mentioning the three possibilities in the case of an eye is to bring out that the use of an X for something other than its natural function may still be use *as an X*.

1246^{a}31-^{b}4

The general structure of the argument of this section is fairly clear. Knowledge may be used in two ways—in the normal way and to make a deliberate mistake (illustrated by the example of writing)

169

(ª32–33). That phenomenon is described as 'using the capacity as ignorance' (ª33), and is therefore presumably represented as analogous to the use of an eye not as an eye at all (as is suggested by the mention of the case of dancing girls who use their feet as hands, and vice versa, ª33–35). It is then observed that, on the Socratic identification of virtues with forms of knowledge, it would be be possible to use (e.g.) justice as injustice (ª35–36), performing unjust acts, and committing injustice, *as a result of* justice (ª37). If that is impossible, the Socratic identification must be rejected (ª38–ᵇ1).

The suggestion is that one who makes a deliberate mistake uses his knowledge but does not use it *as* knowledge, using it as ignorance instead, i.e. uses it in order to act in the same way as the ignorant man would. The phrase 'use justice as injustice' must be understood in a parallel way, so what is in question is the possibility of a just man's using his justice to act unjustly.

In the final section (ᵇ1–4), Aristotle recognizes that someone might baulk at the suggestion that it is genuinely possible that someone might be ignorant as a result of knowledge. Such a person would insist that 'erring' was the only possibility, i.e. acting in the same way as one would through ignorance.

This would mean that the identification of justice with knowledge requires only the possibility of someone's acting in the same way as the unjust man would as a result of justice, not that justice should be capable of leading someone to act unjustly; it is conceded that the man is not actually acting unjustly in the case envisaged. Aristotle seems to regard even this as a *reductio ad absurdum* of the identification of virtue with knowledge. But is Aristotle justified in assuming without argument that every kind of knowledge is capable of misuse?

1246ᵇ4-12

Having argued against the Socratic view that identified courage and justice with knowledge, Aristotle now argues against the identification of *phronēsis* with knowledge (*epistēmē*). *Phronēsis* is here translated simply 'wisdom': he has in mind the intellectual virtue that guides a person's conduct, whatever that may prove to be. The specific conception of *phronēsis* found in *E.N.* VI, with its intimate connection with virtue of character seems to be what he is arguing towards in this chapter, in arguing against Socrates.

He begins (ᵇ4) 'Since wisdom is knowledge . . .', but it is clear from ᵇ35 that Aristotle does not accept this. (Kenny, p. 185 following von Fragstein (p. 184), emends 'since' to 'if', which makes the structure of the argument clearer.) The conclusion drawn from this proposition (ᵇ5) is that wisdom will do the same (i.e. presumably, be capable of misuse): the principle used in ª35–ᵇ1 is now applied to wisdom.

Aristotle concludes that it would then be possible to act foolishly from wisdom, and act just as the foolish person would. (The latter seems to be a weaker alternative, parallel to that mentioned at ^{b}2–3.) Further, if there is only one way of 'using wisdom' in so acting such people would be acting wisely (absurdly, because their behaviour is indistinguishable from that of the foolish) (^{b}7–8).

Aristotle now asks how the distortion or corruption comes about. With an ordinary science like medicine there is another science superior to it (sc. that governing the conduct of life). (Hence a doctor's misuse of medicine can be explained by erroneous beliefs about right conduct which take the place of knowledge in his case.) But the knowledge that *phronēsis* is, is supreme; so such a corruption of wisdom is ruled out. ^{b}10–12 then briefly consider the view that wisdom is subordinate, not to a higher form of knowledge, but to virtue of character; this would mean that the distortion of knowledge could be explained by vice in the non-rational part of the soul; i.e. a state in which the agent's desires are misdirected. Aristotle replies that knowledge 'uses' virtue (sc. and is therefore superior to it). The rejected suggestion is not Socratic: Socrates held that knowledge was supreme, and would not have accepted a distinction between wisdom and virtue.

1246^{b}12–18

The conclusion at ^{b}17–18 is that it will be possible to use justice in an unjust way, virtue badly, and wisdom foolishly. All these are later argued to be impossible. Presumably using wisdom foolishly is represented by the case of incontinence. He treats incontinence as a vice of the non-rational part of the soul, which acts upon the rational part, the possessor of wisdom, and causes it to reverse its judgement (^{b}15). This could, without too much strain, be described as 'using wisdom to act foolishly'.

The case of incontinence, where it is supposed that reasoning is overmastered by bad desires, is presented as an occurrence that Aristotle had claimed his opponent was committed to allowing at ^{b}9–12. Since incontinence is a familiar phenomenon, this seems a plausible case. His opponent, however, has to assume a particular account of what goes on in cases of incontinence: he has to assume that vice in the non-rational part of the soul actually affects the judgements made by the rational part. It is far from clear *what* these judgements are that the incontinent man makes. Many cases of incontinence are naturally described as ones in which someone does what he knows or believes to be wrong. Presumably, therefore, Aristotle thinks his opponent would claim that, in cases of incontinence, a man's judgement is distorted so that he judges to be right

171

what normally (or previously, before the onset of desire) he judges to be wrong. This, of course, involves some qualification of the description of the incontinent man as someone who does something that he believes to be wrong, since that will not be his opinion at the time that he acts. With this interpretation, we can explain the remark, at ^b13-14, that some say that the incontinent man (*akratēs*) is wicked (*akolastos*) (or, with another reading 'in some way *akolastos*'). It is characteristic of the *akolastos* that he has a bad character, and, in Aristotle's view, this means that the wrong sort of life appears a good one to him; this picture supposes that such a man acts badly, believing that he is acting rightly, it being a settled belief of his that acting in that way is right.

The conclusion drawn at ^b17-18, that it will be possible to 'use justice' (or virtue in general) in an unjust, or generally vicious, way, is inferred from the occurrence of a phenomenon, described in ^b16-17, that comes about when there is virtue (of character) in the non-rational part of the soul, and ignorance (or, with an alternative textual reading, stupidity) in the rational part of the soul.

Although the state of the text creates problems, this second phenomenon, like the first, involves a bad state in one part of the soul and a good state in the other, but this time it is the non-rational part that is in a good state, and the rational in a bad one; but, as in the case of incontinence, the bad state distorts the good. In line with uses of the notion of employment earlier the chapter, 'using justice unjustly' must be understood as *acting unjustly as a result of justice*: Aristotle is supposing that a person might possess justice in the non-rational part, and then act unjustly because of ignorance (or, on another reading, folly) in the rational part of the soul.

Aristotle's view in *E.N.* VI, cc 12-13 is that genuine justice could not coexist with the absence of the intellectual virtue, *phronēsis* – at best such a person would have 'natural' virtue (*phusikē aretē*) (cf. *E.N.* VI, 1144^b1-16). Aristotle may thus be seen as arguing in favour of the distinction drawn in *E.N.* VI; if the present interpretation is correct, he is not here arguing against Socrates.

What I have said so far does not depend on any controversial emendation; although the text is uncertain at ^b17, any satisfactory emendation will introduce the notion of change or alteration. But there is a question about the structure of ^b14-19, as a whole: if an emendation adopted in the translation at ^b16 is correct, the whole conditional sentence, asserting what the effect of a strong desire on the rational part of the soul will be itself is the antecedent of a conditional. If so, Aristotle says that, if incontinence as described, occurs, so must the other phenomenon, with virtue in one part, and ignorance or foolishness in the other. On one reading, both phenomena are independently allowed to be possible by Aristotle's opponent; on the other, the second possibility is one his opponent is committed to allowing once he accepts the first.

1246^{b}18–25

Aristotle now goes on to argue that if the two possibilities mentioned in the last section are admitted 'the opposite cases will be possible'. This is then treated as a *reductio ad absurdum* of the position under discussion. Thus the argument of ^{b}19–24 is of the form 'It would be strange if X were possible and Y not'. It is fairly clear that what is described in ^{b}19–21 is the case of incontinence, as understood by Aristotle's opponent. The possibility that Aristotle finds especially paradoxical is that someone should act wisely from ignorance, and it is apparent that that is what is described in ^{b}22. If we keep something like the reading of the manuscripts, the subject of the verbs in ^{b}22 will be 'virtue in the non-rational soul', which is accompanied by ignorance or stupidity in the rational part of the soul, and has a beneficial effect on it. If so, this case will be the converse of the second case in the sense that we have a good state in the non-rational soul acting on the bad state in the rational part, instead of the other way round.

If so, symmetry would suggest, as a fourth case, one like the first case (incontinence), except that rationality overmasters vice in the non-rational part of the soul. This, too, seems a perfectly reasonable reading of ^{b}23–24. Moreover, he explicitly describes this as a case of continence (*enkrateia*). This interpretation is in essentials Jackson's.

The four cases may be conveniently set out as follows:

		In the rational part of the soul		In the non-rational part of the soul	
(Incontinence)	(1)	practical wisdom	acted on by	vice wickedness (^{b}14–15, 19–21)	leading to using wisdom unwisely
	(2)	Ignorance (? stupidity)	acts on	virtue (of character) (^{b}16–17)	leading to using virtue viciously
	(3)	Ignorance (? stupidity)	acted on by	virtue (of character) (^{b}21–22)	leading to judging wisely
(Moraux)	(3)$^{'}$	Ignorance (? stupidity)	acted on by	vice	leading to judging wisely
(Continence)	(4)	practical wisdom	acts on	vice (^{b}23–24)	leading to acting temperately

173

(4) is the opposite of (1), and (2) of (3), in the sense that the direction of influence is different. (1) is the opposite of (2), and (3) of (4) in the sense that in the one case there is a good state in the rational part of the soul and a bad state in the non-rational part of the soul, whereas in the opposite cases it is the other way round. It has been argued in the previous section that if (1) is possible, so also must (2) be, and Aristotle regards (2) as evidently absurd. In the present section it is argued that the respective opposites of (1) and (2), viz. (4) and (3) will also have to be possible, and here it is (3) that Aristotle regards as an absurdity.

Moraux objects to this interpretation on the grounds that a good state in the non-rational part of the soul would obey reason and not rebel. He therefore proposes considerable alteration to the text, so as to yield the following translation: 'For it is strange if ever badness, when it comes to be present in the non-rational part of the soul, *will* change the virtue in the rational part, and will cause it to be ignorant, yet virtue in the non-rational part will be persuaded differently by ignorance in the rational part, although the vice of the non-rational part, when ignorance is present in the rational, will *not* change it and make it think wisely and as it should.' The effect of this is to make Aristotle recapitulate not only (1) but also (2), and then describe the action of one bad state upon another to produce a good one ((3)' in the text), in its turn followed by (4): on this interpretation, (3)' and (4) are not *alternative* cases, but successive stages in a single phenomenon. But Moraux's reading seems unnecessary, and requires considerable alteration to the text, unlike Jackson's.

1246^{b}25-32

The general line of argument of this passage is fairly clear, in view of what preceded. Moral vice can pervert (e.g.) knowledge of medicine, but cannot, conversely, convert ignorance of medicine into knowledge. The reason for this is an asymmetry between knowledge and ignorance: knowledge is a capacity, ignorance an incapacity; as Aristotle puts it at ^{b}32, the incapacity is included in the capacity. In ^{b}18-25, a conditional has been put forward, that if certain cases are possible, certain others will be, and in this section Aristotle is arguing against the consequents of the conditional; in particular, he is arguing against the idea that acting wisely as a result of ignorance is possible. If so, he is arguing by *modus tollens* that the sort of cases specified in the antecedent of the conditional are not possible; that will in turn be a refutation of the position on practical wisdom accepted by his opponent if it is indeed a consequence of his position that such cases should be possible.

Two questions naturally arise: (i) Against whom is Aristotle arguing? (ii) Why should his opponent accept that, if (1) is possible, so are (2), (3), and (4)? From ^{b}4, Aristotle has been arguing against the identification of practical wisdom (*phronēsis*) with knowledge; but the view of incontinence as the corruption of wisdom by vice in the non-rational part of the soul is hardly Socratic: Socrates' view was that everyone desires the good, all other desires being derivative from that, and so vicious action is always the result of false beliefs that have led to misdirected derivative desires. So Socrates would hardly have allowed the possibility of knowledge in the rational and vice in the non-rational soul, or, in general, of a good state in one part affecting or being affected by a bad state in the other (the common feature of all the cases described in ^{b}18-25). Aristotle's opponent seems to be someone who identifies wisdom with knowledge, but concedes that it can be misused, making knowledge or ignorance in the rational part vary independently of virtue or vice in the other; he will thus deny that 'nothing is stronger than knowledge'; whereas Socrates would exclude the overmastery of knowledge, holding that it was always guided by desire for the good, in his view the only non-derivative desire.

Against such an opponent, who held that the good or bad states of the two parts of the soul can vary independently, Aristotle can fairly argue that, on such a view, the good or bad state of either part can each lead to action; so four possibilities exist when a good state in one part is accompanied by a bad state in the other. He can also reasonably claim that it is absurd that a person should, despite ignorance, act intelligently, because his action was determined on this occasion by a good state of the non-rational soul. The fundamental error, as Aristotle seems to recognize (see Commentary on next section) is to suppose that the intellectual and appetitive elements of virtue can vary independently. The connection between that and the argument of this section is not very clear; perhaps it is that the view under attack does not make enough allowance for the fact that the ignorant person *lacks* something, in supposing that a good state in the non-rational soul could lead to the right choice despite ignorance in the rational. Once the possibility of independent variation is excluded, and practical wisdom is seen to require the virtues of character, it can no longer be knowledge (*epistēmē*), and open to misuse.

1246^{b}32-36

This passage draws the following conclusions: (i) that someone who has practical wisdom possesses also *all* the virtues of character. (ii) Nothing is stronger than practical wisdom (and hence, on this Socrates was right). (iii) Practical wisdom is not knowledge but a virtue, and on this Socrates was wrong. (i) seems fairly clearly to be the purport of b32-33, despite textual problems.

For the connection between (i) and (ii) and the preceding argument, see Commentary on last section. (i) and (ii) are equivalent in that, if practical wisdom is always accompanied by virtue of character, there is no room for practical wisdom to be overmastered by vicious desires. Although, as Aristotle allows, Socrates accepted (i) and (ii), he was able to do so, identifying wisdom and virtue with knowledge, only because for him the only underivative desire was the desire for the good. Aristotle, by accepting (iii), was able to place (i) and (ii) on a firmer foundation. The position he accepts here is that of *E.N.* VI, cc. 12 and 13.

It is, however, puzzling that b35-36 says wisdom is a virtue, but not knowledge (*epistēmē*). In *E.N.* VI (1139b12-21) *epistēmē* is one of the intellectual virtues. Presumably it is here implied not to be a virtue because it is capable of misuse, as has been stressed in this chapter, though it would count as one in a broader sense, because it is the source only of truth, as is said in *E.N.* VI (op. cit.).

CHAPTER 2

1246b37-1247a3

The problem of this chapter is that welfare, which is agreed to result from practical wisdom and virtue (of character), seems also to be capable of coming about through luck—the evidence being that those who enjoy good fortune are said to fare well (*eu prattein*). The term here translated 'welfare' (*eupragia*) is a near synonym of 'happiness' (*eudaimonia*) on which see Commentary on I, 1214a1-8. One strand in the notion of *eudaimonia* makes it natural to ascribe it to someone who enjoys good fortune. The 'since' clause gives a reason for the relevance of the discussion of good fortune to the inquiry. Compare *M.M.*, II 1206b30-37.

1247a3-13

Aristotle begins by mentioning two possible explanations of good fortune: that it is a matter of the character-dispositions that a man acquires, and that it is a gift of nature, some people being born lucky, just as some are born blue-eyed. Not surprisingly, the former alternative is not further pursued. The second is said to be the view commonly held. Clearly, what is in question is the explanation of the fact that some people *consistently* enjoy good fortune.

1247a13-31

Aristotle continues to argue in favour of the view commonly held, that good luck is a natural endowment, first disposing (a13-24) of

176

the suggestion that good luck of this kind is due to practical wisdom, on the grounds that the people in question cannot offer any rationale of their success. This argument relies on the assumption that one whose projects prosper as a result of his intelligence will always be able to explain how the result was achieved in an explicit way. That is questionable, since practical intelligence need not be combined with verbal articulateness, and it is later challenged by Aristotle. He then (ª24-29) introduces, and summarily disposes of, the alternative that success is due to having a good guardian deity.

1247ª17-20: The reference is not to Hippocrates of Cos, famous in the history of medicine, but to Hippocrates of Chios (*c*. 470-400 BC), a mathematician.

1247ª31-ᵇ1

Aristotle now begins to argue *against* the position that good fortune is a natural gift. (i) (ª31-35) Nature is the source of what occurs always, or for the most part, in the same way, whereas luck is the opposite (ª33; i.e. what occurs by chance is *neither* always *nor* for the most part thus). So if (*a*) the connection is preserved between good luck and luck (i.e. chance), and (*b*) only prospering that is not a matter of reasonable expectation is a matter of luck, the source of good fortune cannot be something that produces patterns that hold universally or in most cases. (ii) (ª35-ᵇ1) If good luck is produced in the way that dark eyes produce poor eyesight (compare 1247ª10) good luck will recur naturally, and the supposed example of good fortune will really be an example of good natural endowment. So, from both (i) and (ii), the conclusion must be drawn that those whom we call fortunate 'are not so by chance' (or, as Aristotle should have said, they do not have what is erroneously *called* good fortune by chance).

Thus he is saying that good luck must be a matter of chance, but what is a matter of chance cannot have the regular predictable character that the prosperity of those said to enjoy good fortune seems to have.

1247ᵇ2-9

In view of the results of the previous section, Aristotle raises the question (i) whether there is such a thing as luck; and (ii) whether it is a cause. His treatment here is disappointingly dogmatic. The main treatment of luck or chance in the Aristotelian corpus is at *Physics* II, c. 5. However, although he there gives an affirmative answer to both (i) and (ii), his view is the reasonable one that luck is not a cause distinct from the other kinds of cause he there distinguishes.

There, as here, he contrasts chance or luck with what occurs always and of necessity, or for the most part (196^{b}10-13); his position is that '. . . among things which are neither necessary nor for the most part, there are some to which it can belong to be for the sake of something. Anything which might be done as an outcome of thought or nature is for the sake of something. Whenever something like this comes to be accidentally, we say that it results from chance (196^{b}20-24).' (The word translated by 'chance' in the *Physics* passage is the same as that translated as 'luck' in the present passage.) Thus, chance occurrences have the feature that they fall under no law that holds universally or for the most part *under the description under which they are correctly said to occur by chance*, though they will have some explanation under another description. This view has the consequence that it is not open to doubt that there is such a thing as chance, and it will not, strictly speaking, be a cause; to say that something occurred by chance will not be to give an explanation, but to deny that a general explanation is available. (But, both in English and in Greek, certain locutions naturally suggest that chance is an explanatory factor—we say '*X* was *due to* chance' or that chance *led to* a certain occurrence.) In discussing Aristotle's views it is convenient to speak of chance, even though 'luck' has been used in the translation.

Here however, he mentions the view (^{b}4-5) that nothing happens by chance or, with the translation adopted here, luck; the next sentence could be interpreted in two ways: (i) When we see no cause for some occurrence, we say it is due to chance (erroneously, since everything has a cause; hence this view is treated as an elaboration of the doctrine of ^{b}4-5 that nothing is due to chance). This leads to the *mistaken* definition of chance as a cause lying outside human calculation (^{b}7-8). (ii) we say that what happens from a cause unknown to us happens by chance, though nothing happens by chance intrinsically and independently of human knowledge; hence chance is defined as a cause outside human reasoning. (i) would deny that there is such a thing as chance at all (implicitly defining a chance occurrence as an uncaused one), (ii) that chance exists objectively, independently of human knowledge of reality. The phrase 'as if it were some nature' (^{b}8) perhaps supports (i), suggesting that it is wrongly thought that there is such a thing to be defined. It is evident that the use of the term 'chance' by the view he rejects is quite different from its use in the *Physics* passage; for, on the theory propounded there, there will be no incompatibility between something's occurring by chance and its being caused, nor will only those occurrences be attributed to chance that have a cause outside the sphere of human calculation. Compare *Physics* II, 197^{a}8-11;

'necessarily, then, the causes from which an outcome of chance might come to be are indeterminate. That is why chance is thought to be an indeterminate sort of thing and inscrutable to man, and at the same time there is a way in which it might be thought that nothing comes to be as a result of chance.' Compare also *Rhetoric* I, 1369^a32–^b5.

It is important, on either interpretation, that the position alluded to in ^b4-8 should be rejected, if Aristotle is to avoid the conclusion that there is no such thing as good fortune. With the translation and punctuation here adopted, Aristotle says that whether chance does not exist is another problem (sc. one that lies outside the scope of the present inquiry). An alternative would be to translate by 'if' rather than 'whether' in ^b4, and suppose that we have a conditional clause whose apodosis has dropped out of the text; in the apodosis the unacceptable consequences would be developed of supposing that there is no such thing as chance. ^b8-9 'This would be another problem' will then look forward to the issue raised in the succeeding section.

1247^b9-18

If someone has a stroke of good luck on one occasion, why should he not enjoy the same good fortune regularly? Aristotle argues that, since the outcome is (in relevant respects) the same, it must always have the same cause; but then the run of successes cannot be due to chance (^b11). However, where the causes are 'indefinite and indeterminate' there is no room for knowledge; otherwise we should have the absurd consequence that people could learn to have good luck, or that *all* forms of knowledge that explain success were really cases of good fortune.

Is Aristotle saying that whenever someone enjoys a run of good luck, the instances of luck must all have the same explanation? If so, the reasoning is fallacious: each case of good luck may have its explanation without there being explanation of the *run* of successes. In such circumstances, where the explanations of the individual cases are thought to be different, we naturally say that it was a matter of chance that the good fortune was repeated, though not that each individual success was a matter of chance. Aristotle is mis-applying the principle that the same outcome has the same cause.

But it may be that he is specifically considering cases in which the repeated strokes of good fortune have the same explanation, without holding that the same is true of *all* such sequences. Even so, the absurd consequences would not follow; for even if the successes *could have* been ensured by someone who had the relevant causal knowledge, it does not follow that the successes *were* thus secured. So there is no danger of the disappearance of the distinction between good luck and skill, or of the absurdity that good fortune would be something that could be learned.

His problem in this section is that, if the connection is maintained between good fortune and chance, *regular* good fortune would seem to be excluded, if chance is incompatible with regularity.

1247^b15:   The reference appears to be to Plato *Euthydemus* 279C f.

1247^b17:   'because he is of that particular sort'. 1247^a36 f. had argued that if some people have good fortune as an endowment in the way that some have dark eyes, good fortune would not be a matter of luck (and hence would not really be good fortune). He now asks why someone should not enjoy repeated strokes of good luck without our attributing to him a natural endowment, as in the case of the dice-player.

1247^b18-28

Aristotle now argues, *against* the argument of 1247^a31 f, that everyone has an impulse to pursue the good, and some people have a natural instinct or knack of making fortunate choices in most circumstances, although the choice is not made from reasoning, and they cannot give a rational account of it. Their inability to give a rational explanation of their choice means that their choice does not result from practical wisdom, by the argument of 1247^a13 (on which see Commentary). On the other hand their success is due to a natural endowment, not to luck. So this argument challenges the connection, accepted at 1247^a33, between good fortune and luck. However, his example of those who sing well without being taught suggests that he may be conflating the contrast between those whose skill depends on teaching and those whose skill does not, with the contrast between those who can articulate and explain what they do, and those who cannot.

1247^b28-1248^a2

Aristotle now proposes to deal with the problem raised by the intuitive connection between good fortune and luck, on the one hand, and the argument that good fortune is something natural, on the other, by suggesting that some cases of good fortune are natural and some are not.

He begins by distinguishing (*a*) cases in which choice, resulting from a natural impulse, plays a part in producing the results and (*b*) cases where it does not (^b29-30); in the former case, if a good outcome results despite faults in the reasoning, we say that the people are lucky, though their good fortune is due to natural goodness (^{b}34–^{a}1). ^{b}32-33 seem to mention a separate class of cases falling under (*a*), in which, by chance, the person actually gets a good that is different from or greater than he intended, which suggests that the initial case is that in which he is lucky to get the good he was aiming for, despite faults in reasoning. In cases of type (*b*), where the agent's desire plays no part, there is no question of natural goodness, reflected in rightly directed desire on the agent's part (^{b}39–^{a}1).

Certainty about Aristotle's conclusion, as stated in ^{a}1-2, is difficult because of textual difficulties. With the reading adopted in the translation, he is saying that unless we are willing to say that the same sort of good fortune is involved in both (*a*) and (*b*), despite the difference between them, we shall have to distinguish several sorts of good fortune. What Aristotle has done is to distinguish cases where luck, and the way in which an agent's desires are directed, conspire to produce a good result from cases where the happy outcome is *purely* a matter of chance.

1248^{a}2-15

This passage raises perhaps the worst textual problems in the chapter; and it is not possible to reconstruct more than the general sense. The conclusion at ^{a}14-15 is that chance is not the cause of all the occurrences that it is thought to be the cause of, since not all apparent cases of good fortune are really correctly so regarded: some result from nature (^{a}13-14). Leading up to this is a passage discussing cases where someone apparently prospers in defiance of what could have been ascertained by knowledge and reason (^{a}2-5; when he says that something else must be the cause, he means, presumably, something other than knowledge). It is then argued, if the reading adopted is correct, that in such cases the occurrence is not totally non-rational (*alogiston*) since the desire is natural: it is wrongly classified as a matter of chance because chance is thought to be the source of what happens outside the sphere of calculation.

When he says that the desire is natural (^{a}8), he presumably has in mind, as before, the natural direction of desire towards the good. It is not made clear how the sort of case discussed in this section relates to the cases classified in 1247^{b}28-1248^{a}2, but it is hard to see how the present cases fall outside the classification there introduced. Aristotle does not seem to have decided whether to say that some occurrences commonly classified as good fortune ought not to be so regarded, or that the term is ambiguous.

1248^{a}15-30

This section begins by raising a puzzle about the cases under discussion, in which someone prospers as a result of the right direction of his desires: is the right direction of desires *itself* due to chance (ª15–23)? But the answer, that the divine element in the human soul is involved, adds a further feature to the description of instances of good fortune that manifest properly directed desires without any calculation.

The argument of the first few sentences is that if, to avoid an infinite regress, a person is said to desire the right ends by chance, exactly the same argument will show that everything (or at any rate every mental activity) is due to chance. Not every piece of deliberation is preceded by a prior piece of deliberation (sc. on whether to engage in deliberation, or how to begin it) (ª18–19), nor is every act of thinking preceded by a previous thought (sc. on what thought to have) (ª20). He is correct in holding that a vicious regress will result if each mental act is held to originate in another act *of the same type*. But why should it be supposed that each mental act is initiated by another of the same type?

At ª23, he recognizes that the alternative exists of supposing that there is some origin or starting-point (*archē*) that requires no *further*, more ultimate, cause, to explain the changes that it originates, although these changes are not the result of chance. He claims that the divine element in the human soul is the required origin; this is said to be superior to knowledge, reason, and intelligence (*nous*).

The reference to the divine element in the human soul is parallel, in some degree, to *E.N.* X, 1177ª13–17, b27–31. There, however, the divine element is tentatively identified with the intelligence (*nous*), whereas here the divine element is *distinguished* from intelligence. On the subject of the divine element in the human soul, see further c. 3.

Aristotle's view is that souls are origins of change, and this means that a soul has the capacity to engage in thought, desire, deliberation, etc., and that no further explanation need be sought for their occurrence; if there were, the soul would not be the originating cause of change that Aristotle supposes it to be. So no regress threatens, nor will these occurrences in the soul come about through chance, since they will reflect the nature of the soul as an origin of changes.

1248ª29–30:   The point of this observation presumably is that, since virtue of character is the instrument, we cannot suppose that virtue is the factor superior to intelligence that Aristotle is looking for. Compare 1246b10–12. This picture of the relation between virtue and intelligence seems rather less sophisticated than that to be found in *E.N.* VI. Compare, however, 1145ª6–9.

1248ª30–b2

The previous section introduced the theme of the divine element in the human soul as a source of psychic phenomena like desire (and, in particular, as bringing it about that a person's desires are rightly directed). He now refers back to 1247ᵇ18–28, where those who prosper in a regular fashion as a result of rightly directed desires in the absence of calculation are mentioned. It is now made clear that, for such people, reasoning and calculation may actually be disadvantageous, for they have the benefit of divine inspiration superior to reason. There are some whose good fortune is so extreme and consistent that it is reasonable to attribute it to divine power.

Clearly, the role of the divine element cannot simply be to bring it about that desires are rightly directed (as 1248ª5 f. might suggest) but also to cause the agent to make the right choice of action in relation to those ends (as we might say, to make a series of *inspired* choices). Further, although the previous section apparently introduced the divine element in the soul as the source of all psychic activities, it is clear that in this section a divine causation of a rather special kind is in question; instead of initiating a fallible train of reasoning from the desired end to the conclusion, the divine element produces action of the appropriate kind in a manner superior to rational calculation. The power of prophecy is relevant because of the close connection between the right choice and foreknowledge of the future.

1248ª34–36:   The point of this sentence is difficult to recover, on account of textual corruption. As I have translated it, Aristotle alludes to a class of persons who can reasonably be called wise, who almost succeed in dispensing with rational calculation altogether.

1248ᵇ3–7

This final section of the chapter can be regarded as answering the question raised at 1247ᵇ28: 'Are there different sorts of good fortune?' He distinguishes one sort, resulting from divine guidance, that tends to be more continuous than the other; this is clearly the sort mentioned at 1247ᵇ33–38. The other sort, less likely to be manifested in a consistent fashion, seems to be that described at 1247ᵇ39–1248ª1.

Aristotle does not give an explicit answer to the other problems that have been preoccupying him in this chapter; his position presumably is that the first sort of good fortune is natural, and not a matter of chance, the second *is* a matter of chance: the connection between good fortune and luck holds in the second case but not in the first.

183

CHAPTER 3

This chapter is one to which there is no parallel in *E.N.* The concept central to the discussion — *nobility* — is almost completely absent from *E.N.*, and not put to any systematic philosophical use. On the other hand, *M.M.* 1207^{b}20-1208^{a}21 parallels this chapter, except perhaps for its final section. The theme of the present chapter is not directly connected with the themes of either of the earlier two chapters of this book, though in places Chapter 2 may be presupposed (see Commentary).

In some respects this chapter draws together the threads of the discussion in all the rest of *E.E.*, and to that extent it may be thought to occupy the same position in *E.E.* that is occupied by *E.N.* X, 6-9. It is from this chapter, if from any, that Aristotle's attitude in this work to the speculative life as the ideal for human beings must be judged. On the other hand, there is no explicit discussion of happiness, nor any reference back to the discussion of that topic in Book I, and in some respects, the chapter is most closely paralleled by certain passages in *E.N.* VI. On one interpretation, here also we find the doctrine of reason as the divine element in the human soul (cf. *E.N.* X, 1177^{a}15, ^{b}26-34). In any case, in the text of *E.E.* as we have it, this chapter is not a concluding chapter, unless the final sentence (1249^{b}24-25) is to be condemned as spurious; its wording makes it clear that the end of the chapter as we have it is only a stage of the discussion that has been reached and there is more to follow. Dirlmeier holds that in fact the discussion of friendship which occupies Book VII should follow this chapter, on the basis of the ordering in the *M.M.*, in which what corresponds to VIII, 2 is followed by the passage parallel to this chapter, and then by the treatment of friendship. Even if we do not follow Dirlmeier in holding that *M.M.* is genuine, the order in that work may be evidence for the original order in which topics were treated in *E.E.* It is certainly true that the present VIII, 1 in no way follows on the end of VII, as we have seen. But there is no clear reason for the present chapter to occupy its present position; the present chapter would perhaps occur most naturally after discussion of individual virtues (including the intellectual ones), and would thus follow on from *E.N.* VI, or from the part of *E.E.* that corresponds to that.

The chapter falls into two halves: in the first section, up to 1249 ^{a}20, the notion of nobility is explained, and a distinction is drawn within the class of goods, between those that are also fine, and those that are not. This is used to define nobility, as an attribute of the completely virtuous man. Such a man is said to be able to use 'natural goods', which for others may not be goods at all, so that for him they are fine. After a brief allusion to the pleasant and its relation to the good and the fine (1249^a17-20), the rest of the chapter, from 1249^a21 onwards, is occupied with the task of specifying the standard which the noble man refers to in deciding how these natural goods should be used. It is in the course of this discussion that some hints are dropped about the place of speculation in the ideal human life, and the role of practical wisdom.

The discussion is incomplete in a number of ways. As already mentioned, there is no attempt to relate the discussion of nobility to happiness, nor is its relation to the particular virtues made clear; there is no discussion of the way in which certain character-states are singled out as being fine, nor is there any discussion of the fine as a motive for action on the part of the virtuous man.

Under discussion in this chapter is a characteristic ascribed to a person by a Greek adjective which has been translated 'fine-and-good'; the word is a portmanteau word, formed out of the words elswhere translated 'fine' and 'good', hence the cumbersome translation. The adjective was common both in philosophical and in non-philosophical Greek long before the time of Aristotle; it is, for example, extremely common in Plato. Although at certain earlier periods the description was sometimes applied on the basis of social status or even physical appearance, the tendency from Plato onwards was to apply it as a term of high moral evaluation. Correspondingly, there is an abstract noun formed from the adjective, which is used in four places in this chapter to denote the quality of character ascribed by the adjective. The translation 'fine-and-nobleness' is not tolerable in English, and I have therefore adopted the translation 'nobility' (following Rackham; Solomon has 'nobility and goodness' which suggests two qualities rather than one). This, unfortunately, obscures the connection between the adjective, used at 1248^b16, 1249^a7, 10, 13 and the noun, used at 1248^b10, 1249^a2, 16, ^b24; but a translation that articulates the components out of which the adjective is constructed is required at 1248^b16, where the argument makes use of the connection with the good and the fine. The English 'nobility' has the merit that it may denote earlier social standing or moral excellence, but its use as a moral term hardly corresponds with the Greek.

In *E.N.* the noun occurs at X, 1179^b10 and IV 1124^a4, but not in a specifically philosophical sense. The noun does not occur in Plato (except in the probably spurious *Epinomis*) nor before the fourth century. The adjective is applied to actions at *E.N.* I, 1099^a22.

1248^b8-16

In this passage it is made clear that the fine-and-good man must have all the virtues. Is their possession also a sufficient condition of being fine-and-good? ^b10 suggests that it is the virtue that results from all of them, as does the contrast implied in the phrase 'particular virtues'. Later, too, at 1249^a16, it is natural to ask how the good man of 1249^a12-13 relates to this. Is he deficient in virtue? It later becomes clear that the fine-and-good man acts from a certain motive: he acts virtuously *because* such acts are fine. This introduces a new factor that is not implied in the earlier account of virtues of character. With ^b13-16, compare II, 1220^a2-4.

1248^b8-9:   The reference to each of the virtues is to the discussion that occupies Book III; but the chapter also presupposes a treatment of justice, and some treatment of practical wisdom.

1248^b16-25

Aristotle now distinguishes, within the class of things that are good in themselves, those that are also fine. For 'fine' (*kalos*), see Commentary on 1214^a1-8. That there is a continuity between its moral and aesthetic uses is apparent from I, c. 8, 1218^a21-24, where Aristotle restricts the application of 'good' to objects subject to change, and implies that 'fine' has a more general application, straddling the division between the changing and the unchanging. In the same chapter, at 1218^b4-6, he seems to use 'good' in the broad sense, and use 'fine' in application to goods not subject to change, but the difference is perhaps only a verbal one. On these passages, see Allan (1971). Allan draws attention to *Metaphysics* M 1078^a31-^b6 and Λ 1072^a26-35, where what Aristotle says is in accordance with the language of the first of the two passages from I, 8 just cited. Similarly in *Politics* VII 1326^a33, *Poetics* 1450^b37, where the beautiful is said to consist in order and being on the right scale.

From these passages, it appears that those things may be described as fine which can be recognized as having merit appropriate to the kind of thing that they are, when viewed from an impersonal standpoint; whereas in Greek thought, when something is called 'good', the question 'good for whom?' always seems to be in place. (Even the notion of being good *simpliciter* (*haplōs*), as opposed to being good for a particular person, seems to be explained in terms of being good for anyone in a normal, natural state.)

None the less, although elsewhere Aristotle seems simply to equate the fine with what is good in itself (cf. *Rhetoric* 1364^b27-28), here he calls only a sub-class of intrinsic goods fine: those which are 'commended'. (I take over this translation from Allan (op. cit.); it seems to have more nearly the right nuance than 'laudable' (Rackham) or 'praised' (Solomon).) Though the virtues and the actions that result from them are fine, health and strength are not (^{b}21–25), and the distinguishing feature seems to be that they are not merely human goods but morally admirable. The word that has been translated 'commended' derives from a verb that has a meaning approximating to the English 'commend'. The same word is used at II 1223^{a}10, and it is there said that we are commended for what we are ourselves responsible for. In support of the fact that 'fine' here means something like 'morally admirable' is the fact that the fine is said to serve as motive for the completely virtuous man. (Compare 1248^{b}36; the difficulties that that doctrine presents for Aristotle's general views will be considered in the Commentary on the next section.) The definition of the fine as what is intrinsically good and also commendable occurs also at *Rhetoric* 1366^{a}33.

The definition offered seems effectively to restrict the class of fine things to the virtues and the actions that they produce (cf. ^{b}36–37). Later, however, he says that some things not intrinsically fine are so when possessed by the fine-and-good man (1249^{a}4–14). This would require a distinction between those things that are commended whenever they occur, without regard to circumstances or to who possesses them, and those that are commended in certain circumstances only.

1248^{b}25–37

Aristotle introduces here the class of 'natural' goods (literally, 'things good by nature'). Such things as wealth, good fortune and physical capacity are given as examples of these (^{b}27–30). It emerges from this section that these goods are not also fine, and they may actually be harmful to those who lack the character to use them correctly. The man who is able to use them in the right way (sc. so that they are beneficial to him) is called 'good' (^{b}25), but is not *eo ipso* a fine-and-noble man. In this passage the natural goods are described as those which men compete for, and which appear to be the greatest goods that there are (^{b}27–28). Similarly, at VII, 1238^{a}17, natural goods and evils are represented as those with which good and bad fortune is concerned. The phrase 'natural good' does not occur in Aristotle outside *E.E.*, and the question arises whether this phrase, as has often been supposed, is equivalent to 'good *simpliciter*' (*haplōs*), which also occurs in this chapter, and is found in *E.N.*, *M.M.*, and *Politics*. On this see Commentary on 1248^{b}37–1249^{a}16.

It seems clear that in this section the criterion for being a good man is solely whether these natural goods are beneficial: the good man is someone who is in a position to act in his own interests. The notion of a good man thus does not have the sort of moral content that is possessed by fine-and-good'. See Commentary on the last section.

187

The main problem in this section occurs at 1248^{b}34-37. The fine-and-good man is said to be the man who possesses intrinsically fine things, and who performs fine actions for their own sake. Since the only fine things considered at the moment are virtues and actions resulting from them (^{b}36-37), it is reasonable to suppose that the intrinsically fine things that the good man possesses are the virtues.

This passage is one of many, in *E.E.*, and *E.N.*, in which Aristotle regards the fine as a motive for action for the truly virtuous man. Thus at III, 1229^{a}4, he says that only the man who is fearless 'on account of the fine' is brave (cf. 1229^{a}9). At 1230^{a}28 f. 'Virtue makes each man choose with a certain motive, and that for whose sake he chooses is the fine ... courage, being a virtue, will make a man stand up to what is fearful for a certain motive, so that he does so not from ignorance ... but because it is fine.' Compare also *E.N.* III, 1115^{b}12-13 (also discussing courage) where the fine is said to be the end of virtue, and IV, 1120^{a}23-25, 1122^{b}6-7, (where this motive is said to be common to all the virtues), 1123^{a}24-25. This has been thought to raise problems for the doctrine that happiness is the final end of human action. Even if we suppose that the conception of the good by reference to which the ideal man orients himself includes virtuous actions, these being integral components of the good life, to act with a view to happiness, even thus understood, seems to have a self-regarding character which is absent from action motivated by the fine. If fine actions are chosen because such action is part of happiness, the agent's ultimate motive is not to perform a fine action. A second difficulty is that some fine actions, including courageous and heroic ones, which for Aristotle are prime examples, seem to require that someone should forgo happiness. For happiness, according to Aristotle, a complete life is required (cf. II, 1219^{a}38), but certain acts of self-sacrifice involve a premature end to one's life and hence the forgoing of any chance of happiness. There are signs that he was aware of the second difficulty, at least. In *E.N.* IX, 1168^{b}25-1169^{b}2, though happiness is not explicitly mentioned, he discusses the question how far the good man ought to be a lover of self, and concludes that a concern to excel others in the performance of fine action is not reprehensible. The virtuous man is concerned with securing good for himself: such a concern may lead him to sacrifice his life, preferring 'intense pleasure for a short time to mild pleasure for a long time, and to live finely for a year to living in a mediocre fashion for many years, and one fine and great action to many insignificant ones' (1169^{a}22-25). See Hardie, pp. 329-33.

Finally, what is the relation between the application of 'fine' to virtuous dispositions and its application to the actions they lead to?

Which application is the primary one? It seems that virtuous dispositions are properly regarded as fine because they lead to fine actions, and not conversely. If the application to the dispositions were the primary one there would be a regress: since virtues are dispositions to act with a view to what is fine, he specification of the motive of a virtuous disposition would include, on further analysis, a reference to that disposition itself. Thus, for Aristotle, actions are not thought of as fine simply because of the character that they manifest; they are admirable independently.

1248^{b}37-1249^{a}16

This section draws out the consequences of the definition of the fine-and-good man, using the notion of 'natural goods', already introduced. Some people aspire to virtue in order to secure such goods as wealth, power, and prestige; such people fail to acquire nobility, as they do not possess the things that are intrinsically fine (^{a}2-3). No grounds are given for this latter proposition, but if it is true, as suggested in the Commentary on the previous section, that the intrinsically fine things that the fine-and-good man must possess are the virtues, the argument is that the dispositions acquired by those who aspire to natural goods are not virtues (in the full sense), since a virtue is necessarily a disposition to act in a certain way for a certain reason (for the sake of the fine). See Commentary on previous section for passages in which Aristotle makes this a requirement for the possession of a virtue.

Aristotle now adds (^{a}5 f.) that, in the case of the fine-and-good man even those goods that are mere 'natural goods' become fine. Thus a distinction is imported between those things that are fine *simpliciter* and those which are fine *for* the fine-and-good man. It is the former that were introduced at 1248^{b}12 f., and in terms of them the fine-and-good man was defined. If Aristotle's position is to be free from circularity, some things must be independently recognized as fine (i.e. the vites and virtuous acts); then, having identified the fine-and-good man, we can identify a further class of natural goods which are fine *for him*.

Aristotle seems to have had two reasons for holding that natural goods become fine in the hands of the fine-and-good man. (i) When he has them they lead to fine acts (^{a}13-14), hence his motive for acquiring them is admirable (^{a}5-6). Presumably, the thought is that wealth, good fortune, personal prestige enable the fine-and-good man to do virtuous actions; for example, generosity requires money, the political virtues are aided by the ability to influence people that goes with personal prestige (*timē*). The natural goods are in fact described at 1249^{a}15 as external goods, and in *E.N.* Aristotle admits the need for external goods for the magnificent man (*megalopsychos*) (IV, 1123^{b}17, 20). (ii) It is just that the fine-and-good man should have these nagural goods: he deserves them, and they are appropriate to him, and what is just is fine (^{a}7–10). This argument perhaps shows that the possession of these natural goods by the fine-and-good man is a fine thing, rather than that these goods themselves become fine.

On the phrase 'good without qualification', used in ^{a}12, and again in ^{a}18, see Commentary on II, 1227^{a}18–30. Now it was characteristic of 'natural goods' like wealth, strength, etc., that they are not invariably beneficial to the person who has them, but only to someone who has the character to make a proper use of them. This suggests that the class of goods without qualification coincides with the class of natural goods, as indeed has been assumed by previous commentators, and as is confirmed by the fact that at the end of the chapter, at 1249^{b}25, he speaks of 'goods without qualification', when a few lines earlier he had spoken of natural goods (1249^{b}17); the run of the argument shows that the same class of goods must be intended in each case.

At ^{a}11, mention is made of things that are beneficial (*sumpheronta*) as if the class of natural goods were a sub-class of those good only instrumentally. It may seem that if something is good for some persons and in some circumstances only, this must be because it has beneficial consequences in some circumstances but not in all. But in view of his example of health (1248^{b}23) as a natural good, which he would certainly count as an intrinsic good, it is clear that natural goods are not to be found only among things that are instrumentally good. But it is difficult to see how there could be something which was intrinsically good, but only 'relative to someone', not in general. Thus, though not all natural goods are intrinsically good, the converse holds.

Unlike natural goods which are not commended, fine things are good in all circumstances. For the notion of 'complete virtue' see Commentary on II, 1219^{a}39.

1249^{a}15–16:   The statement that nobility is complete virtue serves to relate this chapter to the central themes of the *E.E.*

1249^{a}17-20

This summarizing passage offers some evidence of what has preceded in *E.E.* The discussion of what sort of thing pleasure is, and in what way it is a good does not occur in any part of the work that we have, apart from the disputed books. That the class of things that are pleasant without qualification coincides with the class of things good without qualification has been said at VII, 1235^{b}30–1236^{a}6,

1237^{a}4–9, 26–27. What is surprising is that he says that things that are pleasant without qualification will count as natural goods, but not satisfy the conditions for being fine.

In fact, it is doubtful if this section belongs here at all; ^{a}19–20 present an argument that is hardly intelligible as it stands, and is not related in any clear way to the main themes of this chapter, in which happiness is not otherwise mentioned. The thesis that pleasure does not occur except in action is not to be found in either of the discussions of pleasure in *E.N.* VII and X, and conflicts with the position taken there, unless 'action' (*praxis*) is understood in a wide sense as equivalent to 'activity'. If the passage does belong here, the reference to the *happy* (*eudaimōn*) person at ^{a}19 suggests that the fine-and-good man of this chapter is to be identified with him. See Monan, p. 125.

1249^{a}21–1249^{b}6

In this, the second part of this chapter, Aristotle discusses the standard for the use of those goods that count as natural goods but are therefore not fine (^{a}25). Who is envisaged as needing this standard? Is it the good man of 1248^{b}26–27 and 1249^{a}13, for whom the natural goods are in fact good, or is it the fine-and-good man, for whom they are also fine (cf. 1249^{a}5)? At ^{a}24, he says that a standard is needed by the good man (*spoudaios*), but the word used is different from that used at 1248^{b}26, 1249^{a}1, 13, and has therefore been translated 'virtuous'. The word *spoudaios* is the word regularly used for the good man (cf. II, 1219^{b}18, 25, 1228^{a}7, III, 1232^{b}7, VII, 1237^{a}8 (for the *spoudaios* the fine things are also pleasant), 1238^{b}3, 10, 13, 1244^{a}4, 5, 1245^{b}16), and there is no suggestion that there is anyone that Aristotle considers deserving of higher praise. If so, it is natural to regard this section as describing the standard which the fine-and-good man uses; and this is borne out by the last sentence of the chapter, 1249^{b}24–25. If that is correct, what Aristotle is doing here is saying how the fine-and-good man's use of natural goods is such that, in his hands, they also become fine; it in effect elaborates further the observation at 1249 ^{a}13–14 that the fine-and-good man performs many fine actions '*because* of them' (sc. natural goods).

An analogy with the doctor's use of medicaments (^{a}21–24) suggests that what is in question is the proper use of such assets as wealth or good fortune for someone who aspires to nobility of character; but it is clear that Aristotle has in mind also the pursuit and acquisition of such assets as wealth in the first place (cf. ^{b}1–3, 1249^{b}16). Since wealth is not a unqualified good, there are limits to be set to its pursuit; moreover the pursuit of one natural good may compete with the pursuit of another. It is worth noting that a parallel cannot arise for the things that he calls fine—the virtues and virtuous acts; it is not possible to have too much courage or justice, nor can virtue be used in the wrong way. Any employment whatever of a virtue is admirable: virtues lead only to virtuous action, and they are not, like technical skills 'capacities for opposites' (cf. *E.N.* V, 1129^a11-16). Both these propositions about virtues might be disputed by a modern reader. Is it not possible to cultivate generosity at the expense of a sense of justice, or prudence at the expense of resolution? And again, is any act manifesting generosity necessarily immune to criticism? To regard virtues in that way, as perhaps most of us should, is to treat them as natural goods, which are beneficial in most circumstances but not in all; it is also to concede that they may come into conflict: the action prompted by one virtue may conflict with that prompted by another. In *E.N.* VI, $1144^b32-1145^a2$, Aristotle unequivocally adopts the position that the various virtues (in the full sense) cannot be separated from one another; equally, since the possession of (e.g.) courage, in the full sense, involves practical wisdom, there can be no question of courage's prompting someone to make the wrong choice. So there is no need for a standard to be appealed to either in the acquisition or in the use of goods other than natural goods. Thus the latter part of this chapter presupposes a number of characteristic, and connected, Aristotelian doctrines about the virtues. Given these doctrines, it is reasonable that the need for a standard should be thought to arise only in the case of the natural goods. When something is recognized as a virtue, or a virtuous action, such recognition already embodies a standard, and thus does not, once recognized, need some further standard for its appraisal. On the other hand, the question still remains how fine states of character and actions are recognized as such, and to this no answer is offered. Is the standard introduced at the end of this chapter for the use and possession of natural goods also involved in the identification of virtues and actions? If not, what other standard is involved?

1249^b3-6:   Cf. *E.N.* VI, 1138^b21-34. $^b3$ presumably refers to II, 1222^b8 (cf. also 1222^a8). In the translation, the term *logos* has been taken as here meaning 'principle' or 'rule'. It has been held to refer to the faculty of reason. Here, at any rate, the former interpretation seems reasonably certain in view of the recurrence of the same word at $^b5$ in connection with the science of medicine. Verdenius ('Human Reason and Good', p. 286) says that the term here means not 'principle' or 'rule' or 'reason', but 'reasoning'. He cites in support II, 1227^b17 and *E.N.* III, 1114^b29. He may be right about the first of these passages; the second seems perfectly compatible with either of the two traditional renderings.

On this passage and its connection with the passage in *E.N.* VI, already mentioned, see Rowe, pp. 109 f. Does this passage answer the question asked at *E.N.* VI, 1138ᵇ34 'What is the limit (*horos*, i.e. standard) for states of the soul?' If so, then the question raised at the end of the general Commentary on this section is to be answered in the affirmative. Kenny (p. 183) notes that natural goods like wealth are the subject-matter or 'field' of three of the virtues described in *E.E.*; but the other three (courage, temperance, gentle temper) have certain affections as their subject-matter. He holds that Aristotle tells us what the *horos* integral to these virtues is at ᵇ22-24. But is that single sentence all that Aristotle thinks is needed as an answer to this very central question?

1249ᵇ6-25

This section raises major problems of interpretation. The main disagreement of commentators concerns what 'the god' at ᵇ14 and 17 refers to. On one interpretation, the reference is to the supreme divine being of Aristotle's metaphysics, the unmoved mover. The phrase that I have translated non-committally as 'the god' is one used to refer to the supreme divine being. It is thus interpreted by Verdenius (op. cit.) and Rowe (pp. 68 f.). Alternatively, Dirlmeier and Düring hold the reference is not to anything external to the human soul, but simply to theoretical reason, regarded as the divine element as it is in *E.N.* X (1177ᵃ15-16, 1179ᵃ26-27). The crucial passage is ᵇ9-16, as ᵇ16-23 can be interpreted in accordance with either view. It is not in dispute that in the latter section, Aristotle puts forward the activity of contemplation as providing a standard for the choice and possession of natural goods. In ᵇ6-9, he says that the governing element should be adopted as a standard for life, and in general where there are two elements, one naturally subordinate to the other, the subordinate should look to the governing thing in its behaviour (as illustrated by the example of the relation of slave and master, which, for Aristotle, stand in a relation of natural subordination to one another (cf. *Politics* I, 1254ᵃ13 f.)). He then says (ᵇ9) that since a human being (presumably, a human soul) is composed of a governing and subordinate element, each should live looking to what governs it. If 'each' means 'each of the two elements just mentioned' (viz. the governing and subordinate parts of the soul), as Verdenius holds, Aristotle is saying that the governing element must look to the thing which governs it (i.e. some *further* element). If so, it is readily intelligible that in the next few lines (ᵇ11-13), he distinguishes two kinds of governing or ruling, illustrated by medicine and health, the former of which governs medical practice, itself being subordinate to health, which governs it in another sense. But there is some awkwardness in describing the governing and subordinate elements in the soul as each *living*, at any rate if they are identified as the rational and non-rational parts of the soul already familiar from II (cf. 1219^b27 f.), the most natural identification since the language suggests an already established doctrine. Alternatively, 'each' means 'each of us', i.e. every human being; this interpretation is hardly ruled out by the fact that it has already been stated at ^b6–7, since, in the intervening lines it has been argued for on the basis of general doctrine. (It is taken thus by Solomon, Dirlmeier, and Rowe.)

As we have seen, in ^b11–13, Aristotle distinguishes different ways in which medicine and health each govern; medicine prescribes with a view to health, and health serves as a governing principle for medical practice. The same analogy occurs at *E.N.* VI, 1145^a6 f., where Aristotle is discussing practical wisdom. What practical wisdom issues instructions to is the non-rational part of the soul, or rather that part held to be receptive to such prescription, whose virtues are the virtues of character. The general picture of practical wisdom as issuing instructions to the non-rational part of the soul is characteristic also of *E.E.*; also, in *E.N.* VI there is a suggestion that practical wisdom, though it does not employ theoretical wisdom, *does* employ the virtues of character. Similar language occurs at 1246^b11, suggesting that the conception of the relation of practical wisdom to virtue of character that Aristotle has in this part of *E.E.* was not dissimilar to that to be found in *E.N.* VI.

This passage in *E.N.* VI might suggest that Aristotle is here saying that, just as medical science and health are, in different ways, governing factors, so are practical wisdom and theoretical wisdom. But, though practical wisdom is mentioned at ^b14, theoretical wisdom is not mentioned at all. At ^b13, we have a reference to 'the speculative', but the reference must be to a part of the soul. The exact interpretation of the vague remark 'thus it is with the speculative (part)' must await further discussion of the immediate context; but *E.N.* VI would suggest a reference to *part* of the rational soul, that involved in speculation (*theoria*), as distinct from that part whose virtue is practical wisdom.

Aristotle goes on to offer as a reason for his observation about 'the speculative' that the god governs not in a prescriptive fashion, but as that for whose sake practical wisdom prescribes. There is a reference to a distinction of two senses of 'that for which'. Other passages in which such a distinction is made are *Physics* II 194^a35, *De Anima* II 415^b2, 20, and *Metaphysics* Λ 1072^b2 f. From these it is reasonably clear what Aristotle has in mind. In the *De Anima* passage he says: 'It is the most natural function in living things . . . to produce another thing like themselves . . . in order that they may partake of the everlasting and divine; for all desire that, and for the sake of that they do whatever they do in accordance with nature. (But that for the sake of which is two-fold – the purpose for which and the beneficiary for whom) (ibid., 415^{a}26–^{b}2, Hamlyn's translation). '. . . all natural bodies are instruments for soul, and, just as it is with those of animals, so it is with those plants also, showing that they exist for the sake of the soul. But that for the sake of which is spoken of in two ways . . .' (ibid., 415^{b}18–21). What emerges is that X may be 'that for which' in relation to Y in one sense if Y exists (or acts) for X's benefit, in another if Y is an end or standard by reference to which X acts.

In ^{b}14, the god is said to be 'that for which practical wisdom prescribes'. It is fairly clear that the remark that the god has need of nothing has to be taken with the parenthetical observations about the two senses of 'that for which': it certainly does not support the remark that the god is the thing for the sake of which practical wisdom acts (since it could be that in *one* sense, even if it were capable of being a beneficiary), but it does support the unexpressed assertion that it is the thing for the sake of which in the sense which does *not* involve being a beneficiary. The distinction of ^{b}15 is relevant only to make clear the sense in which the god is that for the sake of which practical wisdom acts.

Now health is likewise said to be that for the sake of which medicine prescribes (^{b}12), again evidently in the non-beneficiary sense; further, in ^{b}13–14, it is said that the god governs in a non-prescriptive fashion, whereas practical wisdom prescribes. As that is offered in support of the remark about 'the speculative part' (itself connected with a distinction of two sorts of governing), the god and practical wisdom must be said each to govern in two senses, and these will parallel the two senses of 'that for which' and be illustrated by the different ways in which medicine and health are said to govern: medicine and health are related to one another in a way at least partly analogous to the way that practical wisdom and the god are related. Further, though this is not said explicitly, practical wisdom governs the non-rational part of the soul and its virtues while being itself subordinate to and governed by the thing referred to as 'the god'. Thus practical wisdom governs one thing and is subordinate to something else.

So much seems reasonably certain. Since three things are in play from ^{b}11 onwards, one of them at the same time governing and subordinate, what are the governing and subordinate elements of ^{b}10? If the two things mentioned are practical wisdom and the non-rational part of the soul, 'the god' will be that to which practical wisdom refers in ruling over the non-rational part of the soul. On one view, this is the higher of the two parts of the rational part of the soul, the part that is referred to as 'the better part' in the passage already quoted from *E.N.* VI, c. 13. On this view, that will be the reference of 'the speculative part' in ^{b}13, and he will then be saying that speculative reason (and its activities) will be that for whose sake practical wisdom prescribes, in just the way that medicine prescribes for the sake of health. What is called 'the speculative part' at ^{b}13 is thus, on this view, identical with what is called in this passage 'the god'. As we have already observed, 'the speculative (part)' is most naturally taken to refer to part only of the rational part of the soul.

The alternative, still taking the governing and subordinate elements of ^{b}10 to be practical wisdom and the non-rational part of the soul, is to suppose that by 'the god' Aristotle means God. God serves as a standard for practical wisdom because the standard it uses, elaborated in ^{b}16–24, is given by the end of enabling human reason to engage in that activity in which it approximates as closely as possible to the divine, just as in *De Anima* immortality served as an end to which animals seek to approximate by reproducing their kind. On this view, at ^{b}13, he is saying that the speculative (part of the soul) is like medicine in governing while itself being subject to a higher standard. 'The speculative part' will be simply the whole rational part of the soul, which is thought of as the source of speculation, but also as issuing commands to the non-rational soul through practical wisdom. Thus there is not the distinction between the two parts of the rational soul that is drawn in *E.N.* VI (cf. especially 1139^{a}6 f.) and a single faculty is represented as responsible both for speculation and for controlling desires. This interpretation is favoured by Verdenius and Rowe.

Dirlmeier adopts the first alternative, that 'the god' is the highest element in the human soul, the part of the rational soul that is the source of the activity of contemplation, but unlike the interpretation mentioned above, supposes that the governing and subordinate elements of ^{b}10 are practical wisdom and theoretical reason; as we have seen, on any view, practical wisdom governs one thing and is subordinate to another. This interpretation is open to strong objections, apart from those already mentioned to the identification of theoretical wisdom with the divine element in the soul. At 1249^{b}10, the proposition that the human soul comprises a governing and a subordinate element is presented as if it were an accepted doctrine, to which Aristotle could appeal; and, whereas the notion that practical wisdom prescribes to the non-rational soul has been a pervasive theme of II, there is no clear mention of the subordination of practical wisdom to theoretical reason earlier in the *E.E.*, outside the disputed books. The decisive difficulty, pointed out by Verdenius, is that Aristotle at ^{b}9–10 says that a *human being* comprises a governing and subordinate element, whereas if Dirlmeier were right he should have said that the *rational soul* comprises these elements. Another difficulty is that Dirlmeier relies on the treatment of the rational soul in *E.N.* VI, but has to treat practical wisdom as if it were a part of the soul, whereas in *E.N.* VI it is a virtue of one part of the rational soul. However, as we have seen, it is not necessary to interpret ^{b}10 along Dirlmeier's lines in order to adopt his understanding of the phrase 'the god'.

On any view, ^{b}16–23 enunciate a standard for the fine-and-good man's choice and possession of natural goods which requires that reference be made to the activity of speculation: whatever promotes it is good, whatever hinders it is bad. But how ^{b}17–^{b}20 are interpreted in detail will depend on how the references to the divine are understood. On Dirlmeier's view, in the phrase 'the speculation of the god', the dependent phrase is a subjective one: the divine part of the soul is the subject of the activity of speculation, and 'speculation' has to be taken intransitively. On the Verdenius–Rowe view, in ^{b}17 'speculation of the god' has to be taken as referring to contemplation which has the god as its object, and in ^{b}20 both 'serve' and 'speculate' have 'the god' as their grammatical objects. It is doubtful if there are strong linguistic grounds in ^{b}16–23 for preferring one interpretation of the references to the divine to the other, so this issue must be resolved on the basis of more general considerations.

In favour of Dirlmeier's view are
(i) the passages in *E.N.* X in which human reason is spoken of as the divine element in the human soul; and
(ii) certain passages which, Dirlmeier claims, use 'the god' as a designation of human reason. The passages in question are *Politics* III, 1287^{a}28–31 and *Protrepticus* 10^c Ross (= B 108 – 110 Düring).

But neither gives the support required. In the *Politics* passage, Aristotle says: 'He who recommends that the law should govern seems to recommend that God and reason should govern ...' But there is clearly no need to suppose that 'God' and 'reason' refer to the same thing. In the *Protrepticus* passage all he says is that man seems like a god in comparison with other creatures because of his possession of reason. Moreover, there remains the difficulty of supposing that Aristotle, without explanation, should have used such a phrase as a designation of human reason.

Dirlmeier points out that Aristotle recommends *service* of the god at ^{b}20, whereas his unmoved mover is self-sufficient. If it is a difficulty at all, it is a difficulty for any view that we are exhorted to serve the same thing as has at ^{b}16 been said to be self-sufficient. In fact, there is no need to interpret 'service' too literally. One difficulty for Dirlmeier is that it seems strange to describe human reason as needing nothing. In order to deal with this, he draws a distinction between positive goods, which reason does not need, and absence of hindrance. But that distinction is not in the text, and the language of ^{b}17 suggests that external goods promote the activity of speculation in a more positive way. Moreover, as we have seen, the remark that the god needs nothing must be understood as excluding it from being a beneficiary. This seems to rule out human reason as the referent of the phrase 'the god', for human reason surely *can* be regarded as a beneficiary of the right use of natural goods mentioned in the concluding sentences of the chapter. On this section see, further, Kenny, pp. 174 f.

NOTES ON THE TEXT AND TRANSLATION

In these Notes I have not mentioned emendations adopted in Suse-mihl's Teubner edition and generally accepted subsequently: the intention has been to make clear to any reader using either Susemihl's or Rackham's Greek text what readings have been adopted in the text used for translation. In accordance with normal practice, square brackets indicate excisions of words occurring in the manuscripts, angle brackets material introduced by emendation. The use of the latter is thus different from that made in the Commentary. In the Notes on Book VIII, Chapter 2, the reference to 'the Latin tradition' is to the so-called *De Bona Fortuna*, a Latin version of *Eudemian Ethics* VIII, c. 2 and *Magna Moralia* B, c. 3. Textual proposals made by W. D. Ross and R. Walzer have been marked 'R/W'; 'D. A. F. M. R.' indicates suggestions made by Mr Donald Russell.

BOOK ONE

1214ª11-12: Reading περὶ τὰς κτήσεις καὶ περὶ πράξεις [τοῦ πράγματος].

1214ª13-14: This has been taken as saying simply that problems of theoretical philosophy will be dealt with when their turn comes (i.e. they will not be dealt with in the course of an ethical inquiry). This seems to make rather a lame point, as the passage already pre-supposes the separation of theoretical and practical philosophy. (Cf. Gigon, pp. 97 f.) It seems to be better to construe the sentence as enunciating a methodological principle—one which corresponds to Aristotle's practice—that, in the course of a practical inquiry, matters of a theoretical kind are to be introduced only when they are rel-evant. Cf. *E.N.* I, 1102ª18-28.

On this, see also Rowe, p. 15 and Kenny. I have read ὅτιπερ <ἂν> οἰκεῖον ᾖ (MSS ἦν) τῇ μεθοδῷ.

1214ª18-19: ὡς οὔσης ἐπιστήμης τινος τῆς εὐδαιμονίας With Solomon and Dirlmeier, I have taken εὐδαιμονίας as subject and ἐπιστήμης as complement. An alternative, taken by Rackham, is to construe οὔσης existentially, and make εὐδαιμονίας depend upon ἐπιστήμης ('... there being a science of happiness').

1214^{a}26: Reading ἠ ταύτης παρουσία.

1214^{b}6-14: The reading of the MSS, adopted by Susemihl, raises difficulties both of syntax and sense. Without emendation there are two alternatives: (i) Inserting no comma after ἐπιστήσαντας, construe θέσθαι as an accusative and infinitive depending on it, so that the main clause begins only at μάλιστα δή. It would then be translated: 'On this matter, taking note of the fact that everyone, . . . adopts . . . , we must first, and above all, define . . .' This is open to the following objections: (a) The use of ἐπιστήσαντας (sc. τὴν διάνοιαν) with a dependent accusative and infinitive is doubtful Greek; (b) μάλιστα δή introducing a main clause is unusual; (c) The sense expressed on this interpretation is that everyone does in fact set up some aim to pursue in his life, which is unplausible in itself, and not something we should expect Aristotle to assert. (In fact, ὡς τό γ' . . . ἐστιν, ^{b}9–11 suggests that some foolish people fail to do this). (ii) Taking θέσθαι as part of the main clause, a comma may be inserted after ἐπιστήσαντας, and θέσθαι, made to depend on δεῖ in ^{b}11. He will then be saying that everyone should adopt a final end, not that everyone in fact does. The fact that δεῖ comes so much later on in the sentence is unfortunate, and Gigon may be right in inserting δεῖ before θέσθαι, a reading that has some MS support. I have followed this alternative in the translation. On (i), ἐπιστήσαντας has to be taken as an accusative absolute. It is possible to do the same on alternative (ii), but it is also possible to take ἐπιστήσαντας as a participal phrase, dependent on ἅπαντα, but in the plural because of the sense of ἅπαντα (everyone, having taken note of these things, should . . .'). My translation is intended to preserve the ambiguity of the Greek.

1214^{b}18: Reading τῆς <καλῆς> ζωῆς or something similar, following Gigon.

1215^{a}2: I have translated καὶ μάλιστα περὶ <ταύτης, ἀλλὰ τὰς τῶν ἐπιεικῶν> μόνας. See Dirlmeier, and Gigon. With this reading, ταύτας in ^{a}5 should be taken as referring back to τάς τῶν ἐπιεικῶν rather than the ἀπορίαι mentioned in 3-4.

1215^{a}8-9: I have translated ἔτι δὲ προέργου τὰ τοιαῦτα μὴ λανθάνειν, μάλιστα <δὲ> πρὸς ὅ (MSS ἅ).

1215^{a}28-32: Reading τῶν περὶ τὰς τέχνας τὰς φορτικὰς καὶ τὰς περὶ χρηματισμόν and in 31 χρηματιστικὰς δὲ τὰς πρὸς ἀγοράσεις καὶ πράσεις καπηλικάς R/W.

1216ᵃ2:　Reading ⟨μᾶλλον⟩ ἐξουσιάζει πολλῶν μοναρχῶν.

1216ᵇ18-19:　Alternatively, '. . . health is different from medicine, good government, or something of the sort, is different from political science.'

1216ᵇ37:　Reading τῷ πολιτικῷ (MSS τῶν πολιτικῶν) (R/W).

1217ᵃ20:　Reading ζητοῦντες [ἐπὶ τὸ] σαφῶς εὑρεῖν.

1217ᵃ33:　Reading ὥστε οὐδὲ ⟨πρακ⟩ τῶν ἀγαθῶν (D.A.F.M. R.). Rassow, followed by Allan (1971, p. 65) emends τῶν ἀγαθῶν to πράξεως which' is less easy palaeographically. With the MSS reading two interpretations are possible: (i) 'Some things do not participate in change, so some goods do not, either.' (ii) 'Some things do not participate in change, so they (sc. those things) do not participate in goods either.' (i) is intelligible, but involves an immediate inference that requires justification; (ii) is accepted by Dirlmeier, but is in conflict with the suggestion in the next sentence.

1217ᵇ24-25:　Reading οὐδὲν (MSS οὐδὲ) χρήσιμοι (MSS χρήσιμος) ⟨εἰσι⟩.

1217ᵇ30:　Aristotle says that ἐν ἑκάστῃ τῶν πτώσεών ἐστι τοῦτο. The word πτῶσις is used of the inflexions or cases of a noun but here it seems merely a variant of κατηγορία, and I have translated accordingly. The closest parallel is *Metaphysics* N 1089ᵃ27 (on which see Ross's notes) in which it clearly also has the meaning of 'category'.

1218ᵃ14-15:　The text with the supplementation made by Rassow, Susemihl, Rackham, and Solomon runs: οὐδὲ ⟨τὸ ἀγαθὸν μᾶλλον ἀγαθὸν τῷ ἀίδιον εἶναι οὐδὲ⟩ δὴ τὸ κοινὸν ἀγαθὸν ταὐτὸ τῇ ἰδέᾳ. For reasons given in the Commentary, I think more has dropped out. The argument would be intelligible with some such sentence as ἀλλ' ἦν ἄριστον πάντων ἡ ἰδέα before οὐδὲ δή.

1218ᵃ20:　Reading τἀγαθοῦ ὑπάρχοντος (MSS ἀγαθὸν ὑπάρχον) (D. A. F. M. R.).

1218ᵃ26:　Reading οὔτε γὰρ πῶς (MSS ὡς) ἐφίενται (R/W).

1218ᵃ34: Reading καὶ ἔτι (MSS ὅτι) οὐ χρήσιμον.

1218ᵃ38: Reading αὐτὸ <τ> ἀγαθόν.

1218ᵇ5-6: Reading πρακτὸν δέ τὸ τοιοῦτον ἀγαθὸν, τὸ οὗ ἔνεκα οὐκ ἔστι δὲ τοῦτο (MSS τὸ) ἐν ἀκινήτοις.

1218ᵇ21: Reading καίτοι (MSS καὶ τότε) (R/W).

BOOK TWO

1219ᵃ19: Reading λέγωμεν (MSS λέγομεν) ὅτι <ταὐτὸ> τὸ ἔργον τοῦ πράγματος καὶ τῆς ἀρετῆς (D. A. F. M. R.).

1219ᵃ24: Reading ἔτι ἔστω ψυχῆς ἔργον τὸ ζῆν ποιεῖν, τοῦτο (MSS τοῦ) δὲ χρῆσις καὶ ἐγρήγορσις. Keeping the MSS reading, Aristotle will be saying that the ἔργον of the soul is to produce life, and the ἔργον of living is, in its turn, an employment and waking state. What seems to be needed is some premiss applying the doctrine that, in the case of some things, their ἔργον is their χρῆσις itself, and not something over and above it, to the case of the soul. Kenny (p. 199, note 1) translates 'Let us take leave to posit that the *ergon* of soul is life', appealing to the use of ἔστι to mean 'it is possible'. This makes the argument smoother, but this interpretation of ἔστω . . . ποιεῖν is hard in the absence of parallels.

1219ᵃ30: Reading <τὰ ἐν> αὐτῇ (MSS αὐτή or αὕτη) . . . ἢ ἕξεις (MSS ἕξις) ἢ ἐνέργειαι (MSS ἐνέργεια) (R/W).

1219ᵃ33-34: Reading <ἡ> βελτίστη ἕξις, <δεῖ τὴν> τῆς ἀρετῆς ἐνέργειαν <τὸ> τῆς ψυχῆς (R/W).

1219ᵇ3-4: Where Aristotle says καὶ γὰρ ἡ πρακτικὴ χρηστική ἐστιν, I have taken πρακτική as referring to ζωή, following Solomon and Dirlmeier. The alternative of supplying ἐπιστήμη, in view of the following references to particular skills, is open to the objection that, despite the puzzling features mentioned in the Commentary, we seem to have an argument for the proposition that the life of (virtuous) action is an employment.

1219ᵇ15-16: Reading ἐγκώμιον λόγος τοῦ καθ' ἕκαστον ἔργου, ὁ
δ' ἔπαινος <τοῦ> τοιοῦτον εἶναι καθόλου, ὁ δ' εὐδαιμονισμὸς τέλους.
With Bonitz's insertion of τοῦ, one gets a construction parallel with
that of the previous sentence. Otherwise one has to understand
λέγει with ἔπαινος instead of λόγος ἐστιν. τέλους in line 16 represents Bonitz's emendation of the MSS τέλος. This emendation
produces a sense that is in line with a central thought of this passage,
that happiness is the ultimate end.

1219ᵇ36: Reading ἀλλὰ κατὰ συμβεβηκὸς καὶ οὐκ οὐσίᾳ τὸ αὐτὸ
(MSS τοῦ αὐτοῦ).

1219ᵇ36-1220ᵃ2: Reading ἀφῄρηται δὲ καὶ εἴ ἄλλο ἐστι μέρος
τῆς ψυχῆς, οἷον τὸ φυτικόν, ἀνθρωπίνης δὲ ψυχῆς τὰ εἰρημένα
μόρια ἴδια. (διὸ οὐδ' αἱ ἀρεταὶ αἱ τοῦ θρεπτικοῦ καὶ αὐξητικοῦ). δεῖ
γάρ, εἰ <ἀνθρώπου> ἦ ἄνθρωπος, λογισμὸν ἐνεῖναι ὡς ἀρχὴν
πράξεως (MSS καὶ ἀρχὴν καὶ πρᾶξιν), ἄρχει δ' λογισμὸς οὐ λογισμοῦ
ἀλλ' ὀρέξεως καὶ παθημάτων· ἀνάγκη ἄρα ταῦτ' ἔχειν τὰ μέρη.
This involves amending φυσικόν to φυτικού, an emendation generally
accepted, on the strength of E.N. I 1102ᵃ32, the only other occurrence
of word in Aristotle, and in view of the fact that φυσικόν has no
apparent sense as a designation of a part of the soul. The first clause
then becomes virtually concessive: 'Any other part of the soul that
there is has been excluded, but the parts we have mentioned are
necessary'. The alternatives in ᵇ38-9 mentioned in the Commentary
there are (i) θρεπτικοῦ καὶ ὀρεκτικοῦ (ii) θρεπτικοῦ καὶ αὐξητικοῦ
(iii) θρεπτικοῦ (iv) ὀρεκτικοῦ.

1220ᵃ7-8: Reading ταῦτα δ' οὐκ ἐνέργειαι (MSS ἐνεργεῖ) (R/W).

1220ᵃ14: The meaning of εἰς τοῦτο γὰρ ἀνῆκται is not immediately
clear. The most closely parallel use of ἀνάγειν in E.E. seems to be at
1225ᵃ25. I have translated as if the point is that what virtue is depends
on what its constituents are, but Solomon's 'our enquiry has been
forced on this' may be correct.

1220ᵃ18: The MSS gave ὥσπερ ἀν εἰ καὶ ὑγίειαν. Most editors
have supposed a lacuna after εἰ in order to complete the sense. I
have translated as if Spengel's εἰδείημεν had stood in the lacuna.

1220ᵃ21: Reading αὐτοῖν (MSS αὐτῆς).

1220ᵃ33-34: Reading and punctuating as follows: ... καὶ φθείρεται· πρὸς ἃ <καὶ> βέλτιστα διατίθησιν.

1220ᵃ34-37: For a parallel to this use of σημεῖον ὅτι ... γάρ, see *Politics* VIII, 1338ᵇ42.

1220ᵃ39-ᵇ3: I have translated the following text: ἐπεὶ δ᾿ ἐστὶ τὸ ἦθος, ὥσπερ καὶ τὸ ὄνομα σημαίνει, ὅτι ἀπὸ ἔθους ἔχει τὴν ἐπίδοσιν, ἐθίζεται δὲ τὸ ὑπ᾿ ἀγωγῆς μὴ ἐμφύτου, τῷ πολλάκις κινεῖσθαί πως, οὕτως ἤδη [τὸ] ἐνεργητικόν. This is the same as that proposed by Ross (1915), and involves only the excision of τό at ᵇ3, and appropriate punctuation. There is a mild anacolouthon – a long ἐπεί clause ending with a parenthetical remark, followed by a main clause introduced by διό. The crucial point is the interpretation of ἐνεργητικόν and the preceding οὕτω ἤδη, as the main ground for holding ἦθος to be a ποιότης must occur in that part of the sentence. The word ἐνεργητικόν occurs elsewhere only at *Physics* III, 202ᵃ17 (= *Metaphysics* K 1066ᵃ31) where Aristotle argues that, where one thing acts on something else, there is a single actualization, both of the potentiality for acting in the one thing and of being acted on in the other; there the active party to the transaction is said to be ἐνεργητικὸν τοῦ κινητοῦ. This suggests that the word means something like 'capable of initiating activity'.

1220ᵇ5-6: With Ross, I have read διὸ ἔστω ἦθος τοῦτο, ψυχῆς κατ᾿ ἐπιτακτικὸν λόγον <τοῦ ἀλόγου μὲν>, δυναμένου δ᾿ ἀκολουθεῖν τῷ λόγῳ ποιότης. As Ross points out, τοῦτο can be retained if a comma is inserted after it.

1220ᵇ7: Reading κατὰ τί τῆς ψυχῆς ποῖ᾿ ἄττα τὰ ἤθη.

1220ᵇ9-10: The MSS have πρὸς τὰ πάθη ταῦτα λέγονται τῷ πάσχειν πως ἢ ἀπαθεῖς εἶναι which Dirlmeier regards as acceptable. But if ἢ ἀπαθεῖς εἶναι is treated as part of the τῷ-clause, Aristotle will not say *what* is said of human beings on the strength of these dispositions, hence ἢ ἀπαθεῖς εἶναι must depend on λέγονται and an alternative supplied, with a lacuna supposed either before or after. I have translated as if it were followed by ἢ μή, but if there is a lacuna, it is impossible to reconstruct the text with much confidence.

1220ᵇ11: ἐν τοῖς ἀπηλλαγμένοις: this reading is the closest to the unintelligible ἀπηλαγμένοις of the MSS. It seems clear, however, that the three genitives depend on διαίρεσις, and the ἐν τοῖς ἀπηλλαγμένοις phrase refers to an earlier work of Aristotle containing a relevant description of psychic phenomena, which he proposes to take over for use in the present argument. The translation is intended to follow Dirlmeier's explanation of the meaning of the phrase. See his 'Merkwürdige Zitate', and von Fragstein, pp. 64 f. Compare *E.N.* I, 1102ª26-27.

1220ᵇ16-17:   Reading <οἱ> κατὰ τὰ πάθη [οἱ] ἐνεργοῦντες (R/W).

1221ª19-21:   The text I have translated is: ὁμοίως δὲ καὶ [ὁ] ἀκόλαστος [καὶ] ὁ ἐπιθυμητικὸς <οὗ μὴ δεῖ> καὶ [ὁ] ὑπερβάλλων πᾶσιν ὅσοις ἐνδέχεται. Parallelism with the other descriptions of unvirtuous states, and in particular the ἀναίσθητος in ª21-23, requires that ἀκόλαστος be the predicate and that the subject identify a particular type of person. The insertion of οὗ μὴ δεῖ, proposed by E. R. Dodds, is suggested by μηδ' ὅσον βέλτιον in ª21-22.

1221ª24:   I have translated ὁ μηδαμόθεν ἢ ὀλιγαχόθεν with Dirlmeier.

1221ᵇ11:   κατὰ τὴν ὑπερβολὴν ἢ χρόνου ἢ τοῦ μᾶλλον ἢ πρός τι I have, following Dirlmeier, treated the last phrase as governed directly by κατὰ (i.e. κατὰ τὸ πρός τι); alternatively, with Solomon, we may take it as depending on ὑπερβολὴν. Neither is entirely easy, and Ross has held that the text is corrupt. For the implication of the two alternatives for Aristotle's position, see Commentary.

1221ᵇ19:   Reading ἂν <τὸ> πῶς λαμβάνηται ὡς τὸ (MSS τῷ) μᾶλλον πάσχειν.

1221ᵇ21:   Reading μοχθηρία τις αὐτὴ <ἢ> δη ἐστιν.

1221ᵇ26:   Reading ὁμοίως δὲ ἔχει [ἐπὶ] τὰ ἄλλα τὰ τοιαῦτα. (R/W).

1221ᵇ32:   Inserting ἠθικαί after ἔχοντος δ' ὄρεξιν (οὐ γὰρ ... ἐστιν) with Kapp. This will parallel διανοητικαί in ᵇ29, and seems to be necessary, given that what we have is a recapitulation of 1220ª5, and that the connection between this class of virtues and ἤθη is an essential link in the argument.

1221ᵇ35–36: Reading αἱ μὲν γὰρ δυνάμεις καὶ αἱ ἕξεις τοῖς παθή-μασιν, emending τῶν παθημάτων to τοῖς παθήμασιν with Ross, and taking τοῖς παθήμασιν with διώρισται. With the MSS reading an ἐστι has to be supplied in the μέν -clause.

1221ᵇ39–1222ᵃ1: Reading πάσης γὰρ ψυχῆς (variant reading πᾶσα . . . ψυχή) <ἕξις>, ὑφ᾽ οἵων πέφυκε γένεσθαι χείρων καὶ βελτίων, πρὸς ταῦτα καὶ περὶ ταῦτά ἐστιν ἡ φύσις (MSS ἡδονή) as proposed by Allan. This maximizes the similarity to E.N. II 1104ᵇ18–28, a closely parallel context. The argument applies a general proposition about ἕξεις to the case of virtue, so ἕξις must be introduced somewhere.

1222ᵃ10–11: Reading τὴν ἠθικὴν ἀρετὴν καθ᾽ αὑτὴν ἑκάστην (MSS καθ᾽ αὑτὸν ἕκαστον) μεσότητα εἶναι καὶ (MSS ἤ) περὶ μεσ᾽ ἄττα (R/W).

1222ᵃ17–18: Reading ἐπεὶ δ᾽<οὐκ> ἔστι τις ἕξις ἀφ᾽ ἧς τοιοῦτος ἔσται ὁ ἔχων αὐτὴν ὥστε . . . as suggested by E. R. Dodds.

1222ᵃ19: Retaining the οὗ μέν . . . οὗ δέ of the MSS. Bonitz's alteration to ὁ μὲν . . . ὁ δέ, accepted by Susemihl, seems unnecessary, if we regard it as equivalent to ἔνθα μὲν . . . ἔνθα δέ.

1222ᵃ25: Reading οὐκ ἀεὶ ἐπὶ ταὐτὰ ἡ ἀνισότης ἢ ὁμοιότης πρὸς τὸ μέσον (MSS ἀνισότητος ἢ ὁμοιότητος). The correct text is not recoverable with certainty, but the general sense is clear in this passage, which closely parallels E.N. II 1108ᵇ30 f.

1222ᵃ31–34: Reading ὥστε καὶ αἱ προαιρετικαὶ ἕξεις [αἱ φιλογυ-μναστικαὶ φιλο] ὑγιεῖς μᾶλλον ἔσονται καθ᾽ ἑκατέραν τὴν αἵρεσιν, – ἔνθα μὲν οἱ πολυπονώτεροι, ἔνθα δ᾽ οἱ ὑποστατικώτεροι.

1222ᵇ4: The MSS have διὸ καὶ οὐ κολακικὸν ὁ θυμός ('That is why anger is not given to flattery'). This hardly seems to fit the context, and the word κολακικός is not found elsewhere in Aristotle. Various emendations have been proposed, but certainty is unattainable. Dirlmeier proposes [οὐ] κολαστικὸν ὁ θυμός (which I have accepted) referring to 1221ᵇ15, Topics 156ᵃ31, Rhetoric 1378ᵃ30, and On Virtues and Vices 1251ᵃ5 and ᵇ32, where a tendency to retaliation is said to be characteristic of anger. The thought will presumably be, if so, that, since we tend to go to excess in the case of anger, we have a tendency to act in ways characteristic of that excess.

1222ᵇ5-7: The MSS have ἐπεὶ δ' εἴληπται ἡ διαλογὴ τῶν ἕξεων καθ' ἕκαστα τὰ πάθη, καὶ αἱ ὑπερβολαὶ καὶ αἱ ἐλλείψεις, καὶ τῶν ἐναντίων ἕξεων, καθ' ἃς ἔχουσι κατὰ τὸν ὀρθὸν λόγον. καὶ . . . ἐλλείψεις is difficult if τῶν ἐναντίων ἕξεων is to be made to depend on διαλογή. Bonitz, followed by Dirlmeier, claimed that the text may stand if τῶν ἐναντίων ἕξεων is made to depend instead on αὗται, to be supplied with καθ' ἃς . . . λόγον, which will be coordinate with καὶ . . . ἐλλείψεις, and, like that phrase, in apposition to ἡ διαλογὴ τῶν ἕξεων. I have followed this in the translation.

1222ᵇ13-14: Reading δῆλον τοίνυν ὅτι [αἱ] ἀρεταὶ ἢ πᾶσαι ἤ τινες (MSS τούτων τινες) ἔσονται τῶν μεσοτήτων.

1222ᵇ18: Omitting ὄν after ζῷον, as a dittography, as suggested by Susemihl.

1222ᵇ21-24: Aristotle says τῶν ἀρχῶν ὅσαι τοιαῦται, ὅθεν πρῶτον αἱ κινήσεις, κύριαι λέγονται . . . ἐν δὲ ταῖς ἀκινήτοις ἀρχαῖς, οὐκ ἔστι τὸ κύριον. Both Solomon and Dirlmeier suppose that, with these uses of κύριος Aristotle is singling out those ἀρχαί that are so called in a strict sense, i.e. those that produce κίνησις. This involves seeing no connection between this use of the term and its later use at 1223ᵃ5 and 7. κύριαι λέγονται seems to be an inappropriate way of saying what would be more naturally expressed by κυρίως <ἀρχαὶ> λέγονται, nor is οὐκ ἔστι τὸ κύριον readily interpretable as οὐκ εἰσιν ἀρχαὶ κυρίως λεγόμεναι. A further problem with the alternative view is that it seems inappropriate for Aristotle to explain the notion of an ἀρχή in general, as he does at ᵇ29-41, by reference to what is not strictly an ἀρχή at all. With the use of τὸ κύριον here, compare *Metaphysics* Θ 1048ᵃ10. My view is accepted in Heath, p. 279.

1223ᵃ2-3: Reading καὶ [ὃ] ἐφ' αὑτοῖς ἐστι τοῖς ἀνθρώποις πολλὰ τῶν τοιούτων R/W).

1223ᵃ10-11: Reading ψέγεται γὰρ καὶ ἐπαινεῖται οὐ [διὰ] τὰ ἐξ ἀνάγκης . . . (Fritzsche, R/W).

1223ᵃ30:   The emendation mentioned in the Commentary, proposed by Urmson, involves reading: τὸ γὰρ ἀκούσιον πᾶν δοκεῖ εἶναι βίαιον, τὸ δὲ βίαιον ἀκούσιον, καὶ λυπηρὸν καὶ πᾶν ὃ ἀναγκαζόμενοι ποιοῦσιν ἢ πάσχουσιν.

1223ᵇ11:   Reading καὶ μᾶλλον τοῦ ἀκρατοῦς for μᾶλλον τῆς ἀκρασίας, an emendation first suggested by Solomon and accepted by Ross. Even if the MS reading is retained, the general sense must be the same.

1223ᵇ24-25:   Reading εἰ δὲ ἀδύνατον τὸ αὐτὸ <τὸν αὐτὸν> ... πράττειν ἅμα [τὸ] <καὶ> κατὰ τὸ αὐτό (Bonitz).

1223ᵇ39-1224ᵃ1:   Reading τὸ μὲν γὰρ κατὰ βούλησιν οὐχ ὡς ἀκούσιον ἀπεδείχθη with Rassow. The MSS have ὡς οὐκ ἀκούσιον defended by Dirlmeier. But apart from the reason given in the Commentary, that the thesis has not been proved, but only left unchallenged by the preceding argument, ᵃ2-3 follows more naturally if preceded by a remark to the effect that something else has not been demonstrated. Also, ᵃ1-2 ἀλλὰ μᾶλλον πᾶν ὃ βούλεται καὶ ἀκούσιον seems to fit better with the reading I have adopted.

1224ᵃ18:   Reading ὅταν κατὰ τὴν φύσιν (variant reading, adopted by Susemihl, φύσει).

1224ᵃ29-30:   Reading ἀλλὰ τὸν ἤδη διὰ λογισμὸν πράττοντα with Jackson, Bender, and Susemihl. The MSS have ἀλλὰ ὅταν ἤδη, which, apart from grammatical difficulties, would imply, contrary to Aristotle's doctrines, that animals acquire λόγος. It is impossible to reconstruct the text with certainty, but the meaning is reasonably clear.

1224ᵃ34-35:   ἀπὸ τῶν ἡδέων ἐπιθυμιῶν. This is the reading of the MSS. I have translated ἡδέων as a neuter plural, governed by ἐπιθυμιῶν since the notion of pleasant desires is hardly appropriate.

1224ᵇ1:   Reading ἐφ' ἃ πέπεισται [ἄγει καὶ] πορεύεται as suggested to me by Lesley Brown. ἄγει could easily have crept in from ᵇ2.

1224ᵇ2-3:   The MSS have ὅτι μὲν οὖν δοκοῦσιν οὗτοι μόνοι βίᾳ καὶ ἄκοντες ποιεῖν which is open to the objection that no argument has been presented for the proposition that the continent and the incontinent are the *only* people to act under compulsion. Dirlmeier's suggestion, keeping the MS reading, that μόνοι here means 'in a striking way' is open to the objection that this too goes beyond what has actually been said. At ᵇ3-5, Aristotle says that the reason for this appearance is a similarity with what is done under compulsion, which suggests that the continent and incontinent appear only to resemble (genuine) cases of involuntary action, not to be cases of it. If so, Jackson's μόνον οὐ gives an appropriate sense, and I have adopted it (*Journal of Philology*, 1913).

1224ᵇ5-7: Susemihl's text runs εἴ τις προσθῇ τὸ ἐν τῷ διορισμῷ προσκείμενον, κἀκεῖ λύεται τὸ λεχθέν. With this, the reference of τῷ διορισμῷ is far from clear, and there is the further suggestion that the solution to the problem of the ἀκρατής and ἐγκρατής is a solution to a *further* problem (καί), which is a little strange. Following Dirlmeier, I place a comma before λύεται and replace κἀκεῖ by ἐκεῖ. The reference will be to 1224ᵃ23. The sentence is still puzzling, however: in view of the reference to inanimate objects at ᵇ5, one would expect the reference to be to the definition of compulsion for the case of inanimate objects; but (at 1224ᵃ18-19) there is no mention of the crucial presence of an external factor.

1224ᵇ10: The translation of ἄμφω γὰρ ἔχει raises problems. The most obvious antecedent to ἄμφω would be the ἀκρατής and ἐγκρατής mentioned in the previous line, but then ἄμφω is masculine and must therefore be object of ἔχει, and there is then the question what its subject is. Solomon translates 'He has both tendencies', 'he' being presumably the man in question, ἀκρατής or ἐγκρατής as the case may be, but it is difficult to extract two tendencies from the context, though this is, of course, the key to Aristotle's solution of the paradox. I have, however, adopted this in translation. Dirlmeier takes ὁρμή as subject, and interprets ἄμφω ἔχει as meaning 'is present in both' (sc. the ἀκρατής and the ἐγκρατής), which is linguistically easier, but makes the remark a somewhat banal one.

1224ᵇ15: Reading ἔτι (MSS ἐπεί).

1224ᵇ21: Reading κακῶς πράξειν (MSS κακὸν πράττειν) (D.A.F. M.R.).

1224^b25: Reading ὅταν <ἐπὶ> τῶν ἐν ψυχῇ τι τοιοῦτον ὁρῶσιν.
The MSS have ὅτι; the suggestion of ὅταν is due to D. A. Russell and
the insertion of ἐπὶ to Solomon.

1224^b29: The MSS have ὁ λόγος φύσει ἄρχον. ἔτι (or ὅτι) which
seems unintelligible. I have translated <τῶν> φύσει ἀρχῶν, ὅτι
following E. R. Dodds. An alternative is to emend to ὑπάρχει (Rassow and Dirlmeier).

1224^b35: The MSS have ὥστε μὴ κατὰ φύσιν πράττει which con-
tradicts what is said in the next clause; hence editors have made
various insertions in order to make a suitable contrast with ἀπλῶς.
I have adopted Ross's <πως>μὲν<οὐ> so that the negative governs
the verb rather than the adverbial phrase.

1224^b36: Reading <ἀλλ'> οὐ τὴν αὐτήν (MSS ἔτι)

1225^a8: Reading ἤ. (D.A.F.M.R.).

1225^a9-11: The MSS have ὅσα μὲν γὰρ ἐφ᾽ αὐτῷ τῶν τοιούτων μὴ
ὑπάρξαι ἢ ὑπάρξαι, δεῖ ὅσα πράττει ἃ μὴ βούλεται, ἑκὼν πράττει
which is unintelligible. The simplest emendation is the altering of
δεῖ to ἀεί, proposed by Bonitz and followed by Susemihl; but ἀεί
seems to lack point and to be awkwardly placed. Similar remarks
apply to Dirlmeier's δή. But the clause ὅσα . . . βούλεται is something
of an embarrassment: if ὅσα depends on τοιούτων, as Solomon
supposed, Aristotle will be saying, that, among the things that are
such that the agent does them not wishing to, those that are such
that it is in his power whether they come about or not . . . , which
is intelligible, but there seems no reason why Aristotle should explicitly restrict his remark to actions that the agent does not want to
perform, as the proposition holds quite generally. If τοιούτων is
taken as referring to the sort of action already under discussion
(Dirlmeier), and ὅσα . . . βούλεται is not made dependent on it, we
have an anacolouthon and what seems an absurd restriction of the
class of actions which are voluntary. I have therefore adopted Ross's
palaeographically easy κεἰ [ὅσα] πράττει, making the clause concessive.

1225^a18: Reading ἢ οὐ φύσει <γε>.

1225ᵃ30: ἀλλὰ μὴν οὐδὲ δι' ἐπιθυμίαν. Both Solomon and Dirlmeier suppose that the point is that acts done from desire are not voluntary either. As it was not Aristotle's view that actions done from ἐπιθυμία are in general involuntary, it is necessary to read the sentence as saying not *all* acts done from desire are voluntary, which requires us to supply a good deal. (The possibility that some desires are so strong that the actions they lead to are not voluntary may be mentioned in the passage about superhuman φυσικά at 1225ᵃ21, where, however, ἐπιθυμία is not mentioned specifically.) I have supposed, instead, that the point is only that the actions of divinely inspired prophets, etc. do not result from ἐπιθυμία.

1225ᵃ35-36: The MSS have οἱ γὰρ μάλιστα ἐμποδίζοντες τὸ ἑκούσιον ὡς βίᾳ πράττοντες, ἀλλ' ἑκόντες, which either requires the positing of a lacuna after ἑκούσιον or some emendation. It seems as if λόγοι must be supplied with ἐμποδίζοντες: Aristotle presumably mentions certain arguments as a reason for saying that the discussion of the relation of the voluntary to compulsion is now complete. There is uncertainty about the meaning of ἐμποδίζειν here. Is the allusion to arguments impeding the finding of a satisfactory definition of ἑκούσιον, or to arguments purporting to show that nothing is ἑκούσιον? Dirlmeier simply inserts λόγοι after ἑκούσιον, but more is surely needed.

1225ᵇ4-5: Reading ἢ οἴεται μὲν ὅτι πόμα, ἀλλ' ἦν φίλτρον, ἢ οἶνος, τὸ δ' ἦν κώνειον (R/W). The passage is corrupt, but something like this must be correct.

1226ᵃ3: Reading τὴν διάμετρον <ὅτι> ἀσύμμετρος (cf. *E.N.* III 1112ᵃ22 f.) (D.A.F.M.R.).

1226ᵃ16: Reading βούλεσθαι μὲν <γὰρ> καὶ δόξα (Spengel).

1226ᵃ28-33: The MSS have διὸ οὐ βουλευόμεθα περὶ τῶν ἐν Ἰνδοῖς οὐδὲ πῶς ἂν ὁ κύκλος τετραγωνισθείη· τὰ μὲν γὰρ οὐκ ἐφ' ἡμῖν τὸ δ' ὅλως οὐ πρακτόν. ἀλλ' οὐδὲ περὶ τῶν ἐφ' ἡμῖν πρακτῶν περὶ ἁπάντων. (ᾗ καὶ δῆλον ὅτι οὐδὲ δόξα ἁπλῶς ἡ προαίρεσις ἐστίν). τὰ δὲ προαιρετὰ καὶ πρακτὰ τῶν ἐφ' ἡμῖν ὄντων ἐστιν. διὸ καὶ ἀπορήσειε ... Some transposition seems necessary: the reason for the ἀπορία introduced by διό must be the fact mentioned in the ἀλλ' οὐδ' ...

211

ἀπάντων sentence, that there is not βούλευσις about all πρακτά, which in the received text is too far separated from it, and I have therefore put ἀλλ' . . . ἐστιν immediately before διό. Also, it would be odd for Aristotle, after saying that *not even* all πρακτά are matters for βούλευσις to remark that, all the same, all πρακτά are ἐφ'ἡμῖν.

1226ᵇ2-3: Reading ἐπειδὴ οὖν οὔτε δόξα οὔτε βούλησις ἐστιν ἡ προαίρεσις ὡς ἑκάτερον, οὐδ' ἄμφω.

1226ᵇ17-20: Reading (πάντες γὰρ βουλευόμεθα ἃ καὶ προαιρούμεθα, οὐ μέντοι γε ἃ βουλευόμεθα (MSS βουλόμεθα) πάντα προαιρούμεθα (λέγω δὲ βουλευτικὴν ἦν ἀρχὴ καὶ αἰτία βούλευσίς ἐστιν) καὶ ὀρεγόμεθα (MSS ὀρέγεται) . . . Cf. *E.N.* III, 1113ᵃ2-3 (R/W).

1226ᵇ34-35: Reading τὸ δ' ἑκούσιον μὴ <ἄπαν> προαιρετόν (Susemihl).

1226ᵇ37: The MSS have παθημάτων, which cannot be right, since the notion of a premeditated πάθημα is absurd. Dirlmeier defends it, referring to Antiphon I.27, but the passage is hardly parallel. Bonitz proposed ἀδικημάτων, Ross, ποιημάτων. I have followed Ross in the translation.

1227ᵃ12-13: Reading οἷον εἰ πολεμῶσιν ἢ μὴ πολεμῶσιν [τοῦτο] βουλευομένοις.

1227ᵃ16: Following Dirlmeier, I take the 'if'-clause as conditional and parenthetical, and not as introducing an indirect question, since there seems little point in saying that one who deliberates always engages in a second-order inquiry about his own reasoning.

1227ᵃ21-22, 30: Reading διαστροφῇ (MSS διαστροφὴν) in both places.

1227ᵇ19: Reading λέγωμεν (MSS λέγομεν).

1227ᵇ22-23: Reading πότερον δ' ἡ ἀρετὴ ποιεῖ τὸν σκοπὸν <ὀρθὸν> ἢ τὰ πρὸς τὸν σκοπόν.

1228ᵃ1: Reading τοῦ δὲ τὸ τέλος ὀρθὸν εἶναι τῆς πραιρέσεως

[οὗ] ἡ ἀρετὴ αἰτία. The alternative, keeping οὗ, is to read τό instead of τοῦ.

1228ᵃ13–14: ἡ ἐνέργεια τῆς ἀρετῆς. Dirlmeier takes this not as a genitive of comparison, but as a 'subjective' genitive, i.e. 'the activity of the virtue . But his reasons for rejecting the alternative seem inadequate; further, it seems superfluous to specify the activity by a further genitive, whereas the comparative αἱρετώτερον in ᵃ13 would seem to be most easily understood with an explicit term of comparison. Since, in this context, προαίρεσις is equivalent to ἀρετή, what he says here, with the translation adopted, is virtually the same as is said at ᵃ17–18.

BOOK EIGHT

1246ᵃ26–31: Reading καὶ τοῦτο ἢ <ᾗ> αὐτὸ ἢ αὖ [MSS αὐτὸ ἡδύ] κατὰ συμβεβηκός, οἷον [ἢ] ὀφθαλμοῖς [MSS ὀφθαλμός] <ᾗ> ἰδεῖν ἢ [καὶ ἄλλως] παριδεῖν διαστρέψαντα, ὥστε δύο τὸ ἓν φανῆναι. αὗται μὲν δὴ ἄμφω [ὅτι μὲν] ὀφθαλμοῦ [MSS ὀφθαλμός] <ᾗ> [MSS ὅτι ἦν] ὀφθαλμός [MSS ὀφθαλμῷ]. ἄλλη δὲ κατὰ συμβεβηκός, οἷον πρὸς [MSS εἰ ἦν] ἀποδόσθαι ἢ φαγεῖν. (R/W).

1246ᵃ31–ᵇ4: Emending ἐπιστήμη (MSS, defended by Mrs Mingay in Moraux and Harlfinger, and Kenny) to ἐπιστήμη with Spengler, Jackson, Dirlmeier, and Moraux. In ᵃ32–34, the MSS have καὶ γὰρ ἀληθῶς καὶ ἁμαρτεῖν οἷον ὅταν ἑκὼν μὴ ὀρθῶς γράψῃ ὡς ἀγνοίᾳ δὴ νῦν χρῆσθαι, ὥσπερ μεταστρέψας τὴν χεῖρα καὶ τῷ ποδί ποτε ὡς χειρὶ καὶ ταύτῃ ὡς ποδὶ χρῶνται ὀρχηστρίαδες where the syntax of ὡς χρῆσθαι . . . μεταστρέψας causes difficulty, and the precise meaning of μεταστρέφειν τὴν χεῖρα is uncertain. I have followed Moraux in emending δὴ νῦν to τῇ δυνάμει as an 'Unzialverlesung', χεῖρα to χρείαν and χρῆσθαι to χρήσεται, so that μεταστρέψας depends on it, and transpose ὥσπερ to the beginning of the καὶ τῷ ποδί clause. Jackson's less drastic alternative is simply to emend μεταστρέψας to μεταστρεψάσαι which is then taken with what follows. The passage is discussed by Mrs Mingay, and by Kenny (pp. 184 f.).

The remaining emendations required in this section have secured . general agreement since Spengel.

1246ᵇ4–12:   I see no reason for emending ἐπιστήμη to ἐπιστήμῃ in
ᵇ5, an emendation proposed by Spengel and accepted by Dirlmeier
and Moraux. The remaining emendations required in this section are
relatively slight, and have been generally agreed. Among these is the
reading στροφήν in ᵇ9 for τροφήν of the MSS, following Victorius.
In my translation, I assume, against Solomon, Rackham, and Dirlmeier, that with αὐτῆς δὲ τῆς πασῶν κυρίας τίς we have to understand κυρία ἐστι and not ποιεῖ τὴν στροφήν, and similarly with
ἀρετή in ᵇ11. Aristotle is asking, rhetorically, what is superior to
the supreme science, not what distorts it; this will permit the over-all
interpretation given in the Commentary.

1246ᵇ12–18:   The reading of MSS in ᵇ12–15 is ἢ ὥσπερ λέγεται
ἀκρασία κακία τοῦ ἀλόγου τῆς ψυχῆς καί πως ἀκόλαστος ὁ ἀκρατὴς
ἔχων νοῦν, ἀλλ' ἤδη ἂν ἰσχυρὰ ᾖ ἡ ἐπιθυμία στρέψει καὶ λογιεῖται
τἀναντία, which Jackson keeps, regarding it as a whole sentence in
the form of a question: 'Is there – in the way in which incontinence
is said to be vice of the irrational part of the soul, and the incontinent
man in a manner intemperate – one who is possessed of mind and
yet, if the desire is strong, it will divert him, and he will draw the
opposite conclusion?' This involves supplying ἐστί τις with ἔχων
νοῦν, and an abrupt change in the subject of στρέφει.

After τἀναντία in ᵇ15, the MSS have η σφ with signs of a lacuna.
Jackson, having ended his sentence with a question mark at τἀναντία,
thinks this represents no more than ἤ ἐστι δῆλον ὅτι which introduces
the *second* case, involving ἀρετή in the ἄλογον and ἄγνοια in the
λόγον ἔχον. Jackson's only other emendation in this section is the
alteration of ἕτεραι to ἑτερᾷ, and his over-all reconstruction is intelligible, though awkward in places.

Moraux emends the text as follows: καὶ ὡς ἀκόλαστος ὁ ἀκρατὴς
ἔχων νοῦν; ἀλλ', εἰ δή, ἂν ἰσχυρα ἡ ἐπιθυμία, στρέψει, καὶ λογιεῖται
τἀναντία ἡ <τοῦ ἀκρατοῦ>ς φ<ρόνησις στρεφομένη ὑπὸ τοῦ ἀλόγου>,
δῆλον ὅτι κἂν ἐν μὲν τουτῳ ἀρετη, ἐν δὲ τῷ λόγῳ ἄγνοια ᾖ, <ἢ>
ἑτέρα μεταπείθεται. The crucial feature of this is to end the initial
interrogative sentence at ἔχων νοῦν, emend ἤδη to εἰ δή, and treat all
that follows up to δῆλον ὅτι as the protasis of a conditional. He supposes a lacuna after τἀναντία, thus removing a difficulty over the
change of subject with λογιεῖται and offers a filling *exempli gratia*.
The MSS reading in ᵇ17, ἕτεραι μεταποιοῦνται is hardly possible, but
an emendation introducing a future tense is perhaps preferable to
Moraux's.

In ᵇ17, τ' ο<ὐ> seems a certain emendation, generally accepted since Jackson; the insertion of ἀρετῇ in ᵇ18, first proposed by Spengel, and accepted by Moraux, but not by Jackson or Dirlmeier, seems a considerable improvement and to be necessary for the symmetry of that sentence. I have followed Moraux's reconstruction.

1246ᵇ18-25: In ᵇ20 the emendation of λόγῳ of the MSS is certain: μοχθηρία is a state of the non-rational part of the soul. As explained in the Commentary, Moraux postulates a lacuna at ᵇ21, filled by something like <ὑπὸ τῆς ἐν τῷ λόγῳ ἀγνοίας μεταπεισθήσεται, ἡ μέντοι τοῦ ἀλόγου κακία ἐν τῷ λόγῳ>. On Jackson's interpretation, the text of the MSS hardly requires alteration; though Jackson himself proposed ἐν τῷ λογιστικῷ after ἐν τῷ ἀλόγῳ (and Dirlmeier proposed ἐν τῷ λόγῳ), these are hardly necessary emendations. In ᵇ24 the emendation of κόλασιν ἄν to ἀκολασίαν seems certain.

Should ἄνοια or ἄγνοια be read at ᵇ16, 21, 25, 26, 29? The MSS have ἄνοια at ᵇ16 and 21. There seems to be no good reason not to emend to ἄγνοια in those two places, but very little difference is made if we do not, as presumably ἄνοια includes ἄγνοια. I have followed Jackson, except that I have read ἄγνοια rather than ἄνοια throughout.

1246ᵇ25-32: Reading ἔστι δὲ ταῦτα for ἐπί τε ταῦτα in ᵇ25, τὸ ἀγνοίᾳ χρῆσθαι for καὶ ἀπὸ ἀγνοίας χρῆσθαι in ᵇ26, and ἀλλ' οὖν ο<ὐ> for ἀλλ' ὁ in ᵇ28, and καὶ γὰρ <ἃ> ὁ ἄδικος ταῦτα ὁ δίκαιος δύναται in ᵇ31.

1246ᵇ32-36: Reading καὶ ἀγαθαὶ ἐκείνων (MSS ἐκεῖναι) αἱ ἄλλαι ἕξεις.

1246ᵇ37: Reading ἡ φρόνησις ποιεῖ τὴν εὐπραγίαν καὶ ἀρετή<ν> with Spengel and Dirlmeier.

1247ᵃ1-2: Reading τῆς εὐτυχίας [εὖ] ποιούσης εὐπραγίαν καὶ τὰ αὐτὰ τῇ ἐπιστήμῃ (MSS τῆς ἐπιστήμης). I assume that ἐπιστήμη is here simply equivalent to τέχνη, and Aristotle is making the rather general point that what is produced through skill or knowledge can also come about by chance.

1247ᵃ5: Reading οἱ δὲ καὶ ἐν οἷς τέχνη, following Bekker, Jackson, and Dirlmeier (MSS εἰδέ, Susemihl ἔτι δέ).

1247ᵃ7-10:   It is clear that in these lines *two* possible sources of εὐτυχία are being canvassed: first, that it is a matter of an individual's ἕξις (hence, presumably acquired by his own efforts) and second that it is a matter of φύσις. The punctuation and interpretation (though not the actual text) depend on whether τῷ αὐτοὶ ποιοί τινες εἶναι in ᵃ7-9 refers to the ἕξις or the φύσις alternative. I have followed Dirlmeier in taking the latter option, stressing αὐτοί and hence ending the sentence at εὐτυχημάτων, as Susemihl does. ᵃ9 then says that the current view, attributing good fortune to φύσις, holds that people *are* πρακτικοὶ τῶν εὐτυχημάτων by nature. This is supported by ποιούς τινας in ᵃ10.

1247ᵃ11-12:   Reading τῷ [τὸ] δεῖν <κατὰ τὸ εἶναι τοιονδί> ἔχειν with Dirlmeier, following the Latin tradition.

1247ᵃ15-16:   Reading ἐστι γὰρ (MSS ἔτι δέ) φανερὸν, ὄντες ἄφρονες.

1247ᵃ22-23:   Reading ὁ μὲν οὐδὲν, ἄλλος δὲ βάλλει καθ᾿ ἥν φύσει ἐστι εὐτυχής with Dirlmeier. With this reading, some such word as πτῶσιν or βολήν has to be understood with ἥν. I have followed Jackson against Dirlmeier in putting a full stop after εὐτυχής in ᵃ23, treating the hypothesis of divine favour as a new one, alternative to the φύσις hypothesis.

1247ᵃ25:   Following Susemihl and Dirlmeier, against Jackson, in omitting δέ.

1247ᵃ27:   Reading ἀλλ᾿ οὕτως (MSS οὗτος) <ὁ> εὐτυχὴς τὸν δαίμον᾿ ἔχει κυβερνήτην ἀγαθόν.

1247ᵃ33-35:   Reading and punctuation as follows: εἰ μὲν οὖν τὸ παραλόγως ἐπιτυγχάνειν τύχης δοκεῖ εἶναι – ἀλλ᾿, εἴπερ, διὰ τύχην εὐτυχής – οὐκ ἂν τοιοῦτον εἴη τὸ αἴτιον οἷον ἀεὶ τοῦ αὐτοῦ ἢ ὡς ἐπὶ τὸ πολύ. This involves only the emendation of εἶναι to εἴη, with Spengel and Susemihl.

1247ᵃ36-37:   Reading εἰ ὅτι τοιοσδί, ἐπιτυγχάνει < ἢ ἀποτυγχάνει > ὥσπερ ὅτι γλαυκὸς οὐκ ὀξὺ ὁρᾷ with Jackson.

1247ᵇ1: The MSS have τύχης γὰρ ὅσων αἰτία τύχη ἀγαθὴ ἀγαθῶν, which Susemihl reads and Solomon translates. I have accepted Jackson's εὐτυχεῖς ... ὅσοις (the Latin is *fortunate*), since what is required in support of the conclusion is a reaffirmation of the connection between τύχη and εὐτυχία asserted at ᵃ34.

1247ᵇ8–9: Reading and punctuating as follows: τοῦτο μὲν οὖν ἄλλο πρόβλημ' ἂν εἴη. ἐπειδὴ ὁρῶμεν ...

1247ᵇ9–11: Reading ... ὁρῶμέν τινας ἅπαξ εὐτυχήσαντας, διὰ τί οὐ καὶ πάλιν ἂν διὰ τὸ αὐτὸ κατωρθώσαιεν, καὶ πάλιν. τοῦ γὰρ αὐτοῦ τὸ αὐτὸ αἴτιον. οὐκ ἄρα ἐστὶ τύχης τοῦτο. with Dirlmeier, largely following Jackson.

1247ᵇ12–14: Reading ἔσται μέν τῳ ἀγαθὸν ἢ κακόν, ἐπιστήμη δ' οὐκ ἔσται αὐτοῦ ἡ δι' ἐμπειρίαν (MSS ἀπειρίαν) with Jackson, using the Latin tradition.

1247ᵇ16–17: Reading οὐχ ὅτι τοιοσδί (MSS ὅτι τοῖς δεῖ) with Jackson and Dirlmeier, and adopting, with most editors, Fritzsche's emendation of μακρὰν to μακαρίαν.

1247ᵇ19–21: Reading and punctuating as follows: καὶ πρότεραι αὗταί εἰσι φύσει γε. εἰ γάρ ἐστι φύσει ἡμῖν (MSS ἡ δι') ἐπιθυμία[ν] ἡδέος [καὶ ἡ] ὄρεξις, φύσει γε ἐπὶ ἀγαθὸν βαδίζοι ἂν πᾶσα.

1247ᵇ22: Reading ὥσπερ ἀδίδακτοι ᾠδικοί with Jackson and Dirlmeier.

1247ᵇ23: Reading <ἡ> ἡ φύσις πέφυκε with Jackson and Dirlmeier.

1247ᵇ26: Reading εὖ ᾄσονται for ἔσονται (MSS) with Jackson and Dirlmeier.

1247ᵇ30–32: Reading καὶ ἐν ἐκείνοις <εἰ> (from Latin) ἐν οἷς κακῶς λογίσασθαι δοκοῦσι, κατορθοῦσι, κατευτυχῆσαί (MSS κατορθῶντε καὶ εὐτυχῆσαι) φαμεν.

1247ᵇ32–33: Reading καὶ πάλιν εἰ ἐβούλοντο ἄλλο (MSS ἄν) ἢ ἔλαττον <ἢ> ἔλαβον ἀγαθόν with Jackson and Dirlmeier.

1247^b36–37: Reading τύχῃ (MSS τύχη) δ᾽ αὐτοῦ αἰτία οὖσα ⟨ἐπιθυμία⟩. The insertion of ἐπιθυμία is due to Dirlmeier, but it seems strongly supported by δι᾽ ἐπιθυμίαν in the next sentence: the man is fortunate in this case even though reasoning of a similar kind resulting from desire could result in misfortune in other cases.

1248^a1–2: The MSS have ἀλλὰ μὴν ἢ ἐνταῦθα εὐτυχία καὶ τύχη δίττη κἀκείνη ἡ αὐτὴ ἢ πλείους αἱ εὐτυχίαι, which will hardly do as it stands, but it is hard to restore the text with much confidence, as there is not much evidence of Aristotle's conclusion on the topic outside this sentence. I have followed Solomon's translation in keeping ἤ . . . ἤ, transposing καὶ τύχη δίττη after καὶ εὐτυχίαι as Spengel proposed. Ross's proposal is largely the same.

1248^a5–8: The MSS have ἐκείνη πότερον ἡ εὐτυχία ἢ οὐκ ἔστιν; ἢ ἐπεθύμησεν ὧν ἔδει καὶ ὅτε ἔδει τὸ λογισμὸς ἀνθρώπινος οὐκ ἂν τούτου εἴη. οὐ γὰρ δὴ πάμπαν ἀλόγιστον τοῦτο, οὔτε φυσική ἐστιν ἡ ἐπιθυμία, ἀλλὰ διαφθείρεται ὑπό τινος. It is doubtful if the text can be reconstructed with even moderate plausibility. Jackson reads . . . ἡ εὐτυχία; ἢ οὐκ ἔστιν, εἰ . . . ᾧ λογισμός γ᾽ (Latin *quidem*) ἀνθρώπινος οὐκ ἂν τούτου εἴη ⟨αἴτιον⟩; οὐ γὰρ . . . οὗ γε φυσική. Dirlmeier postulates a lacuna. The effect of Jackson's emendation in the second sentence, is to make τοῦτο and not ἐπιθυμία the subject of διαφθείρεται. I have, with hesitation, accepted Jackson's emendation, as Solomon does, for the following reasons: (i) That a desire is natural would not normally be regarded by Aristotle as disproved by the possibility of διαφθορά. (ii) If the MSS reading is kept, the proposition that the ἐπιθυμία is not φυσική is offered as a reason, co-ordinate with the occurrence's not being ἀλόγιστον, for denying that we have a case of εὐτυχία, yet Aristotle does not, at this stage of the argument, seem to be assuming that all good fortune is due to φύσις (cf. 1247^b39–1248^a1). (iii) The remarks at ^a12 f., that some apparent cases of εὐτυχία due to τύχη are really a matter of φύσις make more sense if the case currently under discussion is one in which the correctness of ἐπιθυμία *is* a matter of φύσις.

1248^a13–15: Reading . . . ἀλλ᾽ ὅτι οὐ πάντες οἱ δοκοῦντες εὐτυχεῖν διὰ τύχην κατορθοῦσιν, ἀλλ᾽ ⟨οὐ⟩ διὰ φύσιν· οὐδ᾽ ὅτι οὐκ ἔστι τύχη αἰτία οὐδένος δείκνυσιν, ἀλλ᾽ ⟨ὅτι⟩ οὐ [τῶν] πάντων ὧν δοκεῖ.

1248ᵃ18-19: Reading οὐ γὰρ δὴ ἐβουλεύσατο βουλευσάμενος πρότερον ἢ ἐβουλεύσατο, with Bussemaker and Dirlmeier, following the Latin tradition.

1248ᵃ23-24: Reading αὕτη δὲ, ὅτι τοιαύτη κατὰ τὸ εἶναι, τὸ τοιοῦτο δύναται ποιεῖν, with Dirlmeier.

1248ᵃ26: Reading δῆλον δή· ὥσπερ ἐν τῷ ὅλῳ θεός κἂν ἐκείνη (MSS καὶ πᾶν ἐκείνῳ) (Spengel, R/W).

1248ᵃ30: Reading ὃ [MSS οἱ] πάλαι ἔλεγον with Jackson.

1248ᵃ32-34: Reading and punctuating as follows: ἔχουσι γὰρ ἀρχὴν τοιαύτην ἢ κρείττων τοῦ νοῦ καὶ τῆς βουλεύσεως (οἱ δὲ τὸν λόγον, τοῦτο δ' οὐκ ἔχουσιν) καὶ ἐνθουσιασμὸν (MSS ἐνθουσιασμοί), τοῦτο δ' οὐ δύνανται· ἄλογοι ὄντες ἐπιτυγχάνουσιν, . . . with Solomon, and postulating a lacuna after ἐπιτυγχάνουσιν.

1248ᵃ35-36: Reading καὶ οὐ μόνον τὴν ἀπὸ τοῦ λόγου δεῖ ὑπολαβεῖν (MSS ἀπολαβεῖν) (R/W).

1248ᵃ36-39: The MSS have ἀλλ' οἱ μὲν δι' ἐμπειρίαν, οἱ δὲ διὰ συνήθειάν τε (Jackson τὸ ἐν, Solomon τοῦ) τῷ σκοπεῖν χρῆσθαι τῷ θεῷ δὲ αὖται (Jackson δύνανται) τοῦτο καὶ (Dirlmeier γὰρ) εὖ ὁρᾷ (Jackson ὁρᾶν) καὶ τὸ μέλλον καὶ τὸ ὄν, καὶ ὧν ἀπολύεται ὁ λόγος οὗτος (Jackson and Dirlmeier οὕτως, Solomon οὗτοι). Dirlmeier begins a new sentence with τοῦτο γάρ, taking τοῦτο to refer to ὁ θεός ('for that sees both the future and the past, as do those . . .'). Again, the text cannot be reconstructed with even a moderate degree of probability, and there may well be a lacuna. I have accepted οἱ δὲ διὰ συνήθειαν τοῦ ἐν τῷ σκοπεῖν χρῆσθαι τῷ θεῷ and then treated the remainder of that sentence as irretrievably corrupt, and made τοῦτο γάρ begin a new sentence, which may then be interpreted in the way suggested by Dirlmeier.

1248ᵇ1-3: The MSS have μνημονεύουσι μᾶλλον ἀπολυθέντος τοῦ πρὸς τοῖς εἰρημένοις εἶναι τὸ μνημονεῦον, where εἰρημένοις, in particular, is difficult. But the point must surely be that, just as the blind man has better powers of memory as a result of lack of pre-occupation with the visible, the power of divination is improved when reason is in abeyance, and the Latin tradition has a reference to *visibilia*. I have therefore followed Dirlmeier in reading τῷ ἀπολυθέντος τοῦ πρὸς τοῖς ὁρωμένοις (sc. εἶναι) σπουδαιότερον εἶναι τὸ μνημονεῦον.

1248ᵇ10:   Reading καλοῦμεν for ἐκαλοῦμεν. καλοκἀγαθία has not been mentioned previously in what we have of the *E.E.*, and the present tense is supported by *vocamus* in the Latin tradition.

1248ᵇ19–20:   Reading καλὰ ὅσα δι᾽ αὐτὰ [ὄντα] πάντα ἐπαινετά ἐστιν, with Verdenius.

1248ᵇ34–35:   The καλοκἀγαθός is said to be recognized first τῷ τῶν ἀγαθῶν τὰ καλὰ ὑπάρχεν δι᾽ αὐτά. The question is whether to take δι᾽ αὐτά with ὑπάρχεν or with καλά. On the first alternative, Aristotle is saying that τὰ καλά belong to the καλοκἀγαθός for their own sake (so Solomon and Rackham). δι᾽ αὐτά is then simply a variant of αὐτῶν ἕνεκα, as in 1229ᵃ4. On the second view, τὰ καλὰ δι᾽ αὐτά has to be taken as a single phrase, which requires interpretation. The word-order of this sentence may seem to favour the first alternative, but the order of 1249ᵃ3, which surely has to be taken in a parallel way, as the definition of the καλοκἀγαθός is appealed to, points in the opposite direction. I have therefore adopted the *second* interpretation, taking δι᾽ αὐτά with καλά.

1249ᵃ2–4:   The MSS have οὐ γὰρ ὑπάρχει αὐτοῖς τὰ καλὰ δι᾽ αὐτά, καὶ προαιροῦνται καλοὶ κἀγαθοί, καὶ οὐ μόνον ταῦτα, which cannot be correct, involving an intolerable shift from those who are not to those who are καλοκἀγαθοί. Rieckhe proposed emendation of καὶ to οὐδέ before προαιροῦνται, which is hardly sufficient, and it seems best, with Dirlmeier, to suppose a lacuna (e.g. ⟨ὅσοις δὲ ὑπάρχει⟩ καὶ προαιροῦνται) and emend to καλὰ κἀγαθά, following Solomon and Ross.

1249ᵃ7:   Reading διὸ instead of διότι, on the basis of the Latin tradition, following Dirlmeier: what is said in ᵃ5–6 is much more easily taken as a reason for the proposition that natural goods become fine in the hands of the fine-and-good man than as supported by it.

1249ᵃ14:   Retaining δι᾽ αὐτά of the MSS, and not emending to δι᾽

αὐτάς with Spengel and Susemihl. The relevant point here is not that the καλοκἀγαθός performs fine actions for their own sake, but that he does so *because* he possesses natural goods like wealth, strength, etc., and they make καλαὶ πράξεις possible.

1249ᵃ23:   Reading [εὖ] ὑγιεινόν with Ross and Dirlmeier.

1249ᵇ1:   Reading ὅρον καὶ τῆς ἕξεως καὶ τῆς αἱρέσεως καὶ φυγῆς χρημάτων πλήθους καὶ ὀλιγότητος with Dirlmeier.

1249ᵇ7:   Reading καὶ πρὸς τὴν ἕξω καὶ (MSS κατὰ) τὴν ἐνέργειαν τὴν τοῦ ἄρχοντος with Ross and Dirlmeier (though not accepting Dirlmeier's translation of ἕξις as 'possession'). Verdenius (op. cit.) keeps the MSS reading, and translates 'the active state of the ruling factor'.

1249ᵇ10:   ἐπεὶ . . . , καὶ ἕκαστον ἂν δέοι . . . ἑαυτοῦ ἀρχὴν ζῆν. If καὶ ἕκαστον is supposed to introduce an apodosis, καὶ must emphasize ἕκαστον. Verdenius (p. 287) says this 'is out of place in the context', and therefore takes καὶ as 'and'; he thus supposes that καὶ . . . ζῆν constitute more of a protasis for which there is no grammatical apodosis, as a parenthetical remark interrupts the syntax, creating an anacolouthon. Similarly Rowe (p. 68). But Verdenius also insists that ἕκαστον means not 'each one of us' but 'each of the two parts' (sc. ἄρχον and ἀρχόμενον), which seems to undermine his reason for denying that καὶ introduces the apodosis. I have accordingly so taken it, emending ἑαυτῶν to ἑαυτοῦ following Spengel, Dirlmeier, and Rowe.

1249ᵇ11-13:   In accordance with the over-all interpretation defended in the Commentary, I insert a full stop after ζῆν, and remove parentheses from what follows.

1249ᵇ15-16:   With Verdenius, in accordance with the explanation given in the Commentary, I end the parentheses at δεῖται instead of ἐν ἄλλοις, as in Susemihl's text.

1249ᵇ16:   Reading εἴ τις rather than ἥτις, with Verdenius.

1249ᵇ21:   Reading ἔχει δ' (MSS τοῦτο) οὕτω τῇ ψυχῇ.

SELECT BIBLIOGRAPHY

1. *Translations and Texts of the Eudemian Ethics*

The best complete English translation of the *Eudemian Ethics* is that by J. Solomon in the Oxford Translation of Aristotle, Volume IX (London, 1915). There is also a translation by H. Rackham in the Loeb Classical Library (*Aristotle, The Athenian Constitution, The Eudemian Ethics, On Virtues and Vices*, Cambridge, Mass., 1935). Solomon's translation of I, II, cc. 6–11, and VIII, c. 3 is printed, with revisions, along with translations of other ethical writings of Aristotle, in *Aristotle's Ethics*, edited by J. L. Ackrill (London, 1973). The Loeb volume has Rackham's Greek text. The Greek text is also available in a Teubner edition edited by Franz Susemihl (Leipzig, 1884, reprinted 1967). The only full-scale modern commentary is the German one of Dirlmeier (*Aristoteles, Eudemische Ethik übersetzt von Franz Dirlmeier*, Berlin, 1962). This also contains a German translation. There is also a French translation by V. Décarie, with brief notes. (Aristote, *Éthique à Eudème*, Librairie Philosophique J. Vrin, Paris and Montreal, 1978.)

2. *Books and articles cited in the Commentary and Notes*

Ackrill, J. L., *Aristotle's Categories and De Interpretatione*, translated with notes, (Clarendon Aristotle Series, Oxford, 1963).
—, 'Aristotle on "Good" and the Categories', in *Islamic Philosophy and the Classical Tradition: Essays presented to Richard Walzer*, ed. S. M. Stern, A. Hourani, and V. Brown (Oxford, 1972) and in *Articles on Aristotle, 2. Ethics and Politics*, edited by Jonathan Barnes, Malcolm Schofield, and Richard Sorabji (London, 1977).
—, 'Aristotle on *Eudaimonia*', in *Proceedings of the British Academy*, 60 (1974).
—, 'An Aristotelian Argument about virtue' in *Paideia: Special Aristotle Issue* (Brockport, 1978).
Allan, D. J., 'Quasi-mathematical method in *Eudemian Ethics*' in S. Mansion (ed.) *Aristote et les Problèmes de Méthode* (Louvain, 1961).
—, 'Aristotle's Criticism of platonic doctrine concerning goodness and the good', *Proceedings of the Aristotelian Society*, 64 (1963/4).
—, 'The fine and the good in the *Eudemian Ethics*', in Moraux and Harlfinger.
Austin, J. L., 'Agathon and Eudaimonia in the *Ethics* of Aristotle', in J. M. E. Moravcsik (ed.), *Aristotle: Critical Essays* (New York, 1967).

Berti, E., 'Unité et multiplicité du bien selon E.E. I 8', in Moraux and Harlfinger.

Brunschwig, J., 'E.E. I 8 et le περὶ τἀγαθοῦ', in Moraux and Harlfinger.

Charlton, W., *Aristotle's Physics I, II, translated with Introduction and Notes* (Clarendon Aristotle Series, Oxford, 1970).

Cherniss, Harold T., *Aristotle's Criticism of Plato and the Academy* (Baltimore, 1944).

Cooper, John M., *Reason and Human Good in Aristotle* (Cambridge, Mass., 1975).

Dirlmeier, Franz, 'Merkwürdige Zitate in der Eudem. Ethik der Aristoteles' SB Heidelberg, 1962. 2.

Düring, I., *Aristoteles* (Heidelberg, 1966).

von Fragstein, Artur, *Studien zur Ethik des Aristoteles*, Amerstam, 1974.

Fritzsche, A. T. H., *Eudemi Rhodii Ethica* (Regensburg, 1851).

Gauthier, R. A. and Jolif, J. Y., *L'Éthique à Nicomaque*, (Louvain, 1958).

Gigon, Olof, 'Das Prooimion der Eudemischen Ethik', in Moraux and Harlfinger.

Greenwood, L. H. G., *Aristotle – Nicomachean Ethics Book VI* (Cambridge, 1908, reprinted 1973).

Grice, H. P., 'Intention and Uncertainty', in *Proceedings of the British Academy*, 57 (1972).

Hamlyn, D. W., *Aristotle's De Anima, Books II and III*, translated with Introduction and Notes. (Clarendon Aristotle Series, Oxford, 1968).

Hardie, W. F. R., *Aristotle's Ethical Theory*, (Oxford, 1968; rev. edn., 1981).

Hart, H. L. A., 'Negligence, *Mens Rea* and Criminal Responsibility', in A. G. Guest (ed.), *Oxford Essays in Jurisprudence*, (London, 1961) and in H. L. A. Hart, *Punishment and Responsibility: Essays in the Philosophy of Law*, (Oxford, 1968).

Heath, Sir Thomas, *Mathematics in Aristotle* (Oxford, 1949).

Irwin, Terence, *Plato's Moral Theory* (Oxford, 1977).

Jackson, Henry, 'Eudemian Ethics VIII 1, 2', *Journal of Philology*, 1912.

—. 'On Eudemian Ethics 1215^{a}29; ^{b}20; 1224^{b}2', *Journal of Philology*, 33 (1913).

Jaeger, Werner, Aristotle: *Fundamentals of the History of his Development*, (tr. Robinson) (Oxford, 1948).

Kapp, Ernst, *Der Verhältnis der eudemischen zur nikomachischen Ethik*', Dissertation Freiburg Br., 1912.

Kenny, Anthony, *The Aristotelian Ethics*, (Oxford, 1978).

Kirwan, Christopher, *Aristotle's Metaphysics Books* Γ, Δ, E, (Clarendon Aristotle Series, Oxford, 1971).

Leonard, J., *Le Bonheur chez Aristote*, (Brussels, 1948).

Mingay, Jean M., 'Some controversial passages in the Eudemian Ethics', in Moraux and Harlfinger.

Monan, J. Donald, *Moral Knowledge and its Methodology in Aristotle* (Oxford, 1968).

Moraux, Paul, 'Das Fragment VIII 1, Text and Interpretation', in Moraux and Harlfinger.

Moraux, Paul and Harlfinger, Dieter, *Untersuchungen zur Eudemischen Ethik* (Berlin, 1971).

Owen, G. E. L., 'Logic and Metaphysics in some earlier works of Aristotle', in Düring and G. E. L. Owen (eds.), *Aristotle and Plato in the Mid-fourth Century*, Studia Graeca et Latina Gothoburgensia, 11 (Göteborg, 1960).

—, '*Tithenai ta phainomena*', in S. Mansion (ed.), *Aristote et les Problèmes de Méthode*, (Louvain, 1961).

Pears, D. F., 'Aristotle's analysis of courage', in *Midwest Studies in Philosophy, Volume III: Studies in Ethical Theory* (Minnesota, 1978).

Robinson, David B., 'Ends and means and logical priority', in Moraux and Harlfinger.

Ross, W. D., 'Emendations in the *Eudemian Ethics*', *Journal of Philology*, 34 (1915).

—, *Aristotle's Metaphysics* (Oxford, 1923).

—, *Plato's Theory of Ideas* (Oxford, 1951).

Rowe, Christopher J., *The Eudemian and Nicomachean Ethics: a Study in the Development of Aristotle's Thought* (Cambridge, 1971).

Smith, J. A., 'Aristotelica', *Classical Quarterly*, 14 (1920), pp. 18–22.

Stocks, J. L., 'On the Aristotelian use of λόγος: a Reply', in *Classical Quarterly*, 8 (1914).

Urmson, J. O., 'Aristotle's doctrine of the Mean', *Philosophical Quarterly*, 10 (1973).

Verdenius, W. J., 'Human reason and God in the Eudemian Ethics', in Moraux and Harlfinger.

Walzer, Richard, *Magna Moralia und Aristotelische Ethik*, Neue Philologische Untersuchungen, 7 (Berlin, 1927).

Wiggins, David, 'Deliberation and Practical Reason', in *Proceedings of the Aristotelian Society*, N.S. 76 (1975/1976).

3. *Other works*

Flashar, Helmut, 'The Critique of Plato's Theory of Ideas in Aristotle's Ethics', in *Articles on Aristotle, 2. Ethics and Politics*, edited by Jonathan Barnes, Malcolm Schofield, and Richard Sorabji (London, 1977).

Kenny, Anthony, *Aristotle's Theory of the Will*, (London, 1979).

Kraut, Richard, 'Two Conceptions of Happiness' in *Philosophical Review*, 88 (April 1979).

Moreau, Joseph, 'τέλος et ἀρετή d'après EE II 1 et la tradition platonicienne', in Moraux and Harlfinger.

Wiggins, David, 'Weakness of Will, Commensurability, and the Objects of Deliberation and Desire', in *Proceedings of the Aristotelian Society*, 79, (1978/9).

GLOSSARY

αἴτιος, αἰτία	cause, reason, responsible
αἰρετός	worth choosing, worth having
ἀκολασία, ἀκόλαστος	intemperance, intemperate
ἀκούσιος, ἄκων	involuntary
ἀκρασία, ἀκρατεύεσθαι,	incontinence, act incontinently,
ἀκρατής	incontinent
ἄλογος	non-rational (unreasoning 1247^{b}25,
	1248^{a}34)
ἁμαρτάνειν, ἁμαρτία	err, error
ἀναγκάζειν	force
ἀνάγκη	necessity, force (various translations in
	inferential contexts)
ἄνοια	stupidity
ἀπόδειξις	demonstrative
ἀρετή	virtue, excellence
ἠθική —	virtue of character
διανοητική —	intellectual virtue
ὅλη —	total excellence
ἄρχειν	govern
ἀρχή	start, starting-point (principle 1214^{a}28,
	governing principle 1249^{b}9 f.)
ἀτελής	incomplete, unfulfilled
ἀφροσύνη, ἄφρων	folly, foolish
βία	under compulsion
βίαιος	compelled
βούλεσθαι, βούλησις	wish (for)
βουλεύεσθαι, βούλευσις,	deliberate, deliberation
βουλή	
γνώριμος	perspicuous
γνῶσις	understanding
δεικνύναι	demonstrate
δῆλος	evident
διάθεσις	disposition
διάνοια	thought
δόξα	opinion, reputation
δύναμις	capacity

ἐγκράτεια, ἐγκρατεύεσθαι, ἐγκρατής	continence, act incontinently, incontinent
ἐκούσιος, ἐκών	voluntary
ἕνεκα	for the sake of, with a view to (τὸ οὗ ἕνεκα, that for which 1249ᵇ15)
ἐνέργεια	activity, actualization (actual exercise, 1227ᵃ13, 17)
ἐξαίφνης	in a flash
ἕξις	state
ἐξωτερικοὶ λόγοι	external discussions
ἐπαινετός	commended
ἐπί (with dative)	within the power of, under the control of
ἐπιθυμία	desire
ἐπιστήμη	knowledge, science (*plural*, forms of knowledge)
ἐπτακτικός, ἐπιτάττειν	prescriptive, prescribe
ἔργον	function, deed, work
εὐδαιμονία	happiness
εὐτυχεῖν	enjoy good fortune, be fortunate
εὐτύχημα	success
εὐτυχής, εὐτυχία	fortunate, good fortune
ἡδόνη, ἡδύς	pleasure, pleasant
ἦθος	character (*pl.* traits of character)
θεωρεῖν	apprehend, look into, examine, investigate (speculation 1249ᵇ20)
θεώρημα	inquiry
θεωρία	speculation, inquiry
θεωρητικός	theoretical (1226ᵇ26, capable of discerning, 1249ᵇ13 speculative [part])
θυμός	anger, spirit
ἰδέα	form
κακία	vice
καλοκἀγαθία	nobility
καλοκἀγαθός	fine-and-good
καλός	fine (attractive 1215ᵇ10)
κατὰ συμβεβηκός	incidentally
κίνησις	movement, change, process
κύριος	controlling, decisive, important, superior

λέγεσθαι – ὡς	be [so] called in – ways
λογισμός	reasoning, calculation
λυπεῖν	distress
λυπή	pain
λυπηρός	unpleasant
μακάριος	divinely-happy
μεθοδός	discipline
μέσον	mean
μεσότης	mean state
μοχθηρία, μοχθηρός	vice, vicious
νοεῖν	think, understand
νοῦς	intelligence
οὐσία	essence
ὀρέγεσθαι	have an inclination
ὀρεκτικός	appetitive
ὄρεξις	inclination
ὀρθὸς λόγος	right principle
ὀρμή	impulse
ὄρος	limit
πάθημα, πάθος, παθητικός	affection, affectible (experience 1225^{a}8)
πρᾶξις, πράττειν	action, act, do
προαιρεῖσθαι, προαίρεσις	choose, choice
σκοπός	goal
σπουδαῖος	virtuous (good, 1219^{a}27 f.)
συλλογισμός	inference
σωφροσύνη, σώφρων	temperance, temperate
τέλειος	final (1219^{a}20) complete (1219^{a}36, 39, 1249^{a}16)
τέλος	end (complete whole 1220^{a}4)
τύχη	luck
φανερός	clear
φρόνησις	wisdom, practical wisdom
φρόνιμος	wise (intelligent 1248^{a}34)
χρῆσις	employment

INDEX

References in bold type are to passages in the Translation.

Ackrill, J. L. viii, 70, 72, 99, 108, 152, 168, 223

action (*praxis*) 14a12, 30; 15a16 f.; 25; 16a21; 17a37, b25, 40; 19b40; 20b27; 22b19 f.; 23a4; 24a29 f.; 25a31; 26b1; 48b21-2; 49a24; 139

activity (*energeia*) 18b36; 19a31-8, b2, 20; 28a13-17; 95-7, 99, 100

affection (*pathos, pathēma*) 20a1, b8-20; 21a13, b12, 22, 35-9; 22b6, 11; 25a31, b29; 96, 108-10, 115, 119-21

akrasia see incontinence

Alexander of Aphrodisias 83

Allan, D. J. xii, 78, 89, 107, 186, 201, 206, 223

Analytics 17a17; 22b38; 27a10

Anaxagoras 15b6; 16a11

animals (non-human) 17a24; 22b18-20; 24a29; 25b27; 65; 149-50; 155-6

architectonic science 18b11 f.; 90-1

Austin, J. L. 50, 223

being 17b25-35; 70-2

Berti, E. 66, 74, 223

Brown, Lesley 208

Brunschwig, J. 81, 224

capacity 18b36; 20b7-20; 21b17, 35; 108-9, 121

categories 17b25-35; 70-5, 201

causes 91-2, 155-6

change, changing, unchanging things 17a33, b29-33; 18a22, b4-6; 20b2, 26 f.; 22b21-9; 24b9; 48a25 f.; 112, 124-5, 139

character 20a12, 39 f.; 21b32 f.; 27b10 f.; *see also* virtue of character

Cherniss, H. 76, 83. 224

choice (*prohairesis*) 14b7; 23a16-25,

b38-24a7; 25a37, II, c.10; 27b13, 37-28a19; 149-58

completeness 19a37 f.; 98-9, 101-4, 190

compulsion 23a30-5, b20 f.; II, c.8; 131, 138-45

contemplation *see* speculation

continence (*enkrateia*) *see* incontinence

controlling (*kurios*) 18b13; 22b20-5; 23a5; 126-7

Cooper, J. M. 58, 152, 155, 224

courage 16b5, 22; 20b19, 39

Décarie, V. viii, 223

deficiency *see* excess

deliberation 26a22-27a18; 48a18-34; 151-9, 182-3

desire (*epithumia*) 20b13; 23a27-b28; 24a35 f., b17 f., 31; 25a30, b25 f.; 46b15; 47b20 f., 37-48a8, 15 f.; 37-48a8, 15 f.; 130-7, 134-5, 141, 145, 149-50, 180-3

Dirlmeier, F. 84, 107, 113, 125, 127, 145, 158, 169, 184, 193, 194-213, 223

disposition (*diathesis*) *see* state (*hexis*)

Dodds, E. R. 205, 206, 210

Düring, I. 193, 224

employment (*chrēsis*) 19a1-24, b2 f.; 20a33; 95, 97, 99

end (*telos*) 14b10; 16b3, 17; 18b10-18, 35; 19a8 f., 30; 19b16; 26a6-17, b10-30; 27a30; II, c.11; 48b18; 52-3, 89-92, 97-8, 150-2, 155-7, 164-8

error 26a35-b2; 27b2 f.; 46a32-b8; 153, 160-1, 170

Eudemus xi

Euenus 23a31

231